TESTIMONIALS FOR

The Client Connection

"This book is one of the finest collections of insights, information and wisdom collected from the thought-leaders in integrated financial planning. Olivia writes beautifully from her unique vantage point at the intersection of money and psychology. Once again she gives us a gem."

Susan Bradley, CFP®
Founder, Sudden Money® Institute

"Olivia Mellan has more knowledge and insight into how people think about and behave with money than anyone I know. She and co-author Sherry Christie create penetrating pieces that help financial advisors better understand why their clients say and do the things they do, and more importantly, how to help them better handle their finances."

Bob Clark
Publishing Consultant
Former Editor-in-Chief, Dow Jones Investment Advisor

"Olivia Mellan has compiled some of her best work on building rich and lasting client relationships in *The Client Connection*. Traditional financial planning issues are reframed to help us fully appreciate our clients' perspective and discover effective ways to apply healthy motivation and tactfully help clients deal with sensitive issues. The book is packed with stories, strategies and tactics employed by some of the financial advisory industry's greatest thought leaders. There is nothing more important in the advisory business than the connection you have with your client. This book is a graduate-level crash course on the subject!"

Sheryl Garrett, CFP®
Founder, Garrett Planning Network

"Olivia's columns reach out to the community of financial advisors in a way that leads you to believe she can hear what we are thinking and wondering. With empathy, pragmatism and insight, she delivers guidance for the hard work of connecting with clients at those moments that are most trying, critical, and transformational. Through her pithy columns she helps us bridge our technical competence with better communication and advisory skills. With her guidance over the years we become better at how we do what we do for our clients."

Elizabeth Jetton, CFP®
Partner, RTD Financial Advisors
Former FPA President

"Mellan and Christie get to the 'heart and soul' of personal financial planning with this soulful collection of financial wisdom and advice."

Richard S. Kahler, MS, CFP, ChFC, CCIM
Kahler Financial Group

"Olivia has been one of the pioneers and the leaders in the world of Life Planning, the financial planning discipline that treats the meaning in the client's life as the focus and the source of meaningful financial action."

George Kinder, RLP®, CFP®
Founder, Kinder Institute of Life Planning

"These two impressive women are pioneers in this rapidly growing field. Kudos for their unfailing faith and ceaseless efforts to make this information available to all those who can benefit from it."

Ted Klontz, Ph.D.
President, Klontz Coaching

Also by Olivia Mellan and Sherry Christie

The Advisor's Guide to Money Psychology:
Taking the Fear Out of Financial Decision-Making

Overcoming Overspending:
A Winning Plan for Spenders and Their Partners

Money Shy to Money Sure:
A Woman's Road Map to Financial Well-Being

Also by Olivia Mellan

Money Harmony:
Resolving Money Conflicts in Your Life and Relationships

THE CLIENT CONNECTION

How Advisors Can
Build Bridges That Last

Olivia Mellan

OLIVIA MELLAN
SHERRY CHRISTIE

Always Something NU to Discover

1-800-543-0874
www.NUCOstore.com

This publication is designed to provide accurate and authoritative information in regard to the subject matter covered. It is sold with the understanding that the publisher is not engaged in rendering legal, accounting or other professional service. If legal advice or other expert assistance is required, the services of a competent professional should be sought. – **From a Declaration of Principles jointly adopted by a Committee of the American Bar Association and a Committee of Publishers and Associations.**

Circular 230 Notice – The content in this publication is not intended or written to be used, and it cannot be used, for the purposes of avoiding U.S. tax penalties.

ISBN: 978-0-87218-981-2

Library of Congress Control Number: 2008944261

Printed in U. S. A.

Dedication

To our editor and friend Jamie Green, who has made our writing for financial advisors more and more effortless and pleasurable over the years.

About the Authors

Talking about connections that last... The authors were classmates at Mount Holyoke College, but didn't start working together until Sherry Christie interviewed Olivia Mellan for an article about couples and money at their 25th reunion. Since 1995, they've collaborated on more than 150 articles for financial advisors and four "money psychology" books for consumers and advisors.

OLIVIA MELLAN, PRESIDENT, OLIVIA MELLAN & ASSOCIATES, INC.
www.moneyharmony.com

Olivia Mellan is a speaker, psychotherapist, money coach, and business consultant in private practice in Washington, DC. Since 1982, she has been a groundbreaker in the field of money psychology and money conflict resolution. She began her therapy career in 1974 specializing in women's issues, then in couples therapy, and finally in business therapy before realizing that money was the last taboo and deciding to concentrate of improving people's "relationship to money" and "relationships around money."

She is the author of four critically acclaimed books, *Money Harmony: Resolving Money Conflicts in Your Life and Relationships*; *Overcoming Overspending: A Winning Plan for Spenders and their Partners*; *Money Shy to Money Sure: A Woman's Road Map to Financial Well-Being*; and *The Advisor's Guide to Money Psychology* (the last three co-written with Sherry Christie.) *Money Harmony* was named by *Washington Post* columnist Michelle Singletary as one of her top 10 favorite money books.

Olivia's column for financial professionals, "The Psychology of Advice," appears monthly in *Investment Advisor* magazine. She was named one of IA's top 25 in 2006 (those most influential in the planning profession).

She has frequently appeared on *Oprah*, *The TODAY Show*, and ABC's *20-20* and is interviewed often on nationwide radio (*Marketplace*, *All Things Considered*, *Wisconsin Public Radio*), TV, and in the print media. She has hosted a weekly call-in radio show, *Money Harmony with Olivia Mellan* on WWDB-AM 860, Delaware Valley's only money talk radio. Her audio CD set, *The Secret Language of Money*, summarizes the best of her talks for the general public. Her video, "In the Prime: Couples and Money with Olivia Mellan," was produced by WETA-TV.

Recently, she has been training, supervising, and coaching therapists, counselors, and money professionals in money psychology tools and techniques to enhance their relationships with clients through her teleclasses. She conducts family retreats dealing with intergenerational wealth. Her chapter on "Moving Toward Money Harmony" appears in an anthology, *Peak Vitality*, published in 2008, along with chapters by Deepak Chopra, Wayne Dyer, Eckhart Tolle, Alice Walker, and others.

SHERRY CHRISTIE
www.sherrychristie.com

Sherry Christie has been helping people make better financial decisions for more than 20 years. A former advertising agency copywriter and executive, Sherry started her freelance financial writing business in 1991. Her client list includes Bank of America, SunTrust Bank, Nationwide Financial, JPMorgan Chase, and Genworth Financial, as well as wealth management firms and risk & human resource management specialists. She edits a monthly column and occasional features for *Investment Advisor* and *Wealth Manager* magazines.

The Advisor's Guide to Money Psychology: Taking the Fear Out of Financial Decision-Making (Investment Advisor Press, 2002) is her third financial book with psychotherapist Olivia Mellan. Their first two books, *Overcoming Overspending: A Winning Plan for Spenders and Their Partners* (1995) and *Money Shy to Money Sure: A Woman's Road Map to Financial Well-Being* (2001), were originally published by Walker & Company, New York.

Most recently, Sherry wrote *Making Your Company Human: Inspiring Others to Reach Their Potential* with retired CEO F. Leon Herron (LSK Books, 2006).

Acknowledgments

It's hard to know where to start in thanking the people who have played such a large part in making our worklives more satisfying and our personal lives more meaningful and balanced. We hope that anyone left out in this attempt will be forgiving.

This book and *The Advisor's Guide to Money Psychology*, which preceded it, can be traced back to a conversation with Bob Clark, who approached me (Olivia) at the 1995 ICFP retreat in San Diego with an invitation to begin writing a column for *Fee Advisor* and *Investment Advisor*. He had faith in my work and was excited about integrating money psychology into financial advisors' practices. At a conference in Atlanta after 9/11, Bob Veres nudged me to begin writing essays, where I could explore issues more deeply than in a Q&A format. I was reluctant to agree—more time! more work! But now I feel grateful to him for urging me to take the plunge.

I would also like to thank Bill Glasgall, *Investment Advisor*'s former editor-in-chief and advocate of the book that became *The Advisor's Guide*, for his stewardship and his friendship. Thanks, too, to George Gibson at Bloomsbury (originally Walker and Company), my first publisher and a loyal friend who always cheered me on; and to Jackie Johnson, the wonderful editor Sherry and I were fortunate to work with on *Money Shy to Money Sure*.

I'm thankful for all the financial professionals and therapy professionals who supported my work and taught me about areas where I wasn't an expert, including Peg Downey, Dick Vodra, Mary Malgoire, Sheryl Garrett, Susan Freed, Rick Kahler, Dave Drucker, Victoria Collins, Candi Kaplan, and Louise Cole, who began as respected colleagues and ended up as friends. Thanks are also due to Dick Wagner and George Kinder, who helped birth the field of life planning; to Susan Bradley, for her invaluable Sudden Money work and to Mark Tibergien, whose insights into the business of advice are invariably brilliant. A special thank you to Marie Swift for her brilliant marketing savvy and her friendship.

In addition, I'd be remiss not to express my appreciation to all the therapy, counseling, and coaching professionals who have assisted me, many of whom I knew from money psychology teleclasses, speeches, seminars, or my radio show: Lynne Hornyak, my gifted former teleclass co-presenter; Ted Klontz, a source of creative therapeutic help and wisdom; April Benson, Dori Mintzer, and

Barbara Mitchell, who still share the money and relationships journey with me; and Karin McCall, Barbara Stanny, Bari Tessler, Leslie Cunningham, Louisa Foster, Laura Longville, Maggie Baker, and Mikelann Valterra, who contribute richly to the sparsely populated field of money psychology and money conflict resolution. A special "thank you" to Vicki Robin and to Anne and Christopher Ellinger, whose transformational work about the deeper meaning of money and philanthropy has been inspiring.

I'm grateful to the groups that have asked me to speak to them: HSBC, NAPFA, the FPA, the National Underwriter Company/*Investment Advisor*, and others. My spirits soar at the opportunity offered by gatherings like the Students in Free Enterprise (SIFE) Financial Literacy Forum, the Delaware Money School "Purses to Portfolios" conference, and "women and money" conferences in various cities. After all these years, it still gives me tremendous satisfaction to help individuals and couples build stronger relationships with money and to provide financial advisors with the tools to create better connections with clients.

I would also like to acknowledge the families who trusted me to guide them in intergenerational retreats, where we explored wealth issues, values, and building deeper rapport through healthy communication. And to all the clients I've worked with in therapy or coaching: thanks for opening up your lives and your hearts to me.

Certain people have given me unsurpassed support over the years. A fervent "thank you" to the members of the Washington Therapy Guild, my work family: Anne Anderson (who got me started writing in the 1990s), Joe Gorin, Rachel Kaplan, Stephanie Koenig, Ruth Nielsen-Jones, and Don Zuckerman, who have constituted the home base for my psychotherapy practice for more than 30 years; to Sandi England for her professional generosity and her friendship; and to April Moore, and Andy Schmookler, and to Marla Zipin, Nancy Dunn (my son's "fairy godmother"), Ruthie (again!), and Louise Klok, who help me keep my heart open and my spirit committed to "walking my talk."

The lion's share of my gratitude rests with Jamie Green, our wonderful editor, who makes the monthly process of column-writing a joy. It's hard to believe our good luck in also having a terrific editor for this book, Debbie Miner, who has made the project so satisfying. And speaking of good fortune, I couldn't be luckier in having found Sherry Christie, my co-author and editor, who has an extraordinary ability to complete my thoughts and articulate them better than I could ever do myself. Our "work marriage" is now in its 15th year, even though the distance from Washington, D.C., to Jonesport, Maine, means we are rarely face-to-face.

Finally, I want to thank my husband, Michael, my loving life partner and still the best "money mentor" of them all; my son, Anil, whose heart and soul warms mine always; Bennett and Scott, for all that they do and are; and my young grandkids, in hopes that they will achieve some measure of "money harmony" in their lives. – OM

. . .

I offer thanks of my own to Olivia Mellan, whose creative abundance, insight and understanding, generosity of spirit, and sense of humor make our collaboration so illuminating and such fun.

And my deepest appreciation to my husband, Harry, whose integrity, goodness, and wisdom have captivated me for more than 25 years. – SC

Table of Contents

PART II: DEALING WITH DIFFERENCES

PART III: CHANGES

PART IV: MANAGING STRESS

PART V: THE RIGHT THINK TO DO

PART VI: WHO'RE YOU CALLING 'OLD'?

PART VII: PASSING THE TORCH

Introduction

When you press the trigger of money, what happens next is hard to predict. People's financial behavior often has more to do with their fears, anxieties, conflicts, and fantasies than what is rationally in their best interest.

More than 13 years ago, Bob Clark, then editor of editor of *Fee Advisor* and *Investment Advisor*, came to me with the realization that my "money psychology" work deserved a regular platform as an important aspect of financial advice. The more deeply advisors understood their clients' inner worlds, he and I agreed, the more successful they could be in establishing strong, productive relationships that might last for generations.

I joined forces with Sherry Christie, a financial writer whose ability to express my voice makes us a great team, and we began to write for Bob. These articles soon turned into a monthly column in *Investment Advisor*. In 1999, the incomparable Jamie Green became our editor.

During this time we've encouraged many financial advisors to become therapeutic educators, helping clients deal with the whole of their lives instead of just the dollars and cents. Even for those who are not interested in what has become known as life planning, there is value in understanding why a client in an apparently solid relationship may inexplicably stop returning phone calls, why couples may engage in marital mayhem in mid-consultation, why suddenly wealthy clients can be paralyzed by their windfall, and why financial loss and other stresses often make clients behave so badly. From this knowledge can come strategies that work to build a stronger rapport and lead clients to wise actions.

Most of our 150-plus *Investment Advisor* columns have discussed situational questions about topics as wide-ranging as mentoring, fraud, and anger. Many of these were excerpted in *The Advisor's Guide to Money Psychology*. In *The Client Connection*, you're seeing the rest of the story: two dozen essays that go even deeper to give you insight into where clients are coming from. This longer, more thoughtful format allows us to offer more detailed ideas and resources that may become useful additions to your professional toolbox. We've converted the essays into chapters and sorted them into seven subject areas:

1. **All in the Family.** We discuss the power of the mother-daughter bond, the father-son bond, and the intense relationship between

siblings. You'll learn ways to lighten the emotional charge of these connections, so that the past doesn't pollute your clients' attempts to make decisions that will serve them well.

2. **Dealing with Differences.** An examination of money personality types and gender variations will help you understand why some clients behave so differently from others. We'll explore how to talk to both men and women in a way that acknowledges their hard-wired and learned predispositions as well as their individual personalities, so they feel more fully heard and understood. Learning about cultural, religious, national, and ethnic differences in this section will also help you sense when to push, when to step back, and how to understand the power of a client's roots and long-standing traditions.

3. **Changes.** We'll familiarize you with a model of how people change bad habits, which may allow you to develop more patience when clients are not yet ready to abandon their old behavior. You'll learn how to move them toward more action-oriented phases and how to deal with "recycling" to an earlier stage of change. This section also addresses findings from therapy research to help you optimize aspects of your relationship with your clients, creating a more satisfying connection for you both. You'll be able to consider the possibility of integrating other experts into your client work and building resource lists to supplement the assistance you yourself provide. We'll also help you reflect on possible changes in your practice: whether to expand from a sole practitioner to "silos" or an ensemble, and how to run your business in a way that maximizes your strengths and minimizes your weaknesses.

4. **Managing Stress.** Here you'll learn ways to deal with professional and personal stress and trauma, whether your clients' or your own— an especially timely topic in these days of financial upheaval. You'll see how to create a toolkit of stress reduction techniques for your own use and to suggest to clients in need of help. We'll also explore the power of gratitude to heal and combat depression, guilt, and hopelessness.

5. **The Right Thing to Do.** What's ethical and what isn't? This section addresses ethical questions and boundary violations in your practice and among your clientele. We'll discuss setting standards in accord with your integrity and communicating them well to clients and colleagues.

6. **Who're You Calling "Old"?** To help you serve the baby boomer cohort moving into their 50s and 60s, we focus on understanding these clients and creatively addressing their needs and concerns. We also report on research about aging and the amazing brain, so you can help older clients approach the next stage of their lives with greater enthusiasm and verve.

7. **Passing the Torch.** Here we examine the challenge of helping parents and children talk to each other about money and values. You'll see how other advisors have created a framework for older generations to communicate with their children and grandchildren about stewardship of family values and wealth. Finally, we explore the wonderful ways that the power of giving can heal and transform families and the world, and we suggest how to help your clients' children embrace philanthropy.

Through a NAPFA University committee I served on not long ago, I was heartened to see that at least one financial planning organization is beginning to teach what is sometimes called the "softer side" of finance. And just recently, in a teleconference organized by Jamie Green, more than 250 financial advisors discussed ways of dealing with clients' anxiety, panic, and despair over the economic crisis. Participating as a communication expert, I was inspired to hear that many advisors are communicating with clients more than ever and practicing the kind of empathetic listening I've advocated for so long.

By learning to uncover your own talents and flaws and address your clients' deeper needs, you will find it easier to build bridges of understanding, empathy, and trust that last a lifetime. We feel confident that *The Client Connection* will become a powerful guide on your journey to professional fulfillment and success.

PART I

All in the Family

Most clients come into a financial advisor's office with family influences motivating them in powerful ways that are unconscious even to them. When you understand these influences and the effects they produce, you'll have a much better handle on your clients' true needs.

The chapters in this section explore some of the common pressures that family relationships can exert on people's money attitudes. The insights you gain may help you deepen your work with clients, enabling them to forge a healthier relationship with their money (and with you).

The core problem is that talking about money is taboo in many families. When I'm speaking to groups about money and relationships, I often say that my family was typical: my parents didn't talk to my brother and me about money. At this point, someone in the audience usually protests, "In my family, we talked about money all the time. My dad kept saying we were going to the poorhouse, and he and my mom argued about how much she was spending."

This makes everyone smile, but of course it's not what we mean by "talking about money." Most parents don't teach their children how to manage their money—how to save and invest, make wise spending decisions, and give philanthropically. Kids aren't taught what money is and what it isn't. Instead, they learn to equate money with love, power, happiness, self-worth, freedom, or security. By developing such an emotionally charged relationship with money in early childhood, they have difficulty making rational decisions about their moneylife later on.

Children decide at an early age whether to emulate their parent(s) or to be as different as possible from them. Mothers and daughters share a particular form of intensity and identification, as do fathers and sons. Siblings can be raised to be advocates for each other, or to compete for parental love and respect. Genetic similarities can predispose a child to be a spender like Dad or a hoarder like Mom. The result is that most of us imitate one or both parents in the way we deal with money (sometimes careening from one parent's money mode to the other's), or we vow never to be like our parent(s) and go off in the opposite direction. Either way, we are not free to develop a way of being with money in tune with our own values, our life goals, and our integrity—a state of equilibrium I call "money harmony."

The more comfortable you are with discovering your clients' childhood money messages, the more successful you can become as a "therapeutic educator" in the best sense of the word. Some clients will inevitably see you as the "good" parent they wish they'd had as a money mentor, or as a sibling they can trust and open up to. If you understand what family role a client might put you in, you'll find it easier to negotiate a relationship that gives you more impact on his or her financial well-being.

In the next pages, you'll learn what to look for in uncovering long-ago emotional charges that can prevent clients from acting rationally about money. Then we'll suggest ways to guide them toward a future in which they can thrive, financially and emotionally.

CHAPTER 1

Like Mother, Like Daughter

Female clients often bring another person to every discussion with you: their mother

One of my mother's favorite jokes involved a late-night TV program whose host was interviewing a famous star. When this star mentioned hating her mother, the host turned to his largely female audience and asked, "How many of you hate your mother?" Virtually every woman's hand shot up.

Mom thought this was hilarious. Years after the show aired, she had only to mention it for the two of us to go into gales of laughter together.

But as I grew older, I realized that if the host had asked, "How many of you love your mother?" the same hands would have probably gone up. The relationship between daughters and mothers tends to be a complex mix of love and hate. The better you understand this, the more productive your work with women clients will be.

Mothers Are Forever

No relationship is more primal or more far-reaching in influence than the relationship between a mother and her daughter. The mother's fears and anxieties are hard-wired into the daughter, as are the ways she may have damaged her child. As Dr. Christiane Northrup says in her groundbreaking book, *Women's Bodies, Women's Wisdom: Creating Physical and Emotional Health and Healing* (Bantam, 2006), "We carry in our own bodies not only our own pain but that of our mothers and grandmothers—however unconsciously."

As a trained psychotherapist, I have spent many years thinking about, struggling with, and healing a relationship with a difficult mother. I feel I've been able to incorporate many of her strengths and evolve beyond many of her weaknesses. But no sooner had I decided to address this topic than memories of my mother flooded back and an urge to procrastinate gripped me. Although she has been gone for years, the power of our relationship will last all my life.

A mother can have a tremendous influence—constructive, destructive, or both—on her daughter's money style. Girls tend to pick up Mom's money messages and either adopt them wholeheartedly to be like her, or reject them outright in order to dissociate themselves from an attitude or behavior they disapprove of.

Early money trauma involving mothers and daughters can have an especially devastating effect. I once worked with a client who seemed unable to stop overspending. In the course of therapy, she related a memory of having a see-through piggy bank when she was a child. Faithfully saving her nickels, dimes, and quarters, she watched the bank fill up and imagined all the wonderful things she would buy.

One day her mother needed to pay a delivery man and was low on cash. You guessed it: Mom went into her daughter's room, broke the piggy bank, and took the money. When the girl protested hysterically about her lost savings, her mother not only shrugged off the loss but made fun of her for being so emotional. Then and there, the daughter vowed that no one would ever take her money away from her again. To make sure of this, she spent it as quickly as she could. Only with dedicated self-awareness work as an adult was she able to turn this message around and begin finding ways to save money that felt safe to her.

My own mother sent mixed messages about money that I absorbed and incorporated into my own behavior. When she felt lonely and depressed or had an excuse for celebrating, she went shopping for clothes. She would hide her purchases behind the living-room chair until she judged that Dad was in a good mood. At that point she would try on her bargains for him. This process, she felt, gave her permission to integrate them into her wardrobe.

My mother wasn't openly affectionate to me, her only daughter, but one way she did show her caring was to take me out to buy clothes. I liked the clothes, and I understood that they were an expression of her love for me. So in my young adulthood, when I felt sad or unusually happy, I felt compelled to buy myself clothes. Even though I had earned the money for these binge purchases, I would hide the clothing in the trunk of my car (my version of behind the living-room chair) until my husband was in a good mood. Then, just like Mom, I'd bring the clothes in, try them on for him, and finally feel able to hang them up in my closet.

My Mama Done Tol' Me...

Sometimes a daughter replicates her mother's negative financial behavior despite the mother's attempt to steer her away from her own painful mistakes. For example, a woman I know was deserted at age 28 by her wealthy husband, forcing her to find a way to support herself and her young children. It took her four agonizing years to get out of debt, but she is now a financial advisor who owns her own firm. To her consternation, one of her grown daughters has become a spender and money avoider who earns almost nothing and lives in an expensive apartment community. She seems to be waiting for some rich guy to marry her and take care of her—an expectation that boggles her mother's mind, since the girl saw it backfire with her own parents.

The pull to relive a mother's experience is very strong. It can take a lot of maturity and self-awareness for a daughter to develop her own money personality and a healthy sense of autonomy.

Although my mom told me I could become anything I wanted to be, she also insisted in no uncertain terms, "You won't be good at this money stuff, dear, so I hope you find a rich husband who will take care of it all for you." This confidence-sapping advice was particularly odd since I was great at math. But the message went so deep that for years I was intimidated by mortgages, tax forms, investing, and almost everything else involving numbers. It took years to dig myself out of that hole, spurred on by my money psychology work with many clients and workshop participants.

Because money is still a taboo subject in many families, it's often neglected or inadequately addressed in mother-daughter conversations. When it is discussed, mothers may impart lessons based on personal experience and bias: whether or not to merge one's money with a partner's; whether to keep a stash of money hidden from one's husband; whether to trust the stock market; whether to let someone else handle one's investments; and so on.

Investing is an area where moms wield unexpected power. Dr. Tahira Hira of Iowa State University and Cäzilia Loibl of The Ohio State University recently published *Gender Differences in Investment Behavior*, a study of U.S. households with incomes of $75,000 or more, sponsored by the NASD Investor Education Foundation. Dr. Hira told me that when parental influence was a factor in developing investment style and behavior, women tended to report being influenced by their mothers, while men cited their fathers. Sadly, women who reported maternal influence had less confidence and knowledge about investing, while women who were influenced by their dads were more confident and knowledgeable.

This finding is a real disappointment. From older studies and my own clinical experience, I know that women have traditionally been underconfident about their money management and investing abilities. Now that so many women are earning more and filling more positions of responsibility, I hoped for a striking gain in financial confidence.

The sad truth is that when it comes to investing, many women still mirror their mother's lack of confidence and expertise. Ironically, this is true even when a woman is the prime manager of household spending. Old messages die slowly.

Does Mother Know Best?

Raising a money-savvy daughter is fraught with challenges. The goal is to at least be what psychologists call a "good-enough" mother, where the parent gives her child enough healthy nurturing and love to help her develop a sense of self-worth and feel safe in the world.

The mother must also know how much guidance to offer, as well as when and how to begin fostering the daughter's independence. In an excellent article on the Discovery Health Channel titled "Our Mothers, Ourselves: Mother-Daughter Relationships," author Gina Shaw explains how a mother helped her 8-year old daughter sort out the pros and cons of transferring to a school for the arts. This process, which taught the daughter how to make the decision herself, will serve her well when other important choice points arise later in life.

It can be hard for a mother to refrain from trying to mold her daughter in her own image. I'm a good example. I always thought that I wanted a little girl. But when I was pregnant and found out that my child was a boy, I realized I'd be a much better mother to a son. With all the preconceived notions I had about a daughter and all the things I wanted to share with her, I might have weighed her down with the heavy burden of my expectations. By contrast, I had few internal scripts about how to raise a boy. This ended up making me more open to letting my son become his own person.

What keeps so many mothers from helping their daughters become independent? For some women whose sense of self is shaky or whose self-esteem is low, living vicariously through one's daughter is a tempting way to feel better about their own life and choices. On the other hand, a mother who doesn't like or love herself enough may become competitive or feel threatened by a daughter's achievement, especially in an area where she herself lacks expertise. The result can be jealousy and resentment about opportunities available to the daughter that were denied to the mother. Such a climate of negativity hinders the daughter's ability to excel and take pleasure in her own accomplishments.

For their part, daughters may sabotage their success in order to remain close to Mom at all costs. It's a neurotic desire, but a totally human one.

Of course, for all the dysfunctional mother-daughter relationships out there, there are others that are quite healthy and many more that might be called workable. The main thing to understand is that whether or not a woman's mother is alive, she carries that mother inside her as a voice in her head—supporting her, criticizing her, telling her what to do, expressing shame about her, or celebrating her achievements. The more aware your women clients are of these mother-voices, the more power they will have to ignore the negative messages and embrace those that affirm their value as individuals.

Mothering Our Mothers

If a woman reaches her 30s, 40s, or 50s with her mother still living, their relationship becomes still more complex. Who is supposed to take care of whom? Who pays the bills for whom? Who gives advice to whom?

Sometimes the transition is smooth. Peg Downey, president of Money Plans, Inc., in Silver Spring, Maryland, told me that once her daughter Colleen was self-supporting, they would meet for lunch once a week. It became their routine to take turns picking up the tab—a simple example of a relationship moving from parent-child to the greater equality of two grown-ups.

When an adult daughter is financially better off than her mother, it puts extra stress on the mother's

"Mommie Dearest..."

Sometimes a client's sense of self has been badly damaged by her mother, and for one reason or another (the mother's death, for example) the relationship can't be repaired in real life.

I often urge these women to write a letter to their mother sharing all their hurt, anger, love, and longing. Once this letter is done, I suggest that the client write the ideal reply that her mother would have sent her.

Sometimes it's hard to conjure up these healing words and the daughter is blocked. In one instance, a client rewrote the song "I'd Do Anything for You, Dear" from the musical *Oliver!*, replacing the lyrics with a response from her "good" mother. This creative expression helped soothe her wounded soul.

natural desire to take care of her offspring. Peg told me about a time that her mother insisted on treating Peg and her young children to dinner. Knowing her mom was financially stretched, Peg chose an inexpensive restaurant. Even so, her mother gasped, "Wow, this is pricier than I thought!" when she looked at the menu. Instead of embarrassing her with an offer to pick up the check, Peg suggested that Grandma pay for the kids while she herself would buy her mom's dinner. This tactful solution gave her mother the pleasure of "mothering" her grandchildren without worrying about the cost.

A daughter's connectedness to her mother often makes it especially hard to deal with issues of frailty or mortality. When a woman comes to you for advice about how to open a conversation about her mother's financial situation or how to deal with her mother's increasing debility, an understanding of the nature of their relationship will help you decide what advice to give.

One rule you can rely on is that if Mom needs help, a daughter almost always feels she should provide it personally. If she hires professional care, even if it combines the Mayo Clinic and Mother Teresa rolled into one, she often feels selfish and guilty for not having put aside her own family and career. On the other side of the coin, guilt assails many mothers if their needs have cost a daughter her independence. Thankfully, the rise of long-term care insurance offers an emotionally neutral way for a daughter to prearrange care if needed. In many cases, her mother's response will be gratitude and profound relief.

Looking in the Mirror

Daughters with imperfect mothers (i.e., most of us) are often jarred by seeing their mothers in themselves. It can be a relief to recognize differences. Once when I became cold in a restaurant, I asked to borrow my date's jacket. Big deal, right? But my mom would have called over the maitre d' and demanded that he turn off the air conditioning, regardless of what anyone else wanted.

Knowing that I reacted differently in this situation comforted me. On the other hand, my years of mother-daughter work have taught me to appreciate ways that I mirror my mom: in her high energy, her love of dance, her joy in beauty, her desire to make the world a better place. Now that she is gone, the more I can integrate her in myself, the more fully I can claim my own potential.

"It is not essential, or even preferable, that we see mirrors of ourselves when we look at our daughters," says marriage and family therapist Judy

Barber of Family Money Consultants LLC in San Francisco. "Daughters need to meet their own challenges and make their own mistakes without feeling overshadowed by our biases and experiences."

Steve Swartz, an attorney, mediator, and business consultant who is a colleague of Judy's, says that he has "a lot of scar tissue on my tongue from biting it so I don't interfere with my children's lives." This is a hard lesson for any parent to learn.

Working with Mom

Women-owned businesses are a growing segment of the U.S. economy. And like many proud fathers who hope to welcome Junior into the firm, some of these women will invite their daughters to join them.

I greatly admire those mothers who trust their daughters enough to share control, giving them a chance to develop their own expertise and leadership style. Unfortunately, these working relationships are more often fraught with conflict. The mother has difficulty giving up control to her child, while the daughter struggles for her mom's respect and the power to make decisions herself. The clash of these deep-seated behaviors can compromise the health of the business and lead to family explosions.

Some female financial advisors serve as their mother's money manager, like Holly Hunter, a principal of Hunter Advisor LLC in Portsmouth, New Hampshire. But since the complexities of the mother-daughter bond can generate stresses that aren't present in other client relationships, I believe it can be a much more restful solution for an advisor to refer her mother to a colleague.

By the same token, it may benefit a mother-daughter firm to bring in a family business consultant who will have an ongoing advisory role. An independent professional with no ax to grind can help a family-centered system evolve along healthy lines of mutual respect and empowerment.

How You Can Help

In almost all mother-daughter pairs, the struggle for connection and control makes it a real challenge to work out a satisfactory relationship. In *You're Wearing THAT? Understanding Mothers and Daughters in Conversation* (Random House, 2006), linguistics specialist Deborah Tannen notes that mothers and daughters both have a deep desire to be seen for who they really are, and to be fully accepted and cherished. But each person tends to see the other as falling short of who she should be. Tannen believes that each overestimates the other's power to define her, and underestimates her own power to claim her identity. Both mother and daughter also underrate their power to wound each other. Often, neither really knows where the other person is until someone crosses a line and hurts or angers the other.

To resolve a dysfunctional relationship, it's important for each person to become more aware of her own defensive fears, expectations, and longings. Instead of looking for the other individual to meet her every desire, she has to learn to take responsibility for her own needs. By lightening the load they've put on each other, they can develop a more equal relationship.

When this complex dynamic affects a client's well-being, often the most helpful thing you can do is to assist the mother and daughter in communicating with each other. My suggestion would be for you to meet with them individually as well as together, to make sure they feel their needs and concerns are being fully heard and attended to.

While the intensity of their bond makes it possible for some mothers and daughters to have open and intimate conversations, you will find that others are incapable of being honest about their feelings and desires in the presence of one another. This is especially true of daughters who fear losing their mother's love if they displease them or disagree with them too strongly. Regardless of one's age, the yearning for mother-love never disappears.

Failure to Communicate

When a mother visits a grown-up daughter in the daughter's home, can the mother surrender her need to be in charge? Does she criticize the ways her daughter chooses to spend money on herself, her home, or her children? Does the daughter react by attacking her mother's imperfections?

When old patterns like these thwart communication between a mother and daughter, Deborah Tannen, professor of sociolinguistics at Georgetown University, proposes Instant Messaging and e-mail as ways to stimulate new dialogue.

Laura Tracy, a Washington, D.C., family therapist and author who specializes in counseling mother-daughter pairs, sometimes suggests that her clients get together to watch a movie about mothers and daughters. If they have trouble talking to one another without conflict, this can help break the ice by leading to a discussion of the film couple's strengths and weaknesses. If your own clients would like to try this, I'd suggest a movie like *Postcards from the Edge, The Joy Luck Club, Divine Secrets of the Ya-Ya Sisterhood, Steel Magnolias,* or *Terms of Endearment.*

Once you understand the degree of closeness and connection between a mother and daughter, it will be easier for you to help both women find more peace in the relationship and in themselves. As each one gets better at surrendering demands on herself and the other person, she will be able to focus on her own growth and empowerment. In this process, they will become better mothers and better daughters, and healthier individuals.

CHAPTER 2

Child Is Father to the Man

Few money messages are as enduring as the ones a son learns from his dad.

"I'm gonna be like you, dad. You know I'm gonna be like you."

I doubt if there are many parents who can listen to Harry Chapin sing "Cat's in the Cradle" without a shiver of emotion. Whether present or absent, loving or rejecting, fathers have a tremendous influence on what their sons grow up to do and be.

Consciously or unconsciously, a son learns from his dad about work, money, family, and relationships with women and with other men, as well as how to make his way in the world. For good or ill, he will bear the effects of this experience for the rest of his life.

There is good news for fathers who fear they were less than perfect as a teacher or role model when their sons were children: Paternal influence is a lifelong force. "Fathering doesn't end when a son is 21, or 41, or even 61," says Neil Chethik, an author and speaker specializing in men's issues, in "Fathers, Sons, and Loss: What We Can Learn" (UU World, Jan./Feb. 2001). "Throughout our lives, right up until the time of our deaths, we fathers can deepen our relationships with our sons, even when a positive father-son connection failed to form during the son's childhood."

Good fathers provide love and affection, acceptance and respect, and kind and firm limit-setting, so their sons learn the boundaries of acceptable social behavior. They support their sons' unique gifts, values, and personalities, giving up their own desire to be validated by having their offspring follow in their footsteps. This kind of relationship helps a son develop his own healthy autonomy and self-respect, so he's not dependent on his dad's stamp of approval to know that his own life choices have merit.

In this process, both father and son must care for and communicate openly with each other. This helps them learn from each other, in the best possible sense of the word, as men who share mutual respect.

"Just Like You, Dad"

Outside of his clinical setting, a surgeon I know appears very imposing, cool, and remote. But with a patient, he miraculously transforms into the most sensitive guy you can imagine. I was amazed to learn that three of his children had also become physicians or surgeons and had joined his practice. The father smiled happily when I commented on this, and his nurse whispered to me, "He never pushed this on any of them. It's astonishing!"

In families where a father clearly loves his work and is good at it, it's actually not that surprising if his sons (and these days, daughters too) want to follow his example. Unfortunately, a father's bad habits are just as likely to imprint on the younger generation. For example, sons whose fathers are slaves to work may grow up to be workaholics themselves.

Ted Klontz, a life skills coach in Nashville who leads workshops to change people's relationships with money, told me that he was raised on a farm by a father and grandfather who felt that anyone who didn't toil day in and day out was lazy. He grew up believing that if he worked hard enough, the money would take care of itself. As a result, he didn't save much and did no financial planning. In fact, he became what I call a "money monk," believing it was grasping and miserly to think about money.

Vowing not to be like his father, Ted's son Brad paid off his student loans as quickly as possible, saved like a demon, and invested as much as he could in the stock market. After years of building a career as a clinical psychologist with a number of diverse specialties, Brad realized that he had become like his dad, after all. Like Ted, he was working 80 hours a week.

By communicating honestly and vulnerably, and "walking their talk" as they teach others how to have a healthier relationship with money, Brad and Ted have been able to bring about powerful changes in themselves. Ted now pays attention to his finances and has developed a more balanced life. Brad is cutting down his work schedule to spend more time with his fiancée and other loved ones. They're an inspiring duo: a self-aware father and son who are working to correct imbalances in their lives by practicing the nonhabitual and communicating positively with each other.

Fathers and Sons

Fathers' expectations of their sons can lead to instances where the son feels not-good-enough, no matter how successful he is. A West Coast financial planner told me that he had just earned CFP certification when his father inherited a million dollars. Instead of trusting him with this money, his father invested it with two brokers. Not only did the two charge exorbitant fees, but they mismanaged the funds so badly that the $1 million eroded to $350,000. After the young planner got over his hurt feelings, he kept trying to advise his father on how to invest more sensibly. To this day, he told me, his dad refuses to give him any respect or credit for his professional expertise and persists in trusting the questionable competence of the two brokers. In this case, it's starkly evident that the dad's distrust hurt him as well as his offspring.

When you encounter a situation where a father is reluctant to trust and respect his son, anecdotes like these may be useful in educating your client. In some instances, you may be able to intervene with specific advice.

For example, Rich Colman, a principal in the Colman Knight Advisory Group in Carlisle, Massachusetts, told me about a business-owning client who was convinced that his newly graduated son would never succeed in the company. The son, a "social worker-type" in his dad's eyes, hoped to travel in Europe for a while before going to work for a multinational corporation.

Colman suggested that since the client's company imported items from Taiwan, he could send his son to work in that end of the business. The job would allow the young man to travel, while saving the company $250,000 a year. The son was game to try it, and his dad hesitantly agreed. The upshot was that during the three years the client's son spent in Taiwan, he became fluent in Mandarin Chinese and developed skills that complemented his father's. The company's sales tripled, profits zoomed, and now the father and son are business partners. The happy father describes his son as "different from me, but just as effective."

Some fathers refuse to give up authority even if their son's expertise in a particular area is greater than their own. Part of your task is to help sons like these claim their own authority despite their father's failure to acknowledge their gifts. At the same time, you can try to encourage stubborn fathers to let go of their pride and arrogance and be more open to their son's unique qualities.

Absentee Dad Syndrome

When a boy mouths off, acts out, or otherwise rebels against authority, a dad who puts in 70-hour weeks at the office might be tempted to say to the mom, "Don't blame me for the way he's turned out. I wasn't even here!" But growing up without the presence of an accepting, supportive father can cause as many problems as anything a more involved mother may have said or done.

In a landmark *Psychology Today* article titled "Fathers & Sons" (September 1993), Atlanta psychiatrist Dr. Frank Pittman observed that when the Industrial Revolution made it necessary for someone to leave home to work, it was the father who usually ended up bringing home the bacon. Often coming home only at night and on weekends, these "provider" dads became less and less involved in parenting. Instead, they found other roles in the family, such as disciplinarian ("Wait till your father comes home!") or audience ("Tell Daddy what you did today").

Dr. Pittman believes that many fathers have become so fixated on succeeding at work that they have "moved out" of the house emotionally. I would add that divorce, separation, and non-negotiable job pressures swell the ranks of absentee dads. This leaves many sons with what Dr. Pittman calls "father hunger," longing for a closer physical and emotional connection with their dad.

In short, he suggests that the traditional patriarchal presence, which overwhelmed and intimidated sons for millennia, has over the past 200 years become a deficiency in many families: "too little father." Instead of fearing an all-powerful sire, today's sons are more likely to long for their father to love them, bond with them, teach them, and give them approval and validation.

Stepfathers and Sons

These days, the "father" role in many households is filled by a stepfather. It's hard to generalize about the influence of these men on their stepsons. A lot depends on how strong the birth father's relationship is with his son, how long the stepfather has been in the picture, and how active a role the stepfather takes in parenting his stepson. From personal experience, I can testify that my son's birth father was his primary influence in many areas. In financial matters, however, Anil quickly learned that his stepfather was the wisest and best-balanced role model. He now emulates his stepdad not just in money management, but also in his leanings toward a writing or academic career. Sometimes the impact of a stepfather's influence just isn't predictable.

Money and Masculinity

To make up for their absence, some dads overgive money to their sons, though cash is always a poor substitute for time. In many cases, it also leads to boys growing to adulthood knowing that they're expected to be good at managing money, without having had any fatherly coaching on how to do it.

Recent research confirms my clinical experience that young men learn about money mainly from their fathers. There are exceptions, of course, if Dad is absent too much or Mom is the family's primary money manager. But as a rule, sons are deeply affected by their father's views on finances.

These lessons can start at a relatively early age. Rick Kahler, president of Kahler Financial Group in Rapid City, South Dakota, began giving his son Davin an allowance at age 3. At first, Davin spent the money every week. On one trip to a toy store, Rick said, they ran from toy to toy with Davin asking, "How much?" Rick would tell him if he could afford it or, if not, how many weeks it would take to save up the money. "We had many shopping trips that ended in tears as he painfully figured out that there was far more he wanted than dollars in his pocket," Rick says. "I'll never forget the first Saturday he walked out of the store, having bought nothing and with his allowance still in his pocket!"

Paul Feinberg, a retired tax lawyer and estate planner in Cleveland, saw that children of his wealthy clients were often totally in the dark about family assets, and he decided to make sure that wouldn't be the case with his two boys. Starting when they were in high school with a briefing on family assets and income, he progressed to regular meetings to discuss the family's financial status.

Paul viewed each stage in his sons' life as a learning opportunity. When each of them received an inheritance from their grandmother, he coached them about earmarking a small percentage for spending, while saving the lion's share for important long-term goals. In college, they were given each semester's expense money upfront to help them gain experience in budgeting. Now 36 and 31, his money-savvy sons also consult with financial advisors to ensure their plans are on track. With open communication and frequent family money meetings, Paul has helped them grow into knowledgeable financial consumers.

Money messages aren't always communicated through words. Some fathers simply live out their beliefs. Their children often grow up either imitating their behavior, or vowing to be just the opposite. Spender dads may have sons who are spenders or anti-spenders (i.e., hoarders). Workaholic dads may raise sons who either labor as they do, like Ted and Brad Klontz, or react to their work obsession by focusing instead on *la dolce vita*. The rebellious sons of overly controlling fathers may amass enough money to get out from under Dad's thumb, or develop a lifestyle that distances them from money as much as possible. "Like father, like son" is sometimes true, and sometimes just the opposite.

Man to Man

As boys grow into men, they struggle with asserting their independence while still yearning for their father's caring and protection. Since power in our culture often involves money, this ambivalence can show up in a variety of problems and issues that clients bring to your office. By thoughtfully probing the dynamics of the relationship, you may be able to help develop solutions that preserve the dignity of both father and son.

What Women Want

Davin Kahler, five years old and in the throes of a crush on a friend of the same age, recently informed his dad, Rick Kahler of Kahler Financial Group, that he knew what "ladies" liked in a guy. Rick told me that when he asked what that was, Davin informed him, "Well, Dad, they like funny stories" (check); "candy" (check); "flowers" (check); "for you to be smart" (check); "for you to be cute" (check); "good manners" (check), "and for you to have money!" Although Rick says that he and his young son have "just begun our money journey," it sounds like Davin is well on his way there.

For example, when the two meet as adults, who pays? David Mermelstein, Ph.D., a fellow therapist and friend of mine in Bethesda, Maryland, described his almost comic dilemma when meeting his son Mark for lunch. David would offer to pay. Mark would insist on paying for himself. They'd go back and forth about it. Finally, David got the message. Instead of offering to pay at the end of the meal, he just sat there. So did Mark! After asking his son what was going on, the confused dad eventually uncovered the young man's mixed feelings: he wanted to feel and appear competent and self-supporting, but also liked to feel under his father's protective wing. They found a nonverbal solution: when Mark wanted to pay for himself, he would reach for his wallet; if he didn't, David paid. This gave Mark the flexibility to adjust his needs for independence and fatherly nurturing as time went on.

One of the most precious gifts you can offer a male client is your assistance in helping him forge a respectful and loving relationship with his son or father. When a father denies that his son has grown into capable manhood, the wounds can last for a lifetime. Whatever you can do to promote respect, acceptance, and understanding will gain you the gratitude of current and future clients in both generations.

CHAPTER 3

Brother and Sister, Where Art Thou?

So you think kids from the same family should all get along great? Oh, brother!

To judge by the Genesis story of Cain and Abel, sibling rivalry has been going on as long as there have been siblings. Although this rivalry usually stops short of murder and mayhem, there's no question that money can heighten tensions between brothers, not to mention between brother and sister or sister and sister.

Witness an account I recently read of a grudge match between two brothers, heirs to the Singer Sewing Machine fortune. One was a rambunctious bon vivant who settled in Paris; the other a hard-working, sedate businessman from upstate New York. Both were avid art collectors with impeccable taste. They competed fiercely for Impressionist and modern masterpieces, gloating whenever they bested each other. Meeting in a lawyer's office to sort out some money matters, they got into a fistfight and didn't speak to each other for the rest of their lives. What a horrible waste—but what a familiar story!

Sibling relationships can be harmonious, acrimonious, cooperative, competitive, warm, cold, intensely connected, or distant and disengaged. If you had one or more brothers or sisters, you probably learned your place in relation to them. See if any of these phrases apply to you:

- "I was the smart one, but not pretty"

- "I was the good-looking one, but stupid"

- "My sister was the rebel; I was the goody-two-shoes"

- "I was the 'bad kid'; my brother was Mr. Perfect"

Some sibs are raised to cooperate and look after each other, while others are pitted against each other ("Why can't you be as sensible as your brother?").

Mix in each child's individual personality and temperament, and the potential for complications is almost limitless.

These family scripts and roles often pollute sibling relationships well into adulthood. As the fortunes of the individuals involved grow and change, their connections can undergo dramatic ups and downs.

In Money Matters, Siblings Aren't Clones

Siblings may share chromosomes, but often have completely different money personalities. You've probably noticed divergent money attitudes and behaviors among sibs in your own family.

"Since I am in the business of helping others understand their money issues, I often look at my own children," says Chrisanne Cubby, a Money-Path financial life planning coach with Temenos Inc. of Watertown, Connecticut. She noticed early on that the oldest and youngest of her four children were savers like her, while the middle two took after their spender father. Now in their 20s, the middle siblings have significant credit card balances. The oldest and youngest are building up savings and have no debt.

Like Chrisanne's children, some kids follow the example of one or both parents in the way they manage their finances. Others may rebel against a parent's moneystyle—becoming a spender, for example, in reaction to parental frugality. A few seem to develop an independent money personality without being influenced by anyone else. Taking stock of the differences among siblings in your own family can give you more tolerance and compassion for the range of money behaviors your clients display.

When Mom and Dad Play Favorites

Siblings' early perceptions that "Mom loved me best" or "Dad never thought I'd amount to anything" may be reinforced by preferential treatment by parents. For instance, spender children may end up being repeatedly bailed out by Mom and Dad, while sibs who are savers struggle on without any financial aid. If this inequity continues, it may not only create tremendous hostility between the siblings but also make the "neglected" child resent the parents' favoritism.

The worst-case scenario is when unfair treatment occurs after Dad's or Mom's death. At that point, there's no recourse for a child whose feelings have been badly hurt by the terms of the parent's will.

A PBS program some time ago chronicled a lopsided legacy involving three siblings: a doctor, a police officer, and a teacher. Their parents left the bulk of their money to the last two, figuring that the more affluent doctor didn't need it. Unfortunately, they never told their offspring what they were doing, or why. When the will was made public after their deaths, the son who was a doctor felt hurt, angry, and rejected. It seemed to him that his parents had punished him for his success.

If these parents had explained their plans to each child individually, they could have greatly reduced the potential for later resentment between the siblings. If the doctor son had heard them describe their pride in his accomplishments and their concern for his less wealthy sibs, it might not have upset him so much to receive a smaller inheritance than the others.

Jealousy between siblings can also arise when parents try to make up for previous unequal treatment. Ted Klontz, Ph.D., president of Onsite Workshops in Nashville, Tennessee, tells of a client couple who were being emotionally blackmailed by their youngest son, a drug addict who had run away from home and was living with another addict. Guilt-tripping his parents with the argument that "You didn't pay for college, so you owe me," he had squeezed a good deal of cash out of them. After working with Ted, the parents realized that they were feeling guilty about having given less of themselves to this son than to their other children. The money they were heaping on him was actually reparations for their past neglect. Meanwhile, the addict's three siblings were now jostling in line for similar handouts.

Klontz helped this couple get honest with themselves and their children. In family meetings, the four siblings learned exactly how much money their parents planned to leave them. The amount was the same for

When Siblings Want Reparations

It's not uncommon for adult children to feel they were neglected by their parents while a sibling got all the emotional goodies. Intra-family financial disputes are often based on the resulting desire for "war reparations."

The desire to be compensated for past deprivation is understandable, but it is not a realistic goal to pursue. Rather, the neglected sibling needs to work with his anger, hurt, and feelings of rejection, so he can ultimately forgive the other sibling or parents and they can go on to forge more adult relationships.

If a client seems to be seeking an outcome that will make up for past wrongs, I would recommend trying to steer her to some type of therapeutic intervention (see "Refereeing Sibling Bouts"). A trained therapist can help clients learn to let go of the irrational demand to assuage old hurts with money, and to seek a more equitable result based on the current reality of their situation. Family counseling or mediation may be necessary to heal some of the wounds, if they are deep and painful.

each, and each could choose whether to receive it now or later. As the youngest child learns to disengage himself from financial dependence, Klontz's clients no longer have to worry that their children will bankrupt them.

The Importance of Fairness

I'm not recommending that parents should always treat their children with absolute financial equality. Granted, this is an admirable goal, but there are cases where "equal" is not fair. For example, if one child has a severe mental or physical disability, the parents will obviously need to spend more on that child's needs.

David Drucker, an Albuquerque financial planner and principal of Drucker Knowledge Systems, told me about a self-made millionaire who consulted him for planning help. One of the man's three children badly needed financial assistance because of a serious medical condition that affected his ability to work. But the father, who had come from humble beginnings, strongly believed that children should learn to make it on their own. He also wanted to treat his three kids equally. As a result, he refused to favor the physically handicapped son.

In a situation like this, it could be helpful for an advisor to partner with a therapist or counselor and invite the siblings and their father into the office for a talk. The dad's opinion about withholding financial help from his offspring could be explored and even challenged.

He might discover that the two children who didn't need assistance as desperately would encourage him to make an exception for the brother who was more in need. I honestly believe that most siblings will accept an inequality like this. But it's crucial for family members to share their

---

Separate but Equal

Parents often try to "equalize" distributions to avoid upsetting their children, but you may be able to suggest a different solution that will be more beneficial for everyone. For example, clients of Rick Kahler's wanted to give one of their four children $30,000 as a down payment to buy a home. In order not to be unfair to the others, they asked Rick, a financial planner in Rapid City, South Dakota, if they could afford to withdraw $120,000 to make gifts to all four kids.

Feeling that this move would compromise their financial security, Rick suggested instead that they make a no-interest, open-ended $30,000 loan to the child who wanted to buy a house. They could then write a codicil to their will stating that all loans would be forgiven at their death, and that an equal amount (adjusted for inflation) would be distributed to the other children.

The parents enthusiastically endorsed this solution, which honored their desire for ultimate equality while allowing them to support one of their offspring at a time of need. In addition, it had a much smaller impact on their savings than withdrawing $120,000 would have had.

thoughts and feelings with one another, and learn to empathize with each other's situation. Whatever you can do to encourage this continuing dialogue will ultimately benefit your clients, and your own bond with them.

Raised to Fight

Sometimes you may encounter siblings who have been encouraged by a parent to battle each other. The most egregious example I've heard was that of a difficult, bitter man who kept all his money in his own name and refused to make a will. When someone pointed out how unfair this was to his wife and two children, he growled, "Let 'em fight over it when I'm gone."

So much intense emotion can be generated in families—often rooted in the past and exacerbated by more recent actions and decisions—that it is crucial for advisors to help family members learn to communicate clearly and to make simple, well-understood decisions while the parents are still alive. When siblings try to sort this out on their own, terrible rifts can arise.

The mother of a friend of mine constantly pitted her against her sister. My friend attempted to appease her mom's critical nature by pleasing her any way she could. The other daughter reacted to their mother's temperament by moving as far away as possible. When the mother's health failed, my friend became her caregiver and eventually inherited her mom's house. Though she felt she deserved this legacy, the lifelong distrust instilled by her mother made her expect that her sister would be angry and resentful about it. As a result, she was fearful of her sister's attempts to contact her. Years after their mother's death, the unacknowledged subject of the house remained a source of distance between the two siblings.

Here's another case where a financial professional who is a therapeutic educator, or working in tandem with a therapist or counselor, might have helped this mother and her two daughters create a solution that everyone could accept with more serenity.

Help for Battling Brothers (or Sisters)

When tension-prone siblings have a hard time finding common ground on an issue, invite them to revisit the old memories that may be at the root of their difficulty. You could ask them to write out their answers to the following questions at home. Or if you're working with a therapy professional, the siblings may be comfortable talking through their responses with you both.

1. What are your most positive memories involving you and your sibling?

2. What are your most painful, upsetting memories involving you and your sibling?

3. Are there unforgiven hurts that still bother you from the past? If so, what are they?

4. What could your sibling do or say to salve these wounds or heal them completely? What would a heartfelt apology or act of contrition look like or sound like?

5. Do you have any regrets about how you treated your sibling? If so, what could you do to make amends? Be specific.

6. If you could have any kind of a relationship with your sibling, what would it look like, feel like, be like?

7. Describe some aspect of your sibling's personality or character that you really appreciate.

Who Will Take Care of Mom?

Speaking of caregiving, we all know situations where one child in the family bears most of the burden of care for an elderly parent. The caregiver often resents his or her siblings, whose lives aren't impacted by this heavy responsibility. As old folks live longer and longer, you can expect to see more consequences of this in your office.

If it's impractical for the other sibs to contribute time in equal measure, Rick Kahler, president of Kahler Financial Group in Rapid City, South Dakota, suggests a creative solution: the parent(s), the other siblings, or both could pay the sibling who is the primary caregiver. After all, the family would otherwise have to hire someone to provide this service. (Home health aides now earn an average of $20 an hour, according to MetLife research.) This "salary" could make the caregiving sibling feel more valued by the rest of the family. It may also relieve some guilt for the siblings who don't live nearby, or for other reasons haven't been able to take on a share of the burden.

Staying Connected Despite Income Differences

Conflicts often arise when clients are financially better off than their siblings. Ted Klontz described to me a situation involving a client who had prospered despite coming from a poor family where the kids were taught that accumulating wealth was immoral. The client had to work hard to overcome this ingrained belief so he could enjoy his hard-earned money. But when he tried to share his good fortune with his siblings in the form of gifts or tickets to expensive events, they rebuffed his generosity (which may have been tinged with "wealth is bad" guilt).

With Klontz's help, this client learned that he had to give himself enough self-validation to keep on living his own lifestyle in serenity. He needed to give up the fantasy that his siblings would ever accept and approve of his success.

I think unsolicited gifts to less affluent siblings are just fine, if offered with grace ("It would really make me happy if we could take this trip together") and without strings attached. When a brother or sister is truly in need, it can be praiseworthy for their more affluent sibling to help out. But there needs to be ample communication between the siblings about where the giver is coming from and how the givee feels about accepting the gift. (It's never okay to force a gift upon an unwilling recipient.)

There are other situations where family members have developed a parasitical dependence, never repaid loans, and strained marriages by begging for funds that their sibling and her spouse had put aside for their own future security. In these cases, I recommend open communication and a gradual weaning away from such enabling "help."

When a client asks about lending money to a family member, I know many financial advisors would say, "Don't do it!" I advise my own clients that if push comes to shove, make the money a gift—and never part with more than you can afford to lose. In this respect, life is like an in-flight emergency: you have to put on your own oxygen mask before helping others.

Suing a Sibling

Dealing with a sibling isn't like dealing with an acquaintance, or even a friend. You can say no to a buddy and still (in many cases) retain the friendship. But there's a special relationship between members of a birth family. Even in adulthood, older siblings often feel they need to look after younger sisters or brothers. A younger sibling may feel indebted to an older one who took care of her earlier.

A client of mine, whom I'll call Jack, once asked me to help resolve his inner conflict about suing his brother. Born and raised in the Midwest, Jack had moved east and only returned home now and then to see his parents, brothers and sisters, and friends. On one of his visits home, he learned that his younger brother, Steve, had taken over their aging parents' financial affairs.

It had always been Jack's understanding that everything would be shared equally among the five siblings, so he was surprised at the secrecy that now prevailed. Finally his sister Sally told him that Steve had somehow managed to acquire certain mineral rights that paid $1,500 a month, while the other children received mineral rights worth about $35 a month. Sally also revealed that when she challenged Steve about this disparity in front of their parents, Steve agreed to split the $1,500 with her. None of the other siblings was told about this agreement.

When Jack got over his stupefaction, he confronted Steve and Sally. Both of them insisted that they were only honoring their parents' wishes, and that nothing was going to change their minds.

When Jack consulted me, he was trying to decide whether or not to take his brother to court in order to regain what was rightfully his. His older sister, Julie, had warned him that that she would bear the brunt of family conflict and pain if he took legal action, since she lived near Steve while Jack lived a thousand miles away.

I helped Jack become aware that if he sued Steve, he might cause a rift that would end up destroying their connection and stressing other family relationships. He might win the lawsuit and end up with more money, but lose his brother.

In the years since then, Jack has thanked me several times for helping him decide to let go of his anger and leave the matter alone. He believes it was the right decision for him, and for the good of the family as well.

Bringing Siblings Together Again

Many sibling conflicts can only be resolved with the involvement of a third party or an event that transcends old grudges. In the case of the sewing-machine dynasty that I mentioned earlier, granddaughters of the two feuding brothers eventually met at the Metropolitan Museum of Art during an exhibition of the family's acquisitions. Finding common ground, they are reforging connections between the estranged branches of the family. Imagine the years of spite and anguish that might have been avoided if the two brothers had had a good family therapist, working in tandem with a therapeutically sensitive financial advisor, to bridge their differences!

In a similar vein, a friend of mine found herself at odds with her younger sister over a house they had jointly inherited from an aunt. My friend, who had been close to the older woman during her final years, felt it was her aunt's desire to keep the house in the family. The sister, living farther away, disagreed. The intensity of emotions brought on a break between the sisters.

The outside event that changed everything was a cancer scare for the younger sister. Her older sibling rushed to be with her, and they rekindled their relationship during the tense days of waiting for test results. Fortunately, the scare proved to be groundless. To preserve the harmony whose value they both now recognized, my friend agreed to put their aunt's house on the market.

Of course, disputing siblings can't rely on the intervention of a *deus ex machina*, whether in the form of a suspicious lump or an art exhibition, to help them reconcile. That's where you come in. By providing a safe place and a respectful process to air highly charged thoughts and feelings, you may be able to help all parties sit down together and brainstorm creative solutions to a difficult issue. Your presence (perhaps combined with that of a therapist or counselor) will breathe air into a closed family system, allowing problems to be resolved much sooner with less destructive fallout.

Refereeing Sibling Bouts

When you're dealing with sibling friction over money, these guidelines may help steer you toward a satisfying resolution for the parties involved:

1. **Assess the level of good will.** If relationships are impaired but still workable, it may be wise to have a mediator or a trained therapy professional join you to help family members negotiate about the situation at hand. This will free you to exercise your financial and practical skills without becoming tangled in emotional conflict. If hurt, anger, and recrimination have built up to toxic levels, I'd recommend that all parties first seek help from a therapist or counselor to sort out and lighten their emotional baggage.

2. **Try to get the siblings' parents on board.** In general, I advise parents not to make decisions that their kids will have to try to interpret after their deaths. This can lead to

acrimony and escalating conflict. It's far better for a parent to divide assets in advance, fairly and sensibly, having communicated to their spouse and children not only what they are doing but what they hope to achieve.

When sibling money issues are rooted in parental decisions, ask Dad and Mom to explain their wishes and desires. If there are any reasons not to treat all sibs equally, make sure everyone understands them. Discuss what the other sib(s) need or want to feel well taken care of.

3. **Remember the importance of family.** When identifying what you want to accomplish in working with siblings, remember the importance of positive family connections. Try to balance this goal with the desire to save your clients money or maximize their net worth. Ally with the best parts of your clients.

4. **Know when you need professional support.** If siblings are struggling with loaded and difficult issues, such as who will take care of a frail parent or whether to provide financial support to another sib, be aware that elements of this decision may fall outside your area of expertise. If you're worrying about these clients or losing sleep over their problems, consider bringing in a trained professional—a social worker or family counselor, for example—who can help them navigate difficult waters.

5. **Beware of your own prejudices.** If you are grappling with some of these issues yourself (having conflicts with a sibling over money, for example, or struggling with your spouse about whether to help a needy sister or brother), you may unwittingly project your own feelings onto a client in similar circumstances. If it's hard for you to separate your situation from theirs, seek consultative and/or separate help for your clients. And consider working with a therapy professional of your own to help find peace with your personal challenges.

A Sister's Story

When my father was on his deathbed, he spent his last evening with my brother Stu and me, in a sweet communion that is still fresh in my mind years later. Early the next morning he called his caregiver, Bea, to his side and told her how proud he was of his two children. Then he asked her in a troubled voice, "What should I do about these two rings I wear? One is worth much more than the other. How can I decide which one to give to which child?" Bea said, "Your kids have always worked things out. They'll figure out this one, too." My father smiled and said, "You're right." A little while later he died singing—he "sang himself out."

I don't even remember now how we divided the rings. But as co-heirs, we cooperated fully with each other—working together, for example, to coordinate distributions from annuities that we had jointly inherited.

I know Stu and I are extremely lucky. We had our moments—well, make that "years"—of distance when we were younger and developing our adult identities. But as grownups, we have made the effort to communicate honestly and compassionately. That gave me confidence that we would be able to resolve any disagreements arising from our father's legacy.

One of the most important tasks in our lives is to make sure our relationship continues to be close and satisfying. We'll both work hard to make that happen. After all, we're family.

PART II

Dealing with Differences

Most likely, you're an expert on yourself. You have a good idea of how you're apt to think, feel, and act about important things. That probably means you also understand people who are like you. But among your clients, there may be dozens or scores of individuals or couples who are completely different in culture, gender, education, religion, class, or nationality. Even within a family, or between a couple, there can be dramatic contrasts. Somehow, you need to deal with a whole range of unfamiliar and maybe unheard-of differences in order to connect with these folks.

The next chapters will help by exploring how ethnic, cultural, national, and religious backgrounds can influence how people see money. We'll also look at how gender differences—both hard-wired and culturally fostered—tend to affect money attitudes and behavior.

Generalizations like these can be dangerous, of course, if they prompt you to treat a client as a stereotype. At best, they may help you recognize how other people are different from you. With this as a backdrop, you can deepen your understanding of a particular client's attitudes and behavior.

Knowing how and when to use what you learn is a delicate exercise—an art much more than a science. For example, if a client happens to be Chinese and you make a comment that plays off a Chinese stereotype, the client may easily feel pigeonholed and offended (even if your comment is positive). On the other hand, the same client may be grateful if you diplomatically point out that his or her attitude about money is not unusual among other Chinese. As long as your approach is not judgmental or demeaning, you can help clients feel better understood and less lonely, with a stronger sense of belonging to their group of origin.

You might consider using your understanding to help some clients expand beyond the place they're starting from. For example, a man who is accustomed to making unilateral decisions about money may be able to improve the intimacy of a relationship by learning how to share decision-making more equally with his partner. A risk-averse woman who learns to overcome her "bag lady" fears and take intelligent financial risks is likely to gain greater confidence in other areas of her life.

In all cases, remember that understanding differences just gives you a new set of lenses to see more clearly where a client is coming from. Ultimately, each of your clients needs to be viewed as a unique individual who is influenced by a complex mix of factors. The differences in their various backgrounds can simply give you more ways to reach them and help them move toward achieving their goals.

CHAPTER 4

Typecasting

Stereotyping can alienate clients—or get them more on board with you. It's all in how you communicate.

Innate gender differences prevent more women from succeeding in science and math careers. An old stereotype, you say? Just a few years ago this view was put forth by Lawrence Summers, then president of Harvard University, to the outrage of many female academics.

Despite our wishful thinking, stereotypes remain alive and well, and for many reasons they're a phenomenon that fascinates me. We all know that stereotyping can lead to pigeonholing people into categories that may be inaccurate and dehumanizing. Even when the stereotypes are positive (French people are fabulous cooks; Asian kids are super students), they tend to block us from seeing people as the unique individuals they are.

Indeed, generalizing can be downright risky. In my years of studying money psychology, however, I've found that stereotypes sometimes provide a valuable shortcut to understanding clients' attitudes and behaviors. In fact, the compassionate use of stereotypes may actually make clients feel less singled out and stigmatized, and it may suggest ways you can help them become more balanced and rational about money.

Let's start with classification systems. After observing human nature as a therapist and coach, I believe that many people's money behavior puts them into one or more of these categories:

Hoarders. These are people who think that money is security, saving is the most important priority, and spending money on immediate pleasure is bad or wasteful.

Spenders. Those who hate to budget, hate even the word "budget," and love to spend on their immediate desires.

Money Worriers. Those who are constantly beset by anxiety that they can't control their money, or don't have enough of it.

Money Avoiders. Those who avoid dealing with their money and are often in a fog about how much they earn, spend, owe, or have saved.

When I explain these categories in a talk or workshop, the audience's reaction is usually amused relief, not indignation at being pigeonholed. Why don't more people feel annoyed that I have created these "boxes" into which their behavior can be described and placed?

One reason is that I try not to stigmatize anyone in these categories, and I openly admit to being a recovering overspender who loves to buy clothes. That admission allows other spenders to relate to me and feel that I'm not judging them harshly. By sharing my imperfections, I make it easier for clients to own up to theirs.

Also, the use of classifications reassures people that they are not alone in exhibiting certain attitudes and behaviors. I believe this serves as a healing influence, giving them a little more space to decide whether these tendencies are serving them well.

Of course, there are instances (albeit infrequently) when people don't like being classified or put in a box. If I encounter someone like this, I simply dispense with the money category concept. Instead, we proceed on the basis of their self-description, along with their comments about what makes them feel good in their moneylife—my term for the way people feel about and deal with money—and what makes them uncomfortable. After asking them to generate these "good" and "bad" lists, I encourage them to reflect on which list was harder to write. Focusing on the more difficult list makes it possible to help them embrace their strengths or gently confront their weaknesses, which is often a vital step in moving forward.

Remember, however, that this situation is rare. In most cases, giving people "handles" to classify their behavior helps them laugh at themselves and feel more connected to others who are struggling with the same money issues.

Gender Stereotypes

There can be a surprising upside in teaching people about gender-related stereotypes. I often begin by alluding to "Defending the Caveman," the hilarious stage show in which Rob Becker analyzes his marriage through the different lenses of men as hunters and women as gatherers. Becker notes that men shop by going out to kill a shirt. They wear it till it dies, then go out and kill another shirt. For women, shopping means gathering—a scarf for a niece's birthday, great shoes on sale for themselves, something else to give a friend next Christmas.

At this point, people are usually chuckling as they recognize themselves and other men and women they know. By introducing stereotypes in this unthreatening way, I think there is the potential to prevent or mitigate countless marital fights between women who shop and men who think it's an incomprehensible waste of time.

An understanding of social and cultural differences can help clients take other relationship problems less personally. For example, I sometimes cite linguist Deborah Tannen's research showing that men are typically raised to compete with others and try to win, while women grow up learning to cooperate, accommodate, and make decisions as part of a team. Awareness of this distinction (which is changing, but more slowly than some of us might like to see) helps couples develop more empathy with each other when struggles and misunderstandings arise.

As another example of male-female differences, boys tend to develop more rigid boundaries when separating from their mothers, while girls maintain more porous or "merged" boundaries. This can lead to habitual tension in a couple if the man's more autonomous decision-making collides with the woman's expectation of collaborative decisions. The stereotype is the husband who announces excitedly, "Guess what, honey? They gave me a great deal on the trade-in, so I got rid of the station wagon and bought a Hummer!"

The wife's ensuing surprise and hurt at his unilateral decision, countered by his indignation at having to "ask for permission," are natural reactions motivated by these sociocultural (and possibly biological) differences. Once this is understood, clients are often able to cultivate more patience for each other's attitudes and perhaps learn to compromise in a way that acknowledges both their natures.

The most moving instance of a gender stereotype healing tensions and resolving conflict is in the area of merged versus separate money. I have posited for many years that one of the most important reasons for husbands to favor merging the couple's money and wives to resist it has been overlooked or misunderstood. It has to do with the different challenges of intimacy for men and women.

When a man wants to merge their accounts, the woman may counter, "Why? Do you want to control me?" Her hurt partner is apt to retort, "Don't you trust me? Are you planning to leave?" While these unpleasant motives may apply in some cases, I believe that the answer usually lies in the unconscious needs of each gender.

In general, getting and staying connected in an intimate relationship is challenging and difficult for men. As John Gray puts it, they tend to withdraw into their caves when they get uncomfortable. If they desire more connection and closeness with a partner, merging money is something relatively easy for them to accomplish. By contrast, women are prone to overgive and overmerge, sometimes losing their identity in a relationship. Keeping some money separate helps them preserve their individuality in the midst of intimacy.

Once couples understand this difference, solutions can be developed to honor the real, underlying needs of each of them. If they both value autonomy, they can keep all their money in "his" and "her" accounts. Or they can combine most of it, leaving some separate funds for her. Or they can merge a certain amount each month for household expenses and savings, and keep the rest in individual accounts for each of them.

By using generalizations like those mentioned above, you may be able to help heal misunderstandings and teach both sides to take their differences less personally. I know that when I bring out these points, I almost always see the eyes in the room go from hard or angry to soft and vulnerable, as the understanding dawns that both men's and women's needs are valid, not contradictory or mutually exclusive.

Racial and Religious Stereotypes

Stereotyping on the basis of race or religion has become a dirty word, and I would agree that the dangers often outweigh the benefits. In some situations, however, your awareness of cultural or religious beliefs behind clients' attitudes or actions may help you work with them more effectively.

For example, suppose a Jewish couple seeks your help in planning how to send their four children to first-class private colleges and graduate schools. After analyzing the situation, it's clear to you that they will not be able to completely fund the kids' educations unless they forgo their own retirement.

You might feel comfortable explaining this straightforwardly to gentile parents. But a caution flag would go up if you know that according to centuries-old cultural traditions, education is all-important in a Jewish family, and parents are considered responsible for ensuring that their children are well educated, no matter what the cost. To avoid stigmatizing the couple as failures or bad parents (at least in their own eyes), it would behoove you to exercise extreme patience and sensitivity in communicating with them. You might note, for instance, that paying the full tab for higher education could well lead to their becoming a burden on the kids in their old age. Far better for the children to apply for grants, loans, and work-study programs that can help them learn responsibility.

Or consider a situation where a young African-American business owner consults you after a profitable year. Your first impulse might be to suggest an appropriate stock portfolio. However, you know research has found that many black investors are more comfortable putting their money in real estate than in the stock market.

While you could be mistaken in assuming that this stereotype is true for your client, ignoring it entirely might be even worse. I would suggest asking this client about his family's attitudes toward money and investing in order to clarify whether or not he is open to buying equities. If he is uncertain, you might want to broaden his perspective by encouraging him to learn more about these investment vehicles. In any case, understanding the messages he was raised with, and how much weight they carried, will help you decide how to proceed and at what pace.

Class Stereotypes

We Americans pride ourselves on having a classless society, or at least one whose upper strata are accessible to newcomers with ability and persistence. However, stereotypes prevail even here.

For example, it's natural to applaud a client who is a self-made success—graduated with honors, became the company's youngest vice president, or started a business and sold it for millions. It's more difficult to understand why such a client won't follow your advice and go on to achieve even more.

When this happens, it reminds me of the stereotype that people resist succeeding beyond their comfort level. The young client who was the first in her family to graduate from college, or the executive who is at the point of exceeding the highest salary his father ever earned, may have conscious or unconscious conflicts about how successful to be. By keeping this possibility in mind, I can sometimes sniff out self-sabotaging patterns manifest in client decision-making or decision avoidance.

Heirs to family money have stereotypical issues of their own. It's common for them to suffer from guilt ("So many other people are poor; I don't deserve this money"), low self-esteem ("Maybe I wouldn't be able to support myself if I had to"), fear and paranoia ("People pretend to like me because they want my money"), shame ("If people knew I was wealthy, they'd hate/envy/reject me, or consider me corrupt or greedy"). Knowing that one or more of these generalizations may well be accurate, I listen for the story behind the money. Once I become familiar with clients' deeper values and longings and the quality of their family relationships, I help them look for a way to embrace their inheritance and use it to reflect their own integrity.

Handle With Care

After making this case for using stereotypes to help classify client needs, I'm going to contradict myself—or, rather, offer a caveat. It's crucial to cultivate an attitude of deep respect for the individual history and journey of every man and woman you see in your practice.

If you start out by being overly invested in any stereotypical notions, true or not (who's to say what makes a stereotype "true," anyway?), you will be pronouncing judgment before even finding out whether the shoe fits. I therefore advocate listening deeply, fully, and carefully to your clients' concerns, desires, goals, and history. If a generalization comes to mind—"She wants to shop around for a new car; he just wants to go out and 'kill' one"—you can decide whether or not to share it. If you keep it to yourself, use it to infuse your suggestions, interventions, and timing with more empathy.

If a money personality type or other categorization jumps to mind when I'm working with a client, I usually check it out with that client at some point. More importantly, I use it to create assignments for clients who seem ready to try expanding beyond their old habits into the greater flexibility that comes from "practicing the nonhabitual."

For instance, if I meet someone whom I would categorize as a money avoider, I can ascertain which tasks or competencies they avoid and find ways to help them take on one or more, with a reward tailor-made for their personality.

If I work with a couple whose conflict appears to arise from cultural male-female differences, I try to help them see that they are not alone and that others have found creative ways through the impasse they are facing.

Just as stereotypes used insensitively can box in and demean clients, a compassionate understanding of these generalizations can expand one's awareness and ways of building relationships. For example, it's no doubt true that women are underrepresented in math and science. What stirred up the storm of outrage at Harvard was the depreciation of women as less capable of committing themselves to such grueling careers. Instead of generalizing in this negative way, it would have been possible to note that family and feelings of connectedness tend to be more important to women, while men are often more single-minded in their work. The idea that one person must be "down" or deficient so the other can be "up" is, forgive me, a male viewpoint. (Of course, that's a stereotype!)

Take some time to think about how you view patterns of culture, religion, class, race, and gender. The way you understand and talk about "stereotypical" notions and categories can either limit your work with clients by squeezing them into a box, or it can offer new ways to inspire them by honoring the unique influences that make them who they are. The choice is yours.

CHAPTER 5

Impersonal Finance

Think gender distinctions don't matter anymore in financial planning? Sorry, many of your clients beg to differ.

In this brave new world, it's generally assumed that catering to gender differences around money is passé. Worse yet, it's not PC. Everyone is equal now; there's no more need for affirmative action to educate women about finance, and no point in male financial advisors learning "female ways of thinking" or vice versa.

But my experience as a psychotherapist tells me that it ain't necessarily so. Not only are there still strong emotional and cultural differences between the sexes, but neither gender is quite as oblivious to the role of money in relationships as we like to think.

A few years ago, for example, my co-author Sherry Christie and I surveyed two groups of women from Mount Holyoke College: one group from the Class of 1968 and the other from the Class of 1996, young enough to be their daughters. Among those graduates who were in intimate relationships, a remarkable 50% earned more than their partners. We asked whether they or their partners had any problem with this reversal of traditional roles, expecting to find higher comfort levels in the younger group.

The first surprise was that only two-thirds of the younger women said they were comfortable outearning their partner, compared to four-fifths of the older group. Among those who were not okay with the situation, a startling 37% of the younger women admitted that both they and their partner were uneasy with the income disparity. Another 50% told us their partner was bothered about it, but they themselves weren't. By contrast, being the high earner concerned 76% of the women in the older "uncomfortable outearners" group. However, they all insisted that the income imbalance didn't bother their partner.

We might conclude that older men, at least, are fine with being outearned by a woman. But I was reminded of some of the interviews I'd done in 2001 for a book I was writing. During these conversations, several well-known women told me, "I make more money than my husband does, but he's fine with it. He doesn't feel threatened at all. But would you mind not mentioning it in the book?" So possibly, older men aren't really as comfortable with being outearned as their wives like to think!

In matters of mores, change often happens much more slowly than the mass media would have us believe. In societal terms, the 28 years between two college classes is the blink of an eye. Should it surprise us to learn that a woman is still not free to outearn a man without risking their relationship?

Journalist and TV producer Linda Ellerbee has an interesting take on this slow-to-change societal bias. She told me that when a woman dates a man who is richer and better known than she is, people are happy for her: "Congratulations! What a great catch!" But when a man dates a woman who is wealthier and more famous than he is, people say to him in a tone of concern, "Are you okay dealing with this? How are you handling it?" So even if he starts out feeling fine about the money differential, he often ends up feeling weird about it.

Money Still Equals Power

Men and women tend to view the same landscape from different vantage points. Generally speaking, both views are valid. But as the preceding examples indicate, there is one area where the difference in perspective is unbalanced: money and power.

While generalizations can mislead when applied to individuals, they are a useful way to sum up gender differences. In my experience, women typically want to share financial power with their intimate partner, regardless of who earns more. But when a man makes more money than his partner, he usually believes he should have primary authority in making the financial decisions.

As Georgetown University linguist Deborah Tannen points out, men are socialized to succeed by defeating their opponents (win-lose), unlike women, who are trained to be accommodating and cooperative (win-win). In addition to viewing relationships hierarchically, men are more self-contained, in contrast to women's desire to be connected with other people.

These two points of difference explain why a man may come home with a new big-screen TV and say proudly, "Look what I got us!" When his dazed and hurt wife protests, "How could you have done this without consulting me?" he's apt to respond with anger and equal hurt, "Do I have to ask your permission? What are you, my mother?" In his one-up, one-down view, he has gone out in the world, battled store clerks and fellow customers, and returned victorious with his prey. In his wife's view, such an important decision should have been made together after a collaborative discussion.

As financial professionals who are "therapeutic educators," you have an opportunity to help couples learn to make decisions as a team, no matter who earns most of the money. If you can encourage them with sensitivity and patience to share power equally, they will be better able to move forward as partners, with their goals aligned to the fullest extent.

Urge them to talk about it with each other and with you, so they can strategize ways to become more comfortable with jointly sharing financial power. It may be useful to discuss the different contributions each of them makes to the relationship and the family's well-being. Perhaps they would be less conscious of their income disparity if each of them contributes to a joint household account in proportion to his or her earnings.

I'm not saying this is easy. Men, whether younger or older, may view sharing financial power as weakening their masculinity. Women who have been single a long time, or have grown up in a family where developing independence was a survival technique, may be no better at sharing decisions than many men are. I recently received an e-mail from a woman like this, the chief earner in her family. For the sake of her career, her husband had moved across the country more than once without apparent resentment. Now he wanted to use $15,000 of their savings to start his own business. Fearing that his lack of business skills meant the money would be wasted, the wife wrote me in search of support for her "rational" position to deny his request.

Although I empathized with both of them, I told her that in the long run, what they did about the money would be less important than how they did it. Unless she and her spouse could share power and decision-making equally, their relationship would suffer from a lack of mutual respect. I advised her that it was vital to build a bridge of communication, empathy, and esteem, so that her husband could come to feel good about himself and his contributions, both in his work and at home.

Establishing a balance of power is also crucial when one partner is the breadwinner and the other stays home to care for the kids. I often recommend that the stay-at-home parent receive regular pay for this job, which is essential to the family's well-being. It's sad that these parents often feel they have no "right" to ask for money for themselves or their children, or must justify to their wage-earner partner just why they need every nickel. We should value raising children enough to award caregivers the recognition and dignity of an appropriate salary.

Separate but Equal?

The fight goes like this. He says: "Why do you want money of your own?" (He thinks: "She's planning to leave me!") She says: "Why do you insist on putting all our money together?" (She thinks: "He wants to control me!")

Aside from whatever grains of truth may inhabit their more paranoid imaginings, there are often unconscious, positive reasons why men may want to merge their money while women prefer to keep at least some funds separate. Men's greatest challenge in intimate relationships is learning to get connected and stay connected. Merging money is one way they can do that. Women's greatest challenge is not losing themselves in the relationship. For them, having money of their own is a way to maintain a healthy, autonomous self.

When both partners understand these differences, the battle is over. They can forge a truce by choosing a financial solution that works for them both. Totally separate money; partly separate and partly joint: either arrangement is fine if it meets their needs. However, totally merged money makes me uncomfortable. At some point in their lives, most women will be alone. That's no time to have to hunt for the checkbook, or to discover that one's spouse has hocked the investment portfolio to secure a margin loan.

Another common area of misunderstanding arises from men's and women's different relationship responsibilities. Even when a man makes less money than his wife, he usually feels the "provider burden." If she tells him, "Would you stop obsessing about the mortgage? You know my paycheck will take care of it!" she truly doesn't understand his world or his worries. No matter how little he earns, or how much he might secretly want to quit his job and write song lyrics, he has probably been brought up to be the provider.

Most women don't feel similar misgivings about downshifting or quitting work to pursue a personal passion. However, that doesn't mean they have an easier time of it. Women's primary burden centers around what has been called "the second shift" or the "Superwoman syndrome"—the responsibility to be all things to all people. They are the ones who clean, cook, wash, shop, chauffeur, wrap birthday presents, look after aging parents, stay in touch with relatives, return items that don't fit, volunteer at school, supervise home repairs, and much more, usually while holding down a job.

As a therapist, I feel it's vital for both women and men to come to understand each other's burdens and empathize with their partner's struggles. Thankfully, more husbands are willing to help around the house these days, although their assistance usually doesn't come close to covering the variety of roles and tasks that women juggle, or the many priorities they mentally reorganize from moment to moment. For their part, women need to understand that some men focus so intensely on their provider responsibilities that they may neglect to consult with their wives on major financial decisions.

Advisors, too, should be cognizant of these responsibilities. First of all, even if a husband is less vocal in a consultation than his higher-paid wife, take care to talk to both of them equally and address both spouses' needs. From the husband's provider viewpoint, an understanding of financial matters is important, and his wife most likely expects that they will make any key decisions jointly.

Second, time is an immensely valuable commodity to women because they have so little of it to themselves. (When asked what kept them from managing their money better, "lack of time" was the single most important reason given by two-thirds of 1968 Mount Holyoke graduates. Among the Class of 1996, it ranked second only to "Not enough money to do anything with.") Help your women clients strategize ways to save time, or use it more productively.

Men and women have different primal fears that correspond to their different burdens. Men tend to fear failing in their provider responsibility by losing their job or dying prematurely and leaving their family poorly provided for.

Women, whose burden is to take care of so many people, are haunted by "bag lady" nightmares in which there is no one to take care of them. They see themselves out on the street alone and impoverished, with their few remaining possessions in a garbage bag stuffed into an old shopping cart. The prevalence of this fear may be rooted in centuries of dependency on men for economic survival. Worldwide, women earn 90% or less of men's pay for similar work, according to a recent International Labor Organization study. In the U.S., the comparable figure for years has been a meager 75%.

Gender differences around risk add another dimension to the picture. Men tend to be more willing to risk their money, partly due to an upbringing that gives them confidence (rightly or wrongly) about their financial expertise. If they lose money, they're prepared to get up, dust themselves off, and start all over again. Women, who not only earn less but spend less time in the workforce because of childbearing and other factors, are not as sure of being able to replace any money they lose. They may also have been raised to believe that they won't be any good at "money stuff," and, if they're lucky, some man will take care of it for them.

When fears of this kind prevent clients from taking action that is in their best interest, you can help by asking them to write down what they are fearful or anxious about and how they would cope with these bugaboos. This process can rob old fears of much of their power to intimidate.

Many of these gender differences have persisted for centuries, if not millennia. They are unlikely to disappear in our lifetime, which means you can't realistically practice "impersonal finance" that takes no notice of a client's gender. Instead, you need to understand the differences in social conditioning between men and women, while helping your clients learn to share financial power and communicate openly and compassionately with each other.

CHAPTER 6

Gender Matters

Why can't a woman be more like a man—or vice versa? The answer is often in our DNA.

A reporter asked me some years ago if men's greater willingness to bungee-jump and take other big risks might be due to some fundamental difference between their brains and women's brains. While I ducked the question of brain function by saying that I was not a biologist, I said I thought differences in the way girls and boys were raised could explain their different behaviors.

Much more scientific research has been done since then, and it looks as though the reporter's question may have been more on target than either of us knew at the time. New brain studies are helping to deepen our understanding of how the mind works and how people change. In particular, we're learning that men and women are hard-wired in many areas to be as different as night and day.

One of the leading explorers of this landscape is psychologist and family physician Leonard Sax. Most recently the author of *Why Gender Matters* (Doubleday, 2005), Sax has opened my eyes to some of the many ways male and female brains develop differently from birth. He says, "Every step in each pathway, from the retina to the cerebral cortex, is different in females and males.... Girls and boys play differently. They learn differently. They fight differently. They see the world differently."

It's important for advisors to be able to reach male and female clients more effectively. While each individual is unique and will exhibit certain traits to varying degrees, this recently uncovered information can expand our insight into male-female differences, leading to new ways to bridge the gap between men's and women's worlds. Here are some of the research findings, with my ideas on how they may help you work more successfully with clients.

Focus: Gatherers vs. Hunters

Girls' eyes have more P cells keyed to cones, which provide high-resolution details of what they're looking at. Boys' eyes have more M cells keyed to rods, which are more sensitive motion detectors. This difference is apparent even in infancy: baby girls are more likely to focus on people's faces, while baby boys like to stare at mobiles twirling over them. Young girls tend to picture their world in terms of things (Mom, Dad, house) while boys focus on action (jets flying, rockets blasting off, villains getting blown away).

I asked Dr. Sax whether this might suggest that men tend to place more importance on movement and velocity in choosing an investment, while women are more interested in its nature.

Dr. Sax finds this hypothesis quite plausible. And Adam Kanzer, director of stockholder advocacy for the Domini Funds, tells me there are more women investors than men in Domini's socially responsible mutual funds. This fuels my belief that women are more interested in feeling "connected" to their investments, while men are more likely to be interested in performance ups and downs.

But clients' blind spots may keep them from being satisfied later with their investment choices. To help them become better-rounded investors, consider educating women about the importance of past results, risk, portfolio turnover, and so forth, while encouraging men to be more aware of such "softer" issues as product quality and commitment to stakeholders.

Behind the "Strong, Silent Type"

Research as early as the late 1800s began to identify the areas of the brain that control certain kinds of functioning. In 1964, studies showed that there are very real gender differences in brain geography. For example, language resides in the left hemisphere of men's brains, while the right side controls spatial concepts. By contrast, the language function is diffused throughout women's brains, instead of being localized.

This is reflected in the different ways that emotions are handled. A recent study indicates that when adolescent girls experience negative emotions such as anger, humiliation, or sadness, much of the brain activity associated with their feelings moves to the cerebral cortex, an area connected with higher functions such as reflection, reasoning, and language. In boys, negative emotions remain in the amygdala, a more primitive part of the brain. I see this as a reason why men may react more quickly and explosively to negative emotions, while women are more likely to process and discuss these feelings.

A further consequence of this difference in brain structure is that it's harder for men (or boys, for that matter) to talk about their feelings. When you ask a man, "How do you feel about XYZ?" it requires him to connect two parts of the brain that don't normally communicate. Dr. Sax illustrates this with the Garrison Keillor joke about the man who said his marriage worked great because he and his wife rarely talked.

Thus, while it can make sense to ask a new female client, "How do you feel about coming here?" a man may respond better to a question about his thought process. Dick Vodra, an advisor in McLean, Virginia, suggests asking, "What made you pick up the phone and call me this time, after all the times you may have thought of it before?"

Deborah Tannen, a professor of linguistics at Georgetown University and an author whose work I have admired for years, says that when she explored the different ways each sex uses language, she was overwhelmed by the differences separating females and males at every age. Even the second-grade girls she studied were more similar to adult women in their use of language than they were to boys of their own age.

As a couples therapist for many years, I have a lot of compassion for men's challenges. I do believe it's possible for a man to learn to find words to access his feelings, and the men who manage to stretch in this way assuredly have better relationships. An understanding of this difference in brain wiring can also help a woman develop more patience and tolerance in helping a man master this task, which is so difficult for him and comes so naturally to her.

Getting a Rush from Risk

Research shows that boys tend to exhibit riskier behavior when other boys are watching. Girls are less likely to be impressed by risk-taking behavior in their girlfriends, or to enjoy risk-taking for its own sake.

Why? Blame differences in the autonomic nervous system. In boys, risky activities typically trigger a rush that they find intensely pleasurable (think paintball games, demolition derbies, extreme sports). Dr. Sax mentions one study where youthful participants played a video game in which they risked a realistic-looking crash. Most of the boys felt exhilarated by the danger, while most girls said it made them feel fearful. In a related finding, girls tend to underestimate their chances of success in physically risky activities, while boys tend to overestimate theirs.

These different attitudes toward risk appear to have originated millennia ago. I'm fascinated by the conclusion of University of Alberta primate anthropologists Linda Fedigan and Sandra Zohar that male monkeys' risk-taking behaviors cause them to die at a much earlier age than females.

Fast-forward to human investors: no wonder men enjoy taking financial risks that most women shun. And no wonder they take full credit for investment successes, while blaming their failures on outside influences. It's just as obvious why women tend to underestimate their skill as investors, crediting their advisor or good luck when they succeed. In many cases, early socialization reinforces both sexes' genetic predispositions.

Knowing how the male nervous system responds to the thrill of taking chances, you may be able to connect to risk-addicted clients with more insight and help them learn to mitigate these tendencies. By the same token, once you're aware that female clients' investment anxiety is not just acquired but inherited, you may be more successful in encouraging them to take necessary risks.

How We Learn

Given these brain differences, it's no surprise that women and men prefer to learn in different ways. One cue comes from 2004 research on chimpanzees in Tanzania. Female chimps tended to follow their teacher's example, while male chimps preferred to do things their own way. We naked apes may not be as evolutionarily superior as we like to think, since (as Dr. Sax points out) boys are more likely than girls to consult their teacher as a last resort after all other options have been exhausted.

Do You Hear What I Hear?

Wives tend to joke about their husbands' selective hearing. But it's no joke, according to Dr. Sax. Girls hear much better than boys—a difference that persists in adulthood and becomes more marked after age 40.

And it's probably the spouse with XX chromosomes who's going to wake up in the middle of the night hearing a mysterious noise. Girls are distracted by noises 10 times softer than noise levels that would affect boys. In fact, girls and women tend to be much more bothered by extraneous sounds than their male counterparts.

One implication: screen out distracting office sounds (clicking keyboards, ringing phones, distant conversations) while meeting with a woman client. If you have a loud voice, consider toning it down so she won't perceive that you're shouting at her. An advisor with a naturally low voice may want to increase the volume for a male client.

Also, when you're working with a client couple, don't assume you're reaching him just because she appears engaged. He may feel too vulnerable to speak up and say, "I can't hear you." In fact, hearing differences are another good reason to keep checking with clients of both genders to make sure they're on board with you.

This implies to me that women may be more likely to seek a financial advisor's help—and follow through on your recommendations. You might also consider keeping closer tabs on a maverick male client, in case doing things "his way" gets him into trouble.

If men and women see and hear differently, then what's the best way to get through to clients? One tip is to use shock tactics selectively, since the two sexes respond differently to pain, stress, and aggression. Girls and boys don't even feel the pain of a jolt of electricity the same way. If you're a boy, Dr. Sax says, it won't hurt as much.

Educational psychologist Eva Pomerantz found similar reactions to aggression. A confrontational, in-your-face approach often works well with boys, while girls are more likely to be hurt by blunt criticism. So while you may be able to jolt a male client into new behavior by telling him, "You're going to be broke in six months if you keep this up," a woman client is apt to be more compliant if you take a positive, we're-in-this-together approach smattered with praise.

Natural Selection

I have to admit that this particular research made me reexamine my emphasis on supportive, nurturing client interventions. But as a psychotherapist whose awareness has been fine-tuned by men's and women's struggles, I've always known that the anxiety of a more confrontational approach helps some people learn better, while other clients are more successful when they feel calm and safe. When you have a male client (or an atypical female client) whose financial behavior is sabotaging their plans, remember that direct confrontation is one of the options in your toolkit.

Believe it or not, where you sit in your office can also be a factor in working more effectively with clients. Women prefer that you sit across from them so they can look you in the eye and talk about the issues. If you're dealing with a man, sit down next to him shoulder to shoulder and spread out the materials, such as charts and graphs, in front of you both.

Women typically respond well to a small-group learning environment—for instance, a seminar, workshop, or appreciation dinner. Men sometimes learn more effectively when they're moving around. (This may explain their predilection for doing business on the golf course.) If you have a thorny issue to discuss with a male client, you might consider broaching it while the two of you walk to Starbucks for a latte.

Dr. Sax shared with me another interesting finding: Most women learn better at a room temperature of about 75 degrees, while men learn better at about 69 degrees. I wonder how social scientists would interpret this—that cavewomen learned from each other around the fire, while cavemen frantically processed perceptions out on the hunt?

The Will to Work

What about the notorious income differential between men and women? Dr. Sax cites economist Linda Babcock's study of new Carnegie Mellon University graduates. She explains the financial gender gap by noting that the women didn't ask for more money in job interviews, while the men did. Because of this "risk-taking" behavior, the men were rewarded with higher starting salaries.

Gender politics activist, educator, and author Warren Farrell confesses that as a male feminist, he used to wear a pin that said "59¢," alluding to the oft-quoted statistic that women were paid 59 cents for every dollar that men made. Finally he asked himself, "If an employer can hire a woman for 59 cents to do what a man would do for a dollar, why would anyone hire a man?"

Digging deeper, Farrell discovered that among educated full-time workers, women earn $1.17 for every dollar men make. Even among part-time workers, women make $1.10 for every dollar earned by their male counterparts. So much for the 59-cent generalization.

Farrell's research concluded that men and women have different goals for what they want to get out of their work. The opportunity to earn more income usually depends on an individual accepting one or more of these choices:

- More intense work (more responsibility, bigger staff)

- More highly specialized work (e.g., technology, hard sciences)

- More hardship (lots of traveling, relocation)

- More danger (physical hazards)

- More education (extra debt, a late start in your career)

- More work experience (no time off to "find yourself")

Some women choose to earn less in order to achieve a more equal balance between work and personal relationships. Men can benefit from being open to similar choices, instead of conforming to the pressure of providing a more lavish lifestyle than their family really needs.

Apropos of men's choices, *The Wall Street Journal* recently reported that many of the men signing up for an online dating service were looking for women who earned more than they did. It saddens me to think that these guys felt so encumbered by their "provider burden" that they were hunting for someone else to take it over for them.

Farrell's point, which I deeply respect, is that we need to stop viewing women and men as victims, and see clearly that everyone has to make choices and sacrifices in order to create a challenging and rewarding life. This more balanced point of view will help each of us exercise our own choices to live in harmony with our values and integrity.

Practicing the Nonhabitual

Once upon a time, near the beginning of my therapy career, Warren Farrell and I co-facilitated a workshop at Georgetown University titled "Consciousness-Raising for Men and Women." As part of this workshop, participants had to go on a "role-reversal" date with someone of the opposite sex. Each of us was required to embody behavioral stereotypes of the other gender. For example, I was supposed to make remarks about my date's body, open doors, and pay for the meal, while my partner was expected to act compliant, stroke my ego with compliments, and be sexually flirty.

This powerful exercise helped many of us develop more compassion for the constraints that trap women and men in roles not of their own choosing. Its central idea of "practicing the nonhabitual" remains at the core of my philosophy about how people can grow and change.

All this new information about male-female hard-wired differences may help you establish a more effective learning environment for your clients. In addition, I would encourage you to teach them how to counter their own biology when it gets in the way of reaching their goals. For example, explain to a woman investor that it's natural for her to focus on a company's values, but you're there to help her see the other half of the picture. Teach men about their biological tendency to seek more risk than may be wise.

These research findings also suggest that when a couple consults you for advice, it could be a good idea to meet separately with each partner. With what you know about men's and women's innate tendencies, you may be able to help each partner learn and absorb more fully whatever you need to impart. Afterward, you can bring the couple together to finalize agreement about a course of action.

Today, we're beginning to learn just how many gender differences are hard-wired. We need to be focused and vigilant in creating an environment where men and women can overcome this programming to live in a way that reflects their own individuality and uniqueness. Once we stop seeing ourselves as powerless victims, we really can exercise choice in a way that creates balance and fulfillment for ourselves and for our loved ones.

Gender matters to all of us. It's a subject of boundless excitement and fascination to me, as I hope it is to you. Your understanding of male-female differences (and similarities) can give you more insight, more compassion, and more inspiration in helping individuals and couples create the life they envision.

CHAPTER 7

Minority Report

By 2050, minority groups will be the majority of Americans. Are you ready?

Our nation is often described as a melting pot, but I think it's also somewhat like a popcorn popper. People from different cultural backgrounds are likely to pop up anywhere in the country, even in places you might never think to find them. For example, there are sizable communities of Somalis in Lewiston, Maine; Latinos in Fargo, North Dakota; and Pacific Islanders in Des Moines, Iowa.

Clearly, investment advisors who are skilled in dealing with clients of a different ethnic, racial, or cultural background have a competitive edge over those who don't. It's rare, however, to find any guidance on how to talk to and reach clients from different cultures, and rarer still to come across any information on the distinctive attitudes toward money that they may bring to your office.

In exploring this topic, I went to the source: advisors who specialize in cultivating client relationships with specific ethnic or cultural groups. Some are members of these groups themselves; others are not. With the caveat that my research is neither comprehensive nor statistically valid, I invite you to consider what I learned.

In this chapter, I'll concentrate on our nation's two largest minorities: Hispanics (with a particular focus on Mexican-Americans) and African-Americans. In the next chapter, I'll address financial attitudes among Muslims, Jews, Indians, Japanese, and Chinese.

But first a cautionary note. The research for this report reminded me that it's both fascinating and dangerous to examine cultural differences. Fascinating because there is so much that's interesting about a different population's history, values, and behaviors; but dangerous because it can lead to prejudging individuals who are always more complex than any stereotype. Regardless of your clients' cultural or ethnic identity, remember that most of them have the same goals: to create a more secure future for themselves and their loved ones, and to make a difference in the lives of their children and others they care about.

Working to Live

"I don't have everything I love, but I love everything I have," a Venezuelan friend told Rose Carbonell. In "Dinero vs. Money," an article published online at www.cheskin.com, Carbonell, a graduate student in Hispanic marketing communications at Florida State University, contrasts her friend's belief that money is good, but not the most important thing in life, with a typical American attitude that one's life should be used to build wealth.

The difference in these outlooks may have a religious component. Carbonell points out that in *The Protestant Ethic and the Spirit of Capitalism*, Max Weber argues that the capitalistic spirit has its roots in the Protestant Reformation's emphasis on hard work, frugality, and personal responsibility. This conceptual framework encouraged capitalism to flourish in the U.S. In Catholic countries, by contrast, people tend to be wary of unfettered capitalism. (In my view, they may also be more invested in the importance of *caritas*, or caring—the source of our word "charity.")

Carbonell's Venezuelan friend told her, "As long as I'm healthy, my family is around, and I have my friends, I'll be happy, no matter how much money I have…. I'll work to live, not live to work."

Money and Fate

International financial planner Raoul Rodríguez Walters agrees that cross-cultural differences are often rooted in different historical experiences. Rodríguez, whose firm, Mexico Advisor, has offices in Portland, Oregon, and San Miguel de Allende, Mexico, points out that years of dysfunctional regimes have given people in many Latin American countries an adversarial view of government. It's not unusual for legal and accounting professionals to aid citizens in cheating on their taxes. As a result, Latino immigrants to the United States may put up tremendous resistance to the idea of paying their "fair share" to the IRS. Rodríguez often has to educate these clients about the necessity of paying taxes honestly in the U.S.

Repeated political coups and freezing of bank assets in their homeland have made many Latino immigrants equally wary of financial institutions, according to Carbonell. She posits that a discomfort with the concept of interest-bearing debt has its roots in the long domination of Spain by the Moors, whose religious beliefs forbid usury. The association of wealth with iniquity is another legacy of centuries of oppression. Being poor is seen as a better alternative to being wealthy (and hence corrupt).

A fatalistic attitude toward life is also part of the "different mindset" of Hispanic culture, as I was told by Louis Barajas, a financial planner in Santa Fe Springs, California, and author of *The Latino Journey to Financial Greatness: The 10 Steps to Creating Wealth, Security, and a Prosperous Future for You and Your Family* (HarperCollins, 2003). For example, a farewell to a new Mexican client, "I'll see you next week with the rest of the paperwork," is apt to be answered by *"Si Dios quiere"*—"If God wills."

Fatalism is also echoed in the belief that "If I'm poor, God must have intended me to be poor." This may explain why so many Latinos opt to spend their money on present-day needs and wants, instead of investing to improve their situation. Barajas's answer to fatalistic clients is that God wants them to be happy and secure. He tells them about other immigrants who started with nothing and became wealthy, and sometimes shares his own story of achieving success after growing up poor in a Los Angeles barrio.

> **With a Little Help from My Friends…**
>
> The advisors quoted in this chapter and the next were all very generous in providing insights to help others reach clients from minority backgrounds. I also owe special thanks to John Comer of Comer Consulting in Plymouth, Minnesota, a marketing consultant to financial planners, and to Peter Lefferts, chairman of the U.S. Work Group on Personal Financial Planning for the International Organization for Standardization (ISO), who referred me to many of these helpful professionals.

Macho, Macho Man

Hispanic machismo offers unusual challenges to an advisor's ingenuity. The more blue-collar a Latino is, the more macho he tends to be. Louis Barajas, who as "Doctor Dinero" writes a column for Hispanic men in *Open Your Eyes* magazine, handles hombres like this in an interesting way. Sitting across from them in his office, he says, "There was a very wealthy man at this chi-chi firm, interested in me because I was a poor Hispanic, who wanted me to succeed. He told me, 'The difference between the poor and the rich is this: the poor know everything; the rich learn everything.'" Barajas continues, "'I can see that when I work with someone like you, who comes in, willing to learn and wanting to take the best care of his family, and who will listen to me because I was a poor Hispanic who made it, I know I can help you succeed.'" (Because of his skill in aligning himself with his client, I wager that he usually does!)

Another frequently encountered cultural difference, according to Barajas, is dual families. It's not unusual for men to have a wife in one home and a mistress in another, with children by both women. In fact, the civil code of most Mexican states allows a woman from *la casa chica* to share in her lover's estate if she is excluded from his will. This means it's fairly common for a husband to be a financial planning client by himself, while in the U.S. it would be more common to advise a husband and wife together.

Life insurance can be a touchy issue. Barajas told me that a male client often resists buying life insurance, suspecting that the money will go to "El Sancho"—the guy who will take his place when he's dead. Barajas's response is forthright. "I know you may fear your money will go to El Sancho," he tells these clients, "but there are ways we can protect it so it goes right to your kids."

La Familia

I asked Barajas whether it's customary for Hispanics to have a college fund for their children. He told me that when he speaks to a Hispanic audience, he often asks, "How many of you believe that education is the way out?" Everyone in the audience raises their hand. "How many of you are putting away money for your kids' education?" Out of a thousand people, he says, maybe five hands will go up.

This is a serious problem. Although the high-school dropout rate for Hispanics has been declining, the latest data from the U.S. Department of Education shows that it was still over 22% in 2005. In the barrio where Barajas grew up, more than 60% of teens never complete high school. Nationwide, he says, only 7% of Hispanics graduate from college.

Because many Hispanic immigrants are ill-educated themselves, they often aren't aware of their role in motivating their children to get a good education. For example, they may not show up for Parents' Night at school, believing that their kids' success is completely up to the teacher. Barajas encourages these clients to get more involved by requesting them to bring in their kids' report cards. He also asks the children's teachers to write letters home that explain what the child needs to do in order to graduate and succeed. "Sometimes they need tutoring; sometimes they need dental work," he says.

Raoul Rodríguez Walters adds that among Mexicans and other Hispanics, less emphasis is placed on being independent from one's family. In the U.S., he observes, children can't wait to turn 18 and leave home. Even if they go to a nearby college, they often rent an apartment of their own. In Mexico, it's unusual for children to want to leave home, even for college. Most will live at home happily while pursuing their studies, and continue to stay there until they marry. In fact, parents often continue to support their children well after the latter are married. Similarly, older parents often live with *los niños* or very near them. Children who work usually contribute money or pay for services their parents need. The idea of an assisted living facility is scandalous to most Mexicans.

Conspicuous Consumption

When it comes to spending, the stereotypical Hispanic lays out his or her money on fashionable clothes, souped-up cars, and lots of bling—accessories that give their owner status on the street. There's some truth to this stereotype, as Wharton finance professor Nikolai Roussanov and two University of Chicago collaborators recently reported in "Conspicuous Consumption and Race: Who Spends More on What" (found in the Wharton School's online business journal, *Knowledge@Wharton*).

Roussanov concludes that the explanation of this behavior—which is also characteristic of many young African-Americans—is economic, not cultural. The determining factor is the need to appear visibly wealthier or more successful than one's peers. (This display isn't unique to the barrio or the ghetto, I might add; witness the plethora of oversized McMansions, glitzy Lexuses, and the like in high-end neighborhoods populated primarily by European-Americans.)

Whatever the reason, the consequences are serious. Compared to whites at the same income level, Roussanov says, both Hispanics and African-Americans spend as much as 30% more on visible status items, which takes a toll on other budget needs. For example, Latino and black households spend 50% less on healthcare than their white counterparts. Latinos spend 16% less on education than whites do; blacks spend 30% less.

Observing how deeply entrenched status spending is, Roussanov wonders, "How do we promote going to an expensive college rather than buying an expensive watch?"

The Need for Advice

Many Latinos aren't used to paying for advice. When they need counsel, they go to a person in their family who is successful and ask this compadre what they should do. Often, the closest thing to a financial planner in a Hispanic neighborhood is a storefront advisor who will marry you, divorce you, prepare your tax return, notarize your documents, and even plan your travel.

Clearly, planners like Raoul Rodríguez Walters and Louis Barajas are bucking the system. The price they pay is a lot of "handholding" and patient education of their Latino clients. For example, many clients who come from an agricultural background believe in investing only in what they can touch and see: real estate. To help them feel more comfortable with diversification, Barajas says, he rewrote the basic concepts of stock and bond investing so they could be understood by someone like his father, who has a sixth-grade education.

A Matter of Trust

To explore African-Americans' financial attitudes more fully, I spoke with Walter Gray of Ameriprise Financial Services in Edina, Minnesota. Gray, a member of the black community who has been a financial advisor for 23 years, noted that African-Americans as a group are sometimes very extravagant with their money, and yet can be very private about it. Like Hispanics, they don't save as much as the average white American; they also tend to be skeptical of the stock market and wary of people promoting financial products.

The roots of this secrecy and distrust are deep, Gray told me. "Going way back, African-Americans had to hide their money so it wasn't taken from them by the Man. As they accumulated more money, it was stored in a hidden coffee can, buried in the mattress." Today, Gray notes, many African-Americans still do not have checking accounts. Like Latinos and many other immigrants, they use check-cashing stores instead. Working-class black families usually pay their bills with money orders.

In the past, the black community has also been the target of many unsavory practices, from pyramid schemes to insurance scams. As I read the available literature and talked with advisors serving this community, the word "trust" came up over and over again.

Saundra Davis told me, "I watched the insurance saleswoman come to our house for 20 years for a policy for my mother, and I'm thinking, 'She's paying this amount of money for a policy that does nothing.'" Davis is not only executive director of Sage Financial Solutions, a financial planning organization for low- and moderate-income families in San Francisco, but also a black woman raised in a largely Latino community. "When you're in a family that doesn't have a tax preparer or a financial planner, if you don't want to feel like you're dumb or uneducated, you just go along," she says. "You trust someone who sounds educated. You don't know any better." This experience fueled her passion to teach her clients how to take care of themselves financially.

Family and Community

Middle-class black parents tend to be willing to put up some of the money for their children's education. Working to come up with the rest, they feel, will help their kids learn the value of the college experience.

Estate planning is a thornier matter. Most clients want to leave a legacy for their family, but haven't put anything in place to accomplish it. Most do not even have a will. "It's my personal opinion that having a will is your moral and civic responsibility," Gray tells them.

He encourages clients to be philanthropic if they are so minded. Citing a report by John Havens at Boston College's Center for Wealth and Philanthropy, he points out that African-Americans give away a higher percentage of their income than any other ethnic group, mainly to their church.

Kimberly Allers, careers and personal finance editor at *Essence* magazine, observed in a June 2007 *Black Wealth* magazine article by Bruce W. Fraser that many black women make the money decisions in their household. She urged advisors to approach these women with the "understanding that they have more financial pull than other women." They're also expected to help others financially—particularly family members.

In both black and Hispanic families, individuals typically bear a lot of financial responsibility for their relatives, according to Saundra Davis. "One of the glaring differences I notice in working with Latino and African-American clients is the responsibility they feel to support other family members financially," she told me. "In an ethnically diverse family, the first one to go to college doesn't have to do it alone. The whole family rallies around to help them get there." Afterward, she added, the person who "makes it" may feel obliged to place the family's needs ahead of his or her own financial well-being.

The strength of family ties can make it difficult for an advisor to plot a client's future. If someone else in the family has a financial need, the client is expected to liquidate his emergency fund and other resources to help out. Davis asks a client in a situation like this, "What do you believe you owe the family? What can you do that will be truly helpful?" Sometimes, she says, giving money is not the solution.

In one case, Davis worked with a Hispanic woman who was trying to pay down student loans and other debt when she discovered that her brother was in financial distress. She agreed to take over monthly debt payments for him, which meant working an extra shift and postponing paying off her own debts. "We advised her to tell her brother that this support would end in three months," Davis says. "But when we checked with her at the end of the first month, she hadn't done it. Two months, and she still hadn't told him. In the final month, she decided she would extend for another three months." The solution? "It had to hurt enough," Davis explains. "I had to make her need the money." Forced to adjust her spending and cancel a trip she could no longer afford, the client got the message. Instead of continuing to pay endlessly for her brother's money mistakes, she sent him to a financial planner.

Davis helped this Latina woman learn that unless she was living the life she wanted, she couldn't assist anyone else. Now she is more financially secure, and her brother is getting the education he needs to manage his money better.

The Opportunity for You

There's still a perception that the only path to financial success in the black community is through sports or entertainment. Gray tries to dispel this limited thinking as he works with clients and speaks to broader audiences. He feels that better-educated African-Americans are becoming more comfortable with the stock market. He anticipates that, as they realize they can become successful investors, they will pass this knowledge on to their children. (Authors' note: Since the market crash in late 2008, of course, cautious investors of every ethnic background are likely to have returned to their earlier risk-averse stance.)

Unquestionably, the need is there. The average black household earning more than $50,000 a year has saved less than half as much as its white counterpart ($48,000 versus $100,000), according to the 2007 Ariel-Schwab Black Investor Survey.

Gray laments a "have to own it now" mentality among many African-Americans who are weighed down with debt. Despite being financially overextended, they tend to want "the most house they can afford and the most car they can afford," and like to buy and wear trend-setting new clothes. (He reminded me that Bill Blass used to go down to Harlem to see what people were wearing, then redesign these looks for the general public.)

Of course, there are many black individuals who don't fit the generalized picture of status overspenders. Lee Baker, an African-American who is a financial planner with Apex Financial Services in Tucker, Georgia, wrote me, "My experience is that those who seek out the services of a financial advisor do not tend to fall into this category. Most of my clients drive the same car for 5+ years, own a home, have retirement plans, etc." As Nikolai Roussanov's research suggests, these economically secure individuals don't feel as strong a need to flaunt visible signs of wealth.

Still, many other African-Americans are living for today more than for tomorrow. "They don't have as much hope to hope for," Walter Gray says. For all these reasons, the sales cycle is longer with black clients. There's a greater need to educate, nurture, and build trust.

For financial safety, many African-Americans—again like Latinos—prefer to invest in land rather than intangible securities. In 2007, 76% of white families in the Black Investor Survey reported investing in stocks or stock mutual funds, but only 57% of blacks did—the same percentage as 10 years earlier. Baker notes that even when he helps his black clients build a more diversified portfolio, "Quite a few... have additional real estate in the form of unimproved land, rental homes, or apartments."

African-Americans "feel more familiar with real estate through having owned and kept up their own homes," according to John Williams, dean of business administration and economics at Morehouse College in Atlanta. In the *Black Wealth* article mentioned earlier, Williams estimated that 60% of the net worth of black households is tied up in their primary residence, twice as much as the national average.

With greater awareness of the need to fund healthcare, a more comfortable retirement, care for aging parents, and education for their children and grandchildren, African-Americans' interest in the stock market "is greater now because their goals have changed... from an immediate pay-as-you-go attitude to a greater need for investing," according to Jesse Brown, author of *Pay Yourself First* and other books on black wealth-building, who is also quoted in the article. Echoing Walter Gray, Brown says the chief obstacle is "a matter of education and trust."

The Value of Community Outreach

There seems to be a great deal of potential to train more Hispanic, African-American, and other financial advisors who are attuned to the culture of the community where they grew up. But advisors of any background might consider setting up a branch office in a minority neighborhood. If consulting a financial advisor became a visible sign of affluence, more young Latinos and blacks might see it as an alternative to spending on flashy cars and sartorial bling.

How You Can Help

According to the Financial Planning Association's 2004 Attitudes and Impressions survey, 56% of African-Americans believe that financial planning is a high priority, compared to 39% of all survey participants. Yet just 20% of black investors have a financial planner, as opposed to 27% of the general population.

Because of African-Americans' active participation in churches, some advisors are getting involved in religious and other community-related activities to build familiarity and trust. Melvin Smith Sr., a financial planner with First Financial Group in Birmingham, Alabama, finds clients through free financial seminars at churches, colleges, and community organizations, as well as word-of-mouth referrals. He also founded the nonprofit Financial Discovery Forum, where black professionals present 50 to 70 workshops on financial planning every year.

Although I personally believe that any sensitive, nonjudgmental advisor can work well with clients from a variety of cultural and ethnic backgrounds, a good number of people are bound to feel more comfortable dealing with someone from a similar background or culture. Still, that leaves plenty of room for other advisors to learn how to listen and speak to minority clients. If you aspire to be one of them, the following guidelines may help you create more solid relationships.

1. **Consider your biases about the potential client's background.** Are you expecting to meet an overspender with no savings, or someone who will sacrifice her own security to support everyone else in the family? Do your best to drop any limiting beliefs. (It may help to research historical and social aspects of the client's culture, as Raoul Rodríguez Walters suggests.) The important thing is to enter the relationship with an open mind. Remember, your job is to tune into each person's unique fears, hopes, and dreams.

2. **Practice "exquisite listening."** In the initial meeting, devote time to hearing your clients' anxieties and desires, as well as family influences that may be affecting them. As Saundra Davis puts it, she helps them "remember their dreams, what's most important to them, why they go to work every day." The better you understand the forces that drive a client, the stronger a bond you will be able to forge.

3. **Speak in terms they can relate to.** This doesn't necessarily mean tossing off glib references to "El Sancho" (especially if your accent is no better than mine) or "bling." It does mean discerning what your client is really concerned about and longing for, and explaining how you can help them in down-to-earth language (as Louis Barajas did in rewriting the basics of investing).

4. **Cultivate patience.** It may take a while to get some of these clients fully on board with you. Remember, it was months before Davis could motivate her Latina client to set limits on supporting her brother.

5. **Suggest hands-on work to help educate your clients.** For example, to get parents more involved in supporting their school-age children, Barajas asked them to bring in report cards and teachers' comments about the kids' needs.

6. **Develop a resource list, if you don't already have one.** Resources for clients of any background might include consumer credit counseling, low-cost marital therapy, the local Agency on Aging, interventions for addictions, Debtors Anonymous, an Alzheimer's and/or cancer support group, and more.

7. **Know when to refer your clients to someone else.** If, despite your efforts to cultivate a "beginner's mind," you find that working with certain clients makes you impatient, angry, frustrated, or anxious, consider referring them to another advisor (perhaps someone who shares the clients' background) who may be better able to meet their needs. Persuade your clients that your own limitations are at fault, so they don't think there's something wrong with them.

Assimilation Nation

Proponents of cultural diversity may be surprised to learn that many of the nearly 40 million U.S. immigrants are already on the road to assimilation. To determine how similar various immigrant groups are to native-born Americans, the Manhattan Institute for Policy Research, a libertarian think tank, measured three kinds of factors: economic, cultural, and civic. According to a report on the study in the May 13, 2008, edition of *USA Today*, Canadians ranked highest at 53%. Filipinos scored 49%, Cubans 43%, Koreans and Vietnamese 41%, Chinese 21%, Salvadorans 18%, and Indians 16%. Interestingly, the largest immigrant group—Mexicans—is among the most self-contained, with an assimilation rating of only 13%.

You may notice that many, if not all, of these guidelines are valid for your entire clientele, no matter what their backgrounds are. What's different is that when you lack an understanding of a client's history, traditions, and often language, you need to work harder at building a bridge so that the client feels respected, heard, and understood.

Saundra Davis sums it up nicely: "While it is true that people of different ethnicities have differences in the way we perceive and deal with money, a simple truth is that most people have similar financial goals. They want to be able to live in a safe and healthy community, they want to provide for their children and ensure they have opportunities to live their dreams, and they want to retire with dignity knowing they will be able to enjoy their senior years with sufficient financial resources to meet their needs."

I couldn't agree more.

THE CLIENT CONNECTION

ERRATA

Pages 67 and 68, the introduction to "Part III: Changes," was inadvertently placed before Chapter 8 instead of before Chapter 9, "Change of Heart." Chapter 8, "Minority Affairs," is the last chapter of "Part II: Dealing with Differences."

Also, please note that, in the Table of Contents, Part V should be listed as "The Right Thing to Do."

PART III

Changes

In this turbulent world, change is the only thing we can be sure of. Nothing stays the same, even if we want it to.

Many people are afraid of change. Since anything new threatens to sweep them away to places they've never been, they cling to what's old and familiar—even if that happens to be painful and unhealthy. Eventually, these folks may overcome their resistance in order to bring more fulfillment, financial security, intimacy, and creativity into their lives.

Other people become addicted to change, whether or not it's in their best interest. Easily bored with sameness and stability, they may overturn the status quo just for the heck of it. Don't you know someone who is constantly seeking new sensations and experiences? Or who can't seem to stay in an intimate relationship?

Learning how to change your own bad habits and self-sabotaging behavior can be energizing and fulfilling. And by helping clients make changes that improve their lives, you will be able to build a more solid practice.

"Change of Heart," the first chapter in this section, delves into James Prochaska's study of the stages of change. This will give you a perspective on the process people go through when they succeed in letting go of negative habits to create something new and better. You'll see more clearly the interventions you can make at different stages, and may gain more patience when clients seem unready to begin (that's a stage of change, too!). You'll also find out how to deal with relapses to earlier stages of the process ("recycling" may be a more accurate term), and how to encourage a client to move forward again.

Other chapters address what research in the field of psychotherapy can teach you about becoming a better financial coach, mentor, and therapeutic educator for your clients. For example, you'll learn about the importance of asking for feedback on what's working in your relationship and what isn't. Elsewhere, we'll explore what to do when you're in over your head trying to cope with a client's extreme dysfunction or emotional intensity. And if you're contemplating a change in your business structure, you'll find useful questions that help you become clearer on your goals, your strengths and weaknesses, and your preferred working conditions, as well as the ways you like to use your talents and deal with other people.

One of the best things you can do for yourself and your practice is to become comfortable with change. When you learn to craft the kinds of change that benefit yourself, your work, or your clients' lives, you'll discover a new level of personal and professional satisfaction.

CHAPTER 8

Minority Affairs

In this discussion of clients from different cultures, we look east to Riyadh, Tehran, Mumbai, Osaka, Hong Kong... and Brooklyn

Leafing through a typical personal finance magazine, you'll often find tips on getting student loans for a college-bound child, advice on choosing an assisted living center for Grandma, and profiles of young professionals who have saved $250,000 for retirement by the time they're 30. If only everyone were so smart, so sensible, so self-reliant!

Then you hear Saundra Davis, executive director of Sage Financial Solutions in San Francisco, say, "One of the glaring differences I notice in working with Latino and African-American clients is the responsibility they feel to support other family members financially."

As I suggested in the previous chapter, many of us have blind spots in dealing with clients from different cultures. If we want to serve these clients well, we need to understand their background, their history, their attitudes, preferences, and fears.

Let's take time now to address some of the differences you may find among clients of Muslim, Jewish, Indian, Japanese, or Chinese origin. Perhaps some of you will be jarred to learn that the American emphasis on "standing on your own two feet" is the exception, not the norm, and that the charitable giving which many of us view as discretionary is regarded by others as a divinely-ordained duty.

Muslims: Privacy and Sharia

Taking care of extended family members is a top priority in Arab cultures, according to Middle East Institute Scholar David Mack, a former U.S. ambassador and Deputy Assistant Secretary of State.

As Mack explains, Arabs are expected to share the profit from commercial activities with members of their family. In addition, Islam reinforces the social safety net by obliging Muslims to care for widows and orphans and provide charity to less fortunate members of the community. These practices help check unbridled accumulation of riches in the hands of a very few.

However, the emphasis on "sharing the wealth" with kinfolk also results in nepotism and other favoritism to relatives or tribal members. "What looks to Western eyes like non-economic and even unethical behavior is generally tolerated or even encouraged by Arab society," Mack says. "Most of the time, corporations are channels through which the wealthy and powerful take care of their family."

Finances stay under wraps, though. "As private as money can be for Americans, it's more private for Iranians and others from the Middle East," observes Mohammad Vedadi, a financial advisor with Ameriprise Financial in Minneapolis. "It would be taboo for an outsider to ask how much they make, or what they do for a living. Even within the family, you don't talk about it."

Born in Iran, Vedadi grew up in the U.S. Most of his clients are American-born, but he also attracts newcomers from the Middle East. Despite his Iranian heritage, cultural differences make it hard for him to turn immigrants into investors. "There's a stock market in Iran, but only a small percentage of people know anything about it," he says. "Instead, they invest in gold, silver, or property—commodities they've been familiar with for thousands of years. My Middle Eastern clients and prospects, especially those who are older, still have that bias ingrained in them. It's hard to get them to think about investments that are conceptual, like mutual funds, or to place a high emphasis on long-term financial planning."

The precepts of Islamic law present a further difficulty for devout Muslims. Vedadi explains that Sharia, which encompasses the body of Islamic religious law, forbids believers to profit from companies that charge interest or are involved in producing or marketing liquor, gambling, pork, or pornography, among other taboos. Fortunately, he has found some Sharia-compliant funds managed by the Amana Mutual Funds Trust to offer prospective investors.

The mortgage business is thriving for Islamic finance firms, which don't charge interest and aren't involved in the current subprime debacle. According to an article in *The Washington Post*, firms such as Guidance Residential and University Islamic Financial offer a variety of home financing options that Muslims are comfortable with.

These firms give a homebuyer the same opportunities that conventional lenders do, but with a twist: the finance company buys the house, and then resells it to the eventual homeowner at an agreed-upon markup. The markup is kept competitive with the prevailing mortgage interest rate, so the buyer's monthly payment is roughly the same as it would be with a conventional mortgage. An alternative is a lease-to-own contract similar to car leasing. In a third variation, the buyer and the finance company form a limited-liability entity to own shares of the real estate. All of these approaches circumvent the notion of *riba* or excessive gain that would result from "renting" money (i.e., paying interest).

Although not every religious authority thinks these arrangements are necessary to comply with Sharia, the Federal Home Loan Mortgage Corporation bought more than $250 million worth of Islamic home loans in 2007. That's only a drop in Freddie Mac's $1.77 trillion bucket, but it shows that this kind of mortgage is one way you can help Muslim clients integrate their religious values into their financial life.

Jews: Family and Justice

As anyone familiar with "The Merchant of Venice" will remember, Jewish minorities in Christian Europe were often restricted to just a few roles in society, one of which was moneylending. This heritage has certainly contributed to the popular perception of Jews as shrewd businesspeople. Less commonly acknowledged is the importance Jews place on giving back to the community.

Larry Gellman, managing director of Private Wealth Management at Robert W. Baird & Co. in Tucson, Arizona, has worked with Jewish clients since launching his career 28 years ago. Back then, he says, "many of my clients had emigrated from Europe or were born to immigrant parents. They worked hard, made a lot of money, and felt tremendously grateful for the chance to create a new life. Lots of people they'd known, people smarter than they were, had never made it out of Eastern Europe."

These hard-working entrepreneurs had no concept of retirement. They would dismiss as *meshugah* (crazy) the idea of quitting work once they reached some abstract milestone. Play golf for the rest of their life? They wanted to keep working until they died! In the meantime, they gave generously to Jewish organizations and invested in Israel Bonds. Since then, people like these and their families have started foundations and endowments, giving millions of dollars to U.S. colleges, communities, social causes, and medical research.

Stuart Mellan, who heads the Jewish Federation of Southern Arizona (and is also my brother), reminds me that philanthropy has different meanings for Christians and Jews. The Christian word "charity" is rooted in the Latin word for "affection," while the comparable Jewish term *tzedekah* literally means "justice." To Jews, in other words, giving is not so much an act of love toward one's fellow beings as a responsibility handed down by God. In this respect, Judaic and Islamic laws are not far apart at all. Mellan adds that Judaism teaches that even a poor person should try to provide something for those who are needier, but one should never deprive oneself or one's family of the basic necessities in order to fulfill this commandment.

Another commonality between the two cultures is the focus on helping family members. For Jews, this takes the form of ensuring a good education for one's children. In all the Jewish families I ever knew, paying for the kids' college (in full) was nothing short of an obligation. You might not have enough money to do it, but you'd do it anyway. I recall how worried my father was when I applied to college and later to graduate school. We were far from wealthy, but he was ready to pay the fees somehow. When I received full scholarships for both, he was profoundly relieved.

A generation ago, Gellman says, his Jewish clients invested disproportionately in real estate because "investing in stocks felt like a crapshoot." Since then, Jews have become so well assimilated into American culture that he sees virtually no attitudinal differences between Jewish investors and other clients. (Authors' note: Many Jewish investors and charities were so severely burned by losing their money in Bernard L Madoff's Ponzi Scheme, revealed in late 2008, that it may well change their attitude toward investing — or at least toward trusting investment professionals.)

Indians: Money and Karma

In recent decades, India has sent the U.S. a flood of entrepreneurs, high-tech professionals, and other educated immigrants. When I asked Devang Shah, a CFP (India and U.S.) with Right Returns Financial Planning in Mumbai, India, how these newcomers were likely to behave as financial consumers, he described several contrasts between Indians' and Americans' ways of relating to money. "These differences certainly apply to Indians living in America, particularly first-generation immigrants," he cautions. "As they integrate with the mainstream, the differences will become less noticeable."

One of the most notable differences is Indians' huge appetite for saving. They tend to put money aside without compartmentalizing it for a purpose such as education or retirement. Investment choices are usually conservative.

Shah also notes that middle-class Indians aren't quick to spend what they've saved. "Indians are cost-conscious, but not misers," he says. "For example, they may change their cars less often and avoid borrowing for a luxury expense, yet they will spend well for their children's education or a wedding. Overall, the value attached to having financial assets is higher than the value attached to an expensive lifestyle."

If Indians enter your office as prospective clients, don't expect them to divulge personal financial data as readily as most Americans would. On the other hand, it may be easier to elicit qualitative information about family relationships, needs, values, and so on. Also, while an American prospect will often decide whether or not to do business with you in one meeting, Indians often need more time to get a feel for the relationship before they commit.

Shah finishes by saying, "You know, I think this has got to do with the Indian concept of time. Indian philosophy deals with reincarnation as a given. This can be a conversation by itself."

Listening to Clients from Other Cultures

"Listening to clients and asking questions about their goals can help you uncover differences within our culture as well as across cultures," says John Comer of Comer Consulting in Plymouth, Minnesota, a marketing consultant to financial planners. He adds that working with clients from other cultures may also help you become more effective with your American clients.

"All your clients want you to listen to their real goals and help them achieve those goals," Comer points out. He suggests that productive listening can begin by asking these questions of a client from almost any cultural background:

1.   **What does financial independence mean to you?** What would you do all day? Who would you do these activities with? Where would you be in the world? What people and causes would you support during financial independence? What concerns do you have about your ability to achieve financial independence as you have just defined it?

2.   **What are your aspirations for your children?** What type of life would you like for them? What concerns do you have about their ability to have that kind of life?

3. **Tell me about your family.** Who is part of your household? Do you have desires or obligations to provide for your parents, your siblings, or your extended family?

4. **What are some of your early experiences with money?** If we work with investments, how would you expect your money to be invested? Are there any investments that you feel must be included or any that you feel must be excluded? Typically, investment portfolios I recommend include _____. Typically, investment portfolios I recommend do not include _____. Would you be comfortable with an investment portfolio like that?

With appreciation to Comer, I would suggest adding:

5. **What is your greatest fear, and what is your greatest hope?** With this information about your client's desires and emotions joined to what you have already learned, I think you will be able to gain an understanding of their needs on many levels.

Chinese: Savings and Ready Cash

Devang Shah's comment about Indians' commitment to saving also applies to cultures farther east. Former Federal Reserve chairman Ben Bernanke has argued that a global "savings glut" in countries such as China and Japan sends large amounts of capital overseas to the U.S., financing our enormous trade deficit. China in particular has an astonishingly high combined government, corporate, and consumer saving rate of 50% of GDP.

Tom Doctoroff, CEO of one of the largest ad agencies in Asia, says in "Culture influences how many pennies get pinched" on Ezilon.com, "The high saving rate in China is a defense against uncertainty. The Chinese have a deeply entrenched and historically justified sense that the world is unsafe." Contrasting this with Americans' essentially optimistic view of the world, Doctoroff says that we can save more, but we won't have a true "culture of saving" until there's a fundamental change in our worldview. (Authors' note: The cataclysmic upheaval of our economy since then may have been the shock we Americans need to change our saving and spending behavior.)

"Most Chinese, including Chinese-Americans, usually have a good-sized emergency fund in money markets and CDs," Jie (Jane) Huang told me. "They normally don't carry credit card debt, and they'll sometimes prepay their mortgage."

Huang, a financial advisor with Ameriprise Financial Services in Bethesda, Maryland, notes that Chinese tend to be enterprising investors. They may leverage their equity in one property to buy another, which they can then rent out. "I can't speak for all, but they are interested in stock investing on the more speculative side," she observes. "They tend to try for short-term profit, rather than holding a diversified portfolio for the long term."

Marguerita (Rita) Cheng, a financial planner in the same office as Huang, agrees that Chinese are comfortable buying and trading stocks. They're more likely to have a self-directed brokerage account at E★Trade or Charles Schwab than to hire someone else to manage their money, she says.

Part of the reluctance to confide in an advisor comes from a strong sense of privacy. "In my experience, Chinese may be less comfortable discussing touchy-feely emotional issues," explains Cheng, who is of Chinese and American descent. "Chinese people don't even see therapists or marriage counselors. To discuss personal issues with outsiders may be seen as a sign of weakness." She views this attitude as part of the makeup of many native-born Chinese, whom she describes as tending to be "very analytical and skeptical by nature" and gravitating toward left-brain professions such as engineering, computer science, and life science.

Huang seconds Cheng's comment about Chinese skepticism, which underlies many people's unwillingness to give up control of their money. "Americans' view is 'I trust you until you prove otherwise,'" she says. "The Chinese attitude is more likely to be, 'I trust you more as time goes by.' There is a positive correlation between time and trust. You have to earn it."

Asians may not appear to be as philanthropic as their Western counterparts, Cheng notes, but that does not mean they are not charitable. They are more likely to have multiple generations to provide for. "In many Asian families, it is not uncommon to support elderly relatives or for Grandma or Grandpa to live with their grandchildren," she points out. "It is absolutely taboo to put one's parents in a nursing home." If they move to America, Asians routinely budget for the expense of traveling to the old country to reconnect with relatives and ancestors.

Luck and the Chinese

Two huge casinos in Connecticut, Foxwoods and Mohegan Sun, send more than 100 buses every day to pick up customers in predominantly Asian neighborhoods of Boston and New York. The number of buses doubles on Chinese New Year, Thanksgiving, and Christmas.

In a *Washington Post* article titled "Casinos are aggressively courting Asian Americans," I learned that Foxwoods Resort Casino (the world's biggest in terms of gambling floor space) estimates that at least a third of its customers are Asian. Mohegan Sun says Asian spending makes up one-fifth of its business and is growing. The casinos bring in Asian rock stars and entertainment personalities, sponsor the Boston Dragon Boat Festival and an Asian beauty pageant in Toronto, and shower their bused-in customers with coupons for free food and gambling.

If financial advisors knew as much about Asians as the casinos do, they'd have a much better chance of attracting them as clients. Casino dealers know not to touch Chinese customers on the shoulder—a sign of bad luck. They don't say the number 4, which sounds like the word for death. ("Nine" also sounds to the Japanese like the word for pain.) At Pai Gow and baccarat tables, which have numbered seats, Foxwoods has even omitted the No. 4 seat. Talk about cultural sensitivity!

How does a propensity for gambling jibe with the tendency to save? Surely people don't accumulate money just for the pleasure of risking it on games of chance?

The underlying motivation may have a lot to do with *joss*, which has connotations of both "luck" and "fate." It's an important factor in the lives of many Chinese, whose philosophy is often a blend of Christianity and Buddhism/Taoism. Gambling is a way of inviting good joss, which can make a person wealthy in a heartbeat.

By busing in groups of friends and families, the casinos add a social aspect to the possibility of getting rich. Gambling at Mohegan Sun or Foxwoods doesn't require language skills, offers noodle bars and familiar games of chance, and is affordable for even low-income immigrants. "Our Asian blood loves to feel the luck," Ernie Wu, director of Asian marketing at Foxwoods, says in the *Washington Post* article. His customers don't call it gambling, he adds. "We call it entertainment."

Japanese: Risk Aversion and *Gaman*

Rita Cheng, who lived in Japan for four years, points out that in traditional Japanese families, a husband hands over his paycheck to his wife. "Even if she's a stay-at-home spouse, she handles the household finances and controls the purse strings," Cheng says.

There are social and cultural reasons for the tremendously high savings rate that characterizes most Japanese, observes Rick Kagawa, a financial planner in Huntington Beach, California. Socially, there is pressure to amass as much wealth as possible. (In Osaka, he notes, a common greeting is "How's your money today?") The cultural reasons have to do with the tradition of *gaman*: to persevere, tough it out, suffer through it. Even though Kagawa's family didn't normally speak Japanese at home, he would hear, "You must *gaman*."

Despite their dedication to saving, Japanese-Americans tend to have less wealth than many Chinese-Americans. When Kagawa asked about this as a youngster, he was told that his family lost a generation of income during World War II. Forced into internment camps for the duration of the war, his grandparents lost their restaurant and their new car, and his mother's hopes of going to college were dashed. Many Japanese-Americans were so scarred by the camp experience, or by their elders' subsequent accounts of it, that they retain a lingering distrust of the government.

After the war, these families returned to a more normal way of life. In fact, Kagawa compares his upbringing to that of his Jewish friends. Japanese-American parents tend to hover over their children (like Jewish mothers, I guess!). And as in Jewish families, education is everything; parents assume they will finance college for their kids.

Though Japanese tend to be risk-averse, many have learned the advantages of diversifying. Kagawa's clients, who are predominantly Nisei (the first American-born generation), include gardeners, landscapers, and other service workers who have saved enormous amounts of money. One of them, a librarian, has a net worth fifty times her highest annual salary.

"I wish they would enjoy life more," Kagawa told me. He includes his own father, an insurance agent, in his wish that saving-obsessed Japanese-Americans would relax and enjoy their wealth. Ironically, the next generation is more than willing to spend. These conspicuous consumers can be seen zipping around in Porsches, wearing watches that cost more than their parents' first house.

Cultivating a Beginner's Mind

All in all, an advisor should obviously not take for granted that the saving and spending behavior of a Muslim, Jewish, or Asian-American client will mirror that of the "average" WASP. I would also caution you against assuming that every client from a given background will display all the characteristics discussed here.

The best approach to working with clients from a different culture starts with complete awareness and openness to learning, or what Zen practitioners call a "beginner's mind." To help open your mind and heart as fully as you can, consider the following advice:

1. **Be ready to learn, not just to teach.** Don't assume you know all you need to know. Ask yourself what you can discover as a student of your client's culture, not just as a coach and mentor. "If you don't share the same cultural background as your client, these initial discovery conversations become even more important," says Laura Brook, director of international relations of the Financial Planning Association. "It is here that you might learn that for an Indian,

saving for the weddings of children is critical, and that an extended household is often found in Chinese families. These facts will help you better understand the ins and outs of their priorities and goals."

2.   **Try to put yourself in their shoes.** Be sensitive to the way your questions and comments may sound to people from other cultures. If you find you can't demonstrate the same sensitivity to them that you would to someone from your own background, invite the client to help you understand from their perspective. The "disconnect" may be based on something other than cultural differences. You may also want to talk with a colleague whose background is similar to your client's, or who has more experience serving diverse ethnic and cultural populations.

3.   **Develop a longer-term perspective.** As we've seen, many other cultures consider it improper to divulge personal information to strangers. So as you discuss your client's needs, you need to tread lightly and patiently in order to understand the whole picture of their attitudes toward saving, investing, spending, taking care of family, charitable obligations, etc., before recommending actions for them to take.

4.   **Let clients know you've heard them.** Once you've finished listening patiently, reflect their comments back to them to be sure you've heard them as they wish to be heard. If they need to take action that runs counter to their cultural traditions, you'll need to empathize fully with the sadness of facing what feels to them like a painful loss.

5.   **Avoid making assumptions.** Davis of Sage Financial Solutions points out how easy it is to assume that if clients are not responding, there must be something wrong with them. Davis's experience with Latino and African-American clients also prompts her to say, "When people volunteer to work with low and moderate-income clients, they often expect the client to embrace every recommendation they make and move quickly to adopt it. These are expectations they would not necessarily hold for a high-net-worth client." Cultivate an attitude of respect.

6. **Practice tolerance, but know your limits.** It's important to recognize that your own moral standards and ethical views are not the only ones that have value. On the other hand, you don't have to acquiesce to anything that you find wrong, uncomfortable, or repugnant. Learn how to be true to your principles without communicating disapproval or distaste to a client.

FPA Reminder: Practice Good 'Citizenship'

Laura Brook, director of international relations for the Financial Planning Association, points out that advisors should be sure to determine their clients' citizenship status. "Do you ask them if they are American citizens?" she says. "If not, you may unknowingly be working with some people who are resident aliens. Clients who are not U.S. citizens, or who are married to non-citizens, may have cross-border planning issues that result in serious tax or estate planning problems."

To learn more about dealing with these issues, visit FPA's Cross Border Resource Library or one of the advisor discussion groups at **www.fpanet.org/CareerPractice/CrossBorderPlanning/.**

---

7. **Don't be a stranger.** If you want to serve a particular minority group, involve yourself in as many aspects of its culture as you can. For example, set up a neighborhood office, join a local church, or become active in community organizations. If this meshes with your style of doing business, consider stepping outside your current comfort zone to meet prospective clients where they live.

I'm fond of the saying that "The bonds that unite us are stronger than the differences that divide us." That's certainly true when it comes to helping people live richer and more fulfilling lives. "While the specifics of financial planning can differ from country to country or culture to culture, at its foundation, its motivations are global in nature," Laura Brook says. "People want to have the financial resources necessary to achieve their life goals. And everyone wants the peace of mind that planning can bring."

Amen, I say. And *gaman.*

CHAPTER 9

Change of Heart

Ever wish you had a magic wand to transform clients who need to change? Here's the next best thing: a step-by-step guide to help them succeed.

Is change really possible? Chances are good that nearly every week you see clients who want or need to change themselves or their behavior. Why do some succeed and others fail? Are there ways to improve their chances of success?

Executive coach Lynne Hornyak, my partner in conducting teleclasses for financial and counseling professionals, recently introduced me to a remarkable book about change by James Prochaska and two therapist colleagues. *Changing for Good: A Revolutionary Six-Stage Program for Overcoming Bad Habits and Moving Your Life Positively Forward* (Quill Books, 2002) is an exploration of Prochaska's research on what he calls "self-changers": people who have been able to give up smoking or drinking, resolve their destructive emotional habits, and so on.

Prochaska also studied the work of many different kinds of therapists. He found that no matter what kind of specific therapeutic interventions or techniques they used, their clients went through the same stages of change as did the self-changers.

So how do people change? What makes it possible for them to change for good? What interventions are most useful at each stage of working with them?

Prochaska identifies the following six stages of change:

Stage 1: Precontemplation

This is the denial stage: the client hasn't yet admitted that a problem exists.

Consider the overspender who is dragged into your office by a husband who complains, "She spends so recklessly, we'll never be able to save for retirement!"

If the wife is in the precontemplation stage, she may retort, "I don't buy designer clothes or drive a Maserati, so what are you complaining about?" or "You're so tight, you think any spending is frivolous!" In other words, she doesn't think she has a problem.

At this stage, if you ask pointed questions or suggest actions the client can take to change a behavior that she doesn't see as problematic, you will probably join her spouse in becoming a "bad guy." This is a time for gentle exploration, consciousness-raising, and information-gathering about the issue at hand, with the goal of encouraging her to move to the next phase.

Stage 2: Contemplation

At this point, the client is thinking, "Maybe I do have a problem with spending, but I'm not ready to do anything about it. I work hard, and it's a great stress reliever for me. Aren't I entitled to enjoy life a little?"

Once a client begins to contemplate the problem, even if it's embedded in rationalization and self-justification, your intervention can stimulate the process of change. The way to intervene most effectively is to ask consciousness-raising questions. Try to help clients look at their habit or behavior and begin seeing whether or not it serves them well. For example, you might ask the overspender:

- What do you like to spend money on?

- Where do you tend to spend it?

- Do you have an idea of how much you spend every month?

- When you charge things on a credit card, do you tend to buy more often?

- Do you have financial goals that are important to you?

- Do you have money saved for them?

- How do you plan to achieve them?

A process of self-reevaluation also happens during contemplation and the subsequent preparation phase. This involves an emotional and cognitive self-appraisal to see if one's problematic behavior is at odds with some cherished value. In the best case, individuals end up thinking, feeling, and believing that their life would be improved significantly if they changed the behavior or behaviors in question.

You may be able to guide clients into self-reevaluation by helping them ask the right questions of themselves:

- "Why am I behaving like this?"

- "What are my underlying needs?"

- "What is the effect of this habit on me? On others?"

- "How would others around me react if I changed?"

- "How would I feel if I changed?"

From these and similar techniques and questions, a list of benefits and costs can emerge. This is a vital first step in encouraging clients to create a new self-image and to think before they exercise their old bad habits.

In the contemplation and precontemplation stages, Prochaska also identifies emotional arousal as an important factor in motivating change. By this he means what therapists call "catharsis": powerful, intense emotions that inspire us to change habits that are not good for us.

An example of emotional arousal came for me when my soon-to-be-husband realized that I, an overspender, tended to rack up credit card debt. He said, "Honey, it doesn't make sense to pay 18% on your credit card balance. If you can't pay off your bill every month, let me know and we'll deal with it." By healing enough of the shame I felt at being an out-of-control spender, this caring, nonjudgmental intervention moved me and fueled my commitment to change. From that time on, I was able to pay off my credit cards monthly.

The question is why, as a fairly intelligent and math-adept person, did I need someone else's words to persuade me to act sensibly? I think the answer is that I was at the contemplation stage, ready to take this issue on. His compassionate remark helped me turn a corner and prepare to change my habit of credit card overuse for good. I firmly believe that this intervention was crucial to my recovery so many years ago.

Empathy, warmth, and constructive input from others can obviously be very helpful during this phase. But emotional arousal may sometimes mean shocking a client out of complacency. An example would be an overweight person in denial whose doctor informs her that the extra pounds will shorten her life, or a smoker who sees an X-ray of his lungs. As a financial advisor, you might have to tell a client couple that unless they go on a tight budget and increase their savings, they will have to live on 30% of today's income in retirement.

Faced with the overpowering necessity for change, clients may feel anxiety, regret, or deep sadness. These intense emotions may well provide the motivation they need, lighting a fire under their commitment to change and moving them to prepare for action.

Stage 3: Preparation

Emotional arousal and self-reevaluation continue in this phase, and commitment to action begins. The client acknowledges the existence of a problem that needs to be addressed and resolved. In the preparation stage, he or she is getting ready to do something about it, much as athletes visualize or rehearse a move in their heads before committing themselves to act.

A friend of mine recently decided that he was becoming a full-fledged sugar addict and needed to give up processed sugar and desserts, except for fruit. However, he wasn't ready to embark on this plan for three weeks, when he would return from a long-awaited vacation. In the meantime he indulged himself fully, and began seeing himself giving up desserts upon his return. Three weeks later, just as planned, he moved into the action stage.

Another process of change that helps in preparation and later stages is what Prochaska calls "social liberation"—awareness and use of safe zones to control or limit a bad habit. Some examples might be choosing a restaurant with no-smoking rules (for a smoker) or using a credit card with a very low credit limit (for an overspender). These external aids let self-changers put themselves, at least part of the time, in situations that are conducive to change.

Stage 4: Action

This phase is the one that involves beginning a new behavior or eradicating a negative habit. It's the busiest phase of all, because there are many processes of change at work.

For example, let's go back to your client, the overspender. She likes to buy clothes in stores and via mail-order catalogues. Many of her purchases are on Tuesdays and Thursdays, when she has some free time and is not far from her favorite store, Chico's.

What healthier "countering activities" could she substitute for this behavior? Instead of shopping, maybe she could find an absorbing hobby to practice at home, meet a friend for lunch or tea, or take an exercise class or a continuing education course to fill the time.

You could also suggest that your client exercise environment control, or what I call "avoiding slippery places." For instance, she could cut up her Chico's membership rewards card or cancel some or all of her catalogues.

This new behavior is bound to be difficult, and it's helpful for clients to reward themselves for sticking to it. Ask them to come up with a reward that works for them. It needs to be something that doesn't undermine their progress (which rules out a clothes-shopping expedition as a reward for avoiding Chico's for a week).

In this action phase, as well as the maintenance phase that follows it, commitment is essential to sustain the process of change. Helping relationships can be very beneficial, although that doesn't necessarily mean the client needs a therapist. Free 12-step programs like Debtors Anonymous can be effective. So can money mentors. Ideally, you should be on that list, along with good friends who can help the client stay out of slippery places and reinforce positive behavior.

Stage 5: Maintenance

In this stage the self-changer has begun to institute new, healthier behavior. Now he or she needs to learn how to maintain this desirable change.

For many clients, this will entail regular consultations with you to ensure that they are still moving toward their goals. Other reinforcing techniques will vary with the need. For instance, a program for a now-recovering overspender might include weekly Debtors Anonymous meetings and coaching, counseling, or therapy to explore more deeply the roots of the problem. She might put a photo of a dream retirement destination in her wallet to remind herself why she is brown-bagging her lunch or avoiding the Clinique makeup counter (or, for a male overspender, avoiding Brookstone or Best Buy).

When my friend gave up desserts, periodic check-ins with the nutritionist who helped him take the plunge were crucial in sustaining his commitment to change. With her help, he was able to find substitute snacks to satisfy his sweet tooth. His wife's constant encouragement about kicking the sugar habit helped a lot. So did staying away from the pastry shop where he used to buy a snack every afternoon.

Stage 6: Termination

Not everyone reaches this final stage, which occurs only when the change has been so deeply incorporated into one's life that it can be maintained without vigilant work. At that point, it isn't "change" any more—it's part of normal behavior. A consummation devoutly to be wished!

"Recycling," Not Relapsing

Prochaska suggests that when people initiate change and then slip back, "recycle" would be a better term to use than "relapse." That's because self-changers who backslide do not in fact slip all the way back to precontemplation and denial. Instead, they cycle back to contemplation or preparation, then start through the remaining stages of change again. This time they may be equipped with some new tricks or tools, or at least a renewed commitment to move toward their desired goal.

To conclude the overspender example, suppose that after several weeks of successful behavior change, your client confesses to you that while waiting for a delayed flight, she wandered into an airport gift shop and impulsively bought an expensive scarf for herself. All is not lost. In fact, this "slip" may recycle her into more intense preparation and recommitment. To heighten her awareness and reinforce her willpower, you might suggest that she keep a spending diary to track what she spends her money on and how she feels about it.

Why is Prochaska's work so valuable? After many years as a therapist and more recently as a coach, I love the way this simple system provides a road map for change that anyone can use. Designing interventions around these processes—consciousness-raising, social liberation, emotional arousal, self-reevaluation, commitment, countering, environment control, and helping relationships—can promote change when used at the right time.

If clients are in denial about the negative effects of some aspect of their behavior, remember that they may actually be in the first stage of change—

precontemplation. Their initial resistance doesn't mean the task is hopeless. My clinical experience tells me that people who need to change are often weighted down with shame, defensiveness, self-deprecation, fear, or anxiety. Prodding them into action too soon will not effect change. They won't really move forward until their emotional burden is lightened through consciousness-raising, self-reevaluation, and catharsis.

The chances of success are heightened when you help clients gain awareness of the cost-benefit ratio of their actions in the early stages of change, and avoid suggesting behavioral improvements until they are in the preparation or action stage. With your thoughtful assistance and support, they may be able to move more smoothly into contemplation, preparation, action, and maintenance—and perhaps eventually into termination, when the new habit is so deeply ingrained that maintenance is no longer necessary. This understanding of how people change and how you can facilitate the process may be one of the most valuable ways to increase your effectiveness as an advisor.

CHAPTER 10

Therapeutic Finance

Once, finance was finance and therapy was therapy. That's different now—to the benefit of many advisors and their clients.

A while ago, I took part in a committee retreat about teaching communication and counseling-related skills to financial planners. The discussion was sponsored by the National Association of Personal Financial Advisors (NAPFA), which has been particularly open to employing money psychology tools and principles.

But as we discussed how to help advisors communicate more effectively with clients, someone suggested that we avoid using the terms "therapeutic educator" and "therapy." It was a vivid reminder that these concepts still provoke strong reactions in many people. Any approach smacking of therapy rankles some advisors and makes others uneasy.

Despite the many commonalities between financial advisory services and psychotherapy, this wariness has kept lots of advisors from taking greater advantage of what therapy professionals have learned. As someone with a foot in both camps, I thought it might be time to investigate successful therapy principles and techniques that financial advisors can use to enhance their work with clients.

It's How You Do It, Not What You Do

My research began with a summary of therapy techniques by Jay Lebow, Ph.D., a clinical psychology professor at Northwestern University ("A Look at the Evidence: Top 10 Research Findings of the Last 25 Years," *Psychotherapy Networker*, March/April 2007). Dr. Lebow observes that certain psychotherapy modalities seem appropriate for particular problems, such as depression, obsessive-compulsive disorder, and substance-use disorders, to name a few.

Unfortunately no single school or method of therapy appears to stand out as universally effective, but there is one important predictor of across-the-board success: the therapist-client relationship. Dr. Lebow says firmly, "Without a positive alliance, virtually any psychotherapy is ineffective."

In fact, the quality of the relationship is a more potent predictor of outcome than orientation, experience, or professional discipline. The client's perception of the relationship tends to predict its outcome even better than the therapist's.

I think this has a huge implication for financial advisors. Like therapists, you're unlikely to take exactly the same approach with clients who have different needs—say, asset management, life planning, or charitable giving. You use the process that best suits the individual client. But in all cases, your chances of success with that client are enhanced if you can build a connection of trust and respect.

The Power of the Alliance

How can a financial advisor strengthen this connection? Studies in the therapy world suggest these five guidelines:

1. **Listen more empathetically.** Learning to listen carefully and fully is part of every therapist's training. Many advisors think they listen well, but clients often disagree. In a Financial Psychology Corporation/*Investment Advisor* survey reported in December 2001, an overwhelming 69% of individual investors wanted their relationship with their advisor to focus more on their feelings about money.

2. **Focus on clients' strengths and successes.** Confronting and pressuring clients makes them less likely to comply with a plan or sustain a change for the better. In his research into changing self-destructive behaviors, James Prochaska, Ph.D., a clinical psychology professor at the University of Rhode Island, found that positive reinforcement was more powerful than negative comments in helping people change. You don't have to ignore clients' problems, but make an effort to avoid putting the primary emphasis on their faults.

    To tease out strengths and weaknesses, I often suggest asking new clients to write down three things about their approach to money that they feel good about, and three things they feel uncomfortable or regretful about. I call this exercise "finding your baseline." If the "good" list is harder for them to write, it may be useful to spend time shoring up their confidence and feelings of self-worth. If the "bad" list is harder, gently help them turn their attention to one item on the list that they can begin to take action on. To reinforce this new behavior, encourage them to reward themselves for making a change.

3. **Don't rush.** Trying to move things along too fast, or interpret a client's behavior or motivation too early, can compromise the success of the work. Many therapists know that unless they match their pace to the client's own process, emotions, and thoughts, listening deeply and sharing feedback when the client is ready to hear it, progress can easily be derailed.

    Dick Vodra, first vice president of Spire Investment Partners in McLean, Virginia, had an experience with a new client that illustrates this point. Introduced to him by an attorney, she wanted an overview on part of her portfolio. But after years of family conflicts and bad experiences with two other financial advisors, she had great trouble opening up. When Dick asked what she envisioned her life like in a few years once these things were worked out, she said she had no idea and that she could not look ahead. Dick quickly realized that instead of moving toward long-term goals, he had to start slowly, building trust, stanching the wounds, and allowing her to set the pace of future planning. Like many good advisors, while he has a good process for getting to know a client's dreams, goals, and values, he knew when to put that aside and simply be with his client.

4. **Be open to what your clients really need.** When Rick Kahler, president of Kahler Financial Group in Rapid City, South Dakota, recently met with a client for an annual review, he asked, "Before I launch into my agenda, what has changed since the last time that you want me to know?" The client told him she had been diagnosed with breast cancer, talking about her fear of death and her unresolved relationship with her daughter. He listened for over an hour, handing her tissue after tissue as she cried and talked. With about five minutes left, she asked how her portfolio was doing. Although Kahler had prepared more than an hour's worth of charts and graphs, he gave her a one-minute summary that basically said, "Everything is fine." The client thanked him for a wonderfully productive meeting, leaving him stunned. As he said, "In my book, we had accomplished nothing; in hers, everything."

5. **Ask for feedback.** Therapy research has determined that feedback from clients about what's working and what isn't can improve the

outcome, if the practitioner acts on that information to tweak the process. According to Barry Duncan, Psy.D., co-director of the Institute for the Study of Therapeutic Change, therapy that is going badly can change direction and become effective if this feedback loop is created.

If you solicit frequent feedback from your clients and keep adjusting your process to meet their needs, the probability of client satisfaction and success increases exponentially. Ask questions such as:

- Are we meeting frequently enough, or too often?

- Do you prefer face-to-face visits? How do you feel about phone or e-mail contacts?

- Are you getting the kind of help you need?

- Is there any way I can serve you better?

- Is there anything that bothers you about the way we've set up our relationship?

- Do you feel my fee is fair?

- What do you value most about the service I'm providing?

- What would you change?

The answers can help you fine-tune your rapport with clients, improving relationships to create more and more satisfaction.

Lessons from Couples Therapy

Dr. John Gottman, together with his wife, psychotherapist Julie Gottman, has spent decades studying the factors that lead to a successful or a failed marriage. Throughout the 1980s and '90s, this mathematician-turned-psychologist followed couples to see who got divorced, who established parallel lives (living separately, though still married), and who stayed together, happily or not. Using heart monitors and spring-loaded platforms to record fidgeting, he videotaped ordinary people in their most ordinary moments. His research (reported in

Getting Over Therapyphobia

For a number of advisors, even the mention of "therapy" or "therapeutic" evokes a negative reaction. This resistance is often due to concern that they might do or say something wrong to a client who is venting strong feelings.

Reflecting clients' thoughts and feelings back to them with empathy and compassion is good, deep listening, not therapy, and cannot harm them. If the intensity of feelings being directed at you ever makes you feel that you're over your head, it's time to consider referring the client to a therapy professional.

Another sign of being outside your zone is obsessing about particular clients. Thinking about them on weekends, worrying about them, and feeling overly responsible for them are all signs that you need to consult a trained professional, either for supervision or an outright referral. You should never feel you're all on your own. After all, you don't expect to have to do tax audits or draw up a QPRT for your clients. That's why you bring in experts.

If you don't already have a good relationship with a trained therapy professional whom you trust, it could be time to start looking for someone who is comfortable with financial matters. In fact, it's a good idea for all advisors to develop a list of therapists, counselors, coaches, substance abuse counselors, 12-step programs, and so on.

Psychotherapy Networker, March/April 2007) showed that it wasn't only how a couple fought that mattered, but how they made up.

Whether a couple is married or not, Dr. Gottman found three elements that predict success in their relationship: a five-to-one ratio of positive to negative interactions, increased positive interactions during conflicts, and decreased negative interactions during conflicts.

The Gottmans also identified four negative behaviors, which they call the "Four Horsemen of Marital Apocalypse"—contempt, criticism, defensiveness, and stonewalling. This may manifest in your office as couples blaming each other instead of attacking a problem; refusing to acknowledge their own role in creating conflict; sarcasm, belittling, name calling, or withdrawing into stony silence.

You can gently point out to a couple like this that in order to find a solution to their conflict, they need to learn to communicate with more care, respect, and regard for one another. Or you may be able to set an example by referring to their differences with the right kind of humor, which could help them move toward a better way of relating.

In any case, try to notice more quickly when the "four horsemen" are in the room with you, so you can nip these negative interactions in the bud. I usually handle this by teaching clients to mirror (playing back verbatim what their partner just said), validate (saying what made sense about it from their partner's perspective), and empathize (sharing what else they imagine their partner might be feeling). You may be willing to educate some clients on this simple approach taught by psychotherapist and author Harville Hendrix, especially if you practice it yourself.

If you hesitate to intervene in a case of serious marital tension, an alternative is to refer your clients to a couples therapist, counselor, or coach. Meet ahead of time with a professional you may want to recommend and see if you're comfortable collaborating with each other. Your referrals will feel more solid, and your clients will be more likely to end up with someone who can help them learn to build on their strengths, rather than indulging their weaknesses.

Even if you're thinking, "These are deeper waters than I've been trained to handle," try to be aware of negative or positive interactions in couples who consult you. If they snipe at each other in your office, there's a good chance they'll end up in divorce court. When you're approached by couples who interact with respect, affection, and a light touch, you'll know these are clients you'd like to have in your practice.

Forecasting a Positive Outcome

Therapy research has also revealed that if a client's behavior or attitude hasn't improved by the sixth visit, success over the long run is not likely. Clients who are doing worse by the third visit are twice as likely to drop out. The inverse is also true: early progress often predicts a successful longer-term relationship. I suspect that this axiom holds for advisors and clients as well.

If so, it's more important than ever to cultivate a strong relationship as early as possible. According to Barry Duncan, the strength of a therapeutic alliance is responsible for more than 50% of the outcome. He defines the components of this alliance as the relational bond (how connected your clients feel to you), agreement on goals, and agreement on tasks necessary to achieve those goals.

Dr. Duncan's analysis will resonate with many advisors. If you and your clients feel connected and comfortable early in the process, and you help them identify their goals and commit to actions that are in their best interest, you are both likely to feel that the advisory process is a success.

When Planning Meets Therapy

Until recently, little or no information was available about therapeutic treatment of what we might call "money disorders," where someone shows dysfunctional behavior over money matters. Two pioneers in this area are Ted Klontz, Ph.D., and Rick Kahler, who have developed a Healing Money Issues workshop that combines traditional financial planning with experiential therapy.

Klontz, an author, coach, and president of Onsite Workshops in Nashville, Tennessee, ascribes the uniqueness of his program to the extensive historical inventory that clients are asked to create. "Usually we find elements of significant trauma regarding money that prevent them from doing what they know they need to do," he says. During the course of the five-day program, he and Kahler help clients work through these emotional blocks, freeing them to embrace more positive money behaviors.

Kahler focuses on "left-brain stuff" in this process, while Klontz works with the right brain. "When facts and figures are presented, the left side of the brain begins firing, while the right side literally goes quiet, as if asleep," Klontz explains. "However, when the client is told a story or shown a picture, the right side begins firing also." Using anecdotes, photographs, drawings, metaphors, physical exercises, and three-dimensional sculptures, he helps illustrate what Kahler is saying. "The left side is the facts and figures recorder," Klontz says, "but it never decides anything. The emotional or right brain does the deciding."

To test the program's effectiveness, the Klontz Kahler Institute compared 31 workshop participants with a 31-person control group. Participants showed a significantly greater and longer-lasting reduction of depression and anxiety around money issues, as well as lasting improvements in financial well-being.

The Future of Planning?

It makes perfect sense to me that an intensive program integrating money psychology with financial planning can effect real change. By lightening clients' emotional load, it allows them to transform their moneylife, their self-esteem, and their inner sense of security.

Ted Klontz and Rick Kahler have codified their findings about the combined power of these two disciplines into an Integrated Financial Planning Model. In this model, a trained therapist and a trained financial planner work as a team with a client, or sometimes collaborate while counseling a client separately.

It would be easy for many advisors to adopt this model by teaming up with a financially savvy mental health professional—who, however, may not always be easy to find. (See "Helping Therapists Get Over Moneyphobia.") Rick Kahler suggests introducing clients to a financial therapist as part of the team of professionals you call on as needed. This greatly reduces clients' hesitation to talk to a therapist. Even if you don't introduce your therapy pro at the onset of the engagement, the two of you can still get together to strategize an approach to a challenging issue or personality.

Armed with a more solid understanding of your clients' feelings and needs, you'll have a better opportunity to transform your business model from "exterior finance" (traditional financial planning, asset management, accounting) to "interior finance" (life planning, coaching, financial counseling).

In my opinion, this is the direction in which the planning profession will evolve. However, there will always be a place for advisors who prefer to practice solely in the realm of exterior finance. As long as you and your clients see eye to eye on what they want and the services you provide, you can draw your practice boundaries wherever you feel most comfortable.

Helping Therapists Get Over Moneyphobia

The vast majority of psychotherapists are money avoiders. If a client brings up the subject of money, therapists often (consciously or unconsciously) deflect the discussion to another subject. Or, as Ted Klontz notes, they wait impatiently to respond to the client's "real" issues. Thus, money dysfunctions are never directly addressed.

After participating in a Healing Money Issues workshop put on by Ted Klontz and Rick Kahler, Amy West, a therapy professional at a Spring Lake, Michigan, wellness center, has stayed in touch with Rick several times a year. "My business has really taken off since I started working with him," she says. West now counsels clients through a "therapeutic exploration of [their] money beliefs."

Similarly, I include therapists, counselors, and coaches in teleclasses with financial professionals to help them become less moneyphobic and money-avoidant. This intermingling of disciplines also makes advisors more familiar with simple psychological techniques that can improve their clients' ability to hear and integrate the information they impart.

Interior Finance and Problem Clients

It's sometimes hard for advisors to counter their own left-brain bias toward "exterior finance" solutions. But by learning to tune into a client's deeper needs and feelings, you can often build a much stronger bond. In fact, helping clients open up about their deepest concerns and areas of conflict may actually turn a difficult relationship around. That was Rick Kahler's experience with a client we'll call Sam.

Meetings with Sam, who had some off-the-wall ideas about investing and tended to nitpick returns data, often felt draining and unproductive.

This time, Rick knew Sam was gung-ho to convert his portfolio into euro-denominated investments. When Sam arrived after a seven-hour drive, Rick chose a different approach. Instead of pulling out a portfolio summary, he opened the meeting by asking, "What's at the top of your agenda for us to cover today?"

Sam began to talk about his struggle with deciding whether to sell his family farm. He explained its long history and told Rick that he and his father had both been born there. Mirroring Sam's thoughts and feelings to him, Rick understood why this client, who had no wife or kids, no living parents, and a strained relationship with his one sibling, deeply wanted to keep the place that made him feel emotionally and literally grounded.

At the end of a marathon three-hour session, Sam announced that he had decided not to sell the farm. Rick agreed that the decision made sense. They spent 10 minutes talking about the euro, and ended up keeping Sam's investments dollar-denominated. Unlike past meetings, there was no talk of investment returns or quibbling about Rick's fee.

Rick wondered whether his client viewed the 14-hour round trip as a colossal waste of time. But as he left, Sam turned and said, "We sure covered a lot of ground today. This is one of the best meetings we've ever had. Thanks!"

Today, Sam is among the clients that Rick most enjoys working with. Although he still asks tough investment questions, he no longer grills Rick on portfolio decisions or compensation. Rick says, "Allowing him to set the agenda moved our relationship into a whole new territory."

Putting Principles Into Practice

Among the financial advisors and planners who have become more comfortable with incorporating therapeutic techniques are many, I suspect, who have benefited personally from therapy, counseling, or coaching or know friends or relatives who have. Others may have been influenced by such practitioners as holistic planner Dick Wagner, founder of WorthLiving, and George Kinder, founder of the Kinder Institute of Life Planning.

In the olden days, advisors would exit the room as soon as George talked about clients' feelings. Today, many financial professionals sign up for training based on his *Seven Stages of Money Maturity* work. More and more advisors are comfortable referring clients to a therapist, counselor, or coach; others develop partnerships with therapists and similar experts, and many are comfortable inviting a therapist, like me, to speak at client appreciation events. So there's a good chance that insights from the field of therapy are infusing your work, helping you forge deeper connections with your clients.

If you now find therapy less mysterious and stigmatizing, I hope you'll be more open to using its tools to strengthen client relationships. Whatever you can do to increase the strength of the bond with your clients will make successful outcomes more likely than before.

CHAPTER 11

Emotional Rescue

Help—client overboard! When psychological issues lead into water that's over your head, be sure you know where to find expert assistance.

A client calls, demanding to see you immediately. She's just discovered that her husband has been having an affair with a friend of theirs. She not only wants a divorce, she wants revenge. She starts to scream about him in your office, insisting that you help her "clean him out." Then she bursts into tears.

You know they have kids, and you're concerned that she may later regret any decisions made in the heat of rage and hurt. But the intensity of her emotions makes you feel that you're getting into deeper water than you can handle. What can you do to help? How should you respond?

When clients tell you their fears, anxieties, hopes, and dreams, what they say or how they say it can sometimes make you feel uncomfortable and even helpless. Intense behavior is only one kind of symptom. Clients may confide suicidal thoughts, feelings of deep anger toward their boss and coworkers, or fears that they will abuse their children. Or you may notice signs that they are suffering from drug abuse, alcoholism, gambling, serious overspending, or a sexual addiction.

I believe that when clients' attitudes or behavior interfere with their moneylife—my term for the way people feel about and deal with money—it's appropriate for a financial advisor to help them explore the reasons. The irony is that the more empathetic and supportive you are, the more you risk inviting clients to share their deeper feelings in a way that can lead to intense emotions and catharsis. This is the domain of therapy, not financial planning.

Crossing the Line

For many years, I've described my vision of the ideal financial advisor as a therapeutic educator. In this role, you are more than just a money manager. You help clients unearth their deepest goals and desires. You also try to lighten the emotional charge of any conflicts or intense feelings that may prevent them from making rational decisions and taking the wise actions you recommend.

But when you observe behavior or attitudes that make you feel you're in over your head, you may need to consider consulting a mental health professional for advice, or even referring the client to someone who is more comfortable dealing with intense emotion and conflict. A trained therapist or counselor can often help troubled clients understand what is happening and help them learn better ways of coping.

For example, a solution for the wronged wife might be to suggest that before taking any drastic action, she and her husband owe it to their children to seek couples therapy. The assistance of an experienced, objective professional could help them either heal their relationship or give it a respectful burial.

In instances where the emotional distress is not as visibly dramatic, there may still be indications that a client's level of need is greater than your training or expertise can handle. One clue is when you've started worrying about these particular clients after work and on weekends, trying to figure out how best to deal with them. Another indication that you are treading on thin ice could be if you find yourself getting overwrought when dealing with the client, or dreading the next meeting.

In these situations, it's important to know when you can intervene and when it might be better to seek help from a therapist or counselor. If outside support is more appropriate, how should you broach the subject with your client? And how do you find the right professional or support group for a particular client's needs?

Do It Yourself... or Not?

The line between planning and therapy is drawn in a slightly different place for everyone. You may feel equipped to handle many psychological issues by virtue of your own empathy and experience, as well as from ideas I've suggested in *The Advisor's Guide to Money Psychology*, past *Investment Advisor* articles, or other resources. But no matter what your degree of expertise may be, here's a good rule of thumb: If addressing a client's situation feels perilously like sailing into waters that you are unprepared to navigate, get help.

This includes instances when a client's problem coincides with a similar weak spot in yourself, preventing you from providing impartial and rational advice. For example, if you have always had difficulty relaxing and enjoying some of the real-time rewards of financial security, it may be hard for you to counsel a client who faces family unrest because of this same issue.

In fact, if you have an intense response to a particular problem, it may well be a sign that you need to disentangle your own emotions from your work for clients. You may be sufficiently self-aware to analyze your reaction and its roots by yourself. If your weak spot reduces your effectiveness at work but is not intense or debilitating enough to warrant therapy, another option is to consult a business coach who is sensitive to your psychological issues.

Which Approach?

Let's assume you've decided that a client needs more specialized psychological help than you can provide. To make the right referral choice, it's crucial to understand some key differences between counseling, coaching, and therapy.

Counseling usually focuses on suggesting behavioral changes and giving advice, including specific guidance on support groups, volunteer activities, and direct interventions.

Coaching tends to be even more goal-oriented. Clients devise action plans to change their behavior and move toward the goals they've set. Meetings are sometimes face-to-face, but a great deal of coaching is done by phone in weekly, biweekly, or monthly sessions. In these teleconferences, or in an informal get-together, the coach may share details of his or her own journey to help the client learn and stay motivated.

Both of these types of support are oriented toward the present and future. By contrast, deep **therapy** deals with early childhood trauma, deprivation, and conflicts and seeks to resolve these early conflicts and issues by returning to their source. Whatever the method used (psychoanalytic, experiential, gestalt, etc.), it often encourages deep emotional catharsis, and as full an awareness as possible of the unconscious forces that underlie dysfunctional behavior.

Most therapists do not reveal any personal information about their own journeys or conflicts. The course of a client's thrice-weekly, twice-weekly, or weekly sessions usually lasts for months or even years, although some forms of therapy use behavior modification to change patterns of thinking and action over a shorter term.

(For a greater understanding of the distinctions between therapy and coaching, and the niches coaches may develop, see Lynn Grodzki's *The New Private Practice: Therapist-Coaches Share Stories, Strategies, and Advice* [W.W. Norton, 2002].)

I would suggest counseling for people who are open to a hands-on therapeutic approach and don't like the idea of a long-term delving into the childhood roots of their motivations. Coaching is appropriate as a way to encourage powerful life changes in clients who are not severely disturbed or dysfunctional. When addictions are present, the combination of therapy with group support has proved to be more effective. This support can be found in 12-step programs such as Alcoholics Anonymous, Gamblers Anonymous, Overeaters Anonymous, and Debtors Anonymous.

To introduce a client to the ticklish topic of getting assistance, you might begin by saying that you know an expert who is skilled in helping people deal with the kinds of issues your client is facing. If possible, describe similar situations where other clients, friends, or you yourself have found support and insight.

When a client needs therapy but balks at the idea of getting it, you might discuss the stigma wrongly attached to this word and suggest that it's instead a sign of courage and intelligence to seek expert help. There is less of a stigma about counseling, and coaching may seem even more attractive due to its focus on creating action plans. No matter what type of help you propose, your willingness to talk clients through their resistance can work well, as long as you yourself don't see it as a mark of weakness.

Finding the Right Experts

It's important for every financial planner who embraces the role of therapeutic educator to know therapists, counselors, coaches, and support groups to recommend when it seems necessary or advisable. But if you don't already have a list of people and groups that you trust, how do you create one?

Getting recommendations from colleagues and friends is a fine way to start. But this is only the first step. It's important to interview these mental health professionals yourself, because some of them may share vulnerabilities about money that are similar to your clients'. So before putting therapists, counselors, or coaches on your list, sit down with them. See if they are at ease talking about money neuroses, spending compulsions, and other money conflicts, as well as uncovering what money may represent to a client. You might use the following questions to guide your interview:

1. How much experience have you had in dealing with the issue at hand? With clients' money dysfunctions in general? Can you give me examples?

2. What areas do you specialize in? Addictions, marital therapy, children and adolescents, wealthy clients, other?

3. If I referred an overspender to you, how would you work with this client?

4. If I referred a client who is extremely risk-averse because of a past financial trauma, how would you work with him or her?

5. How often do most clients see you? Twice a week, weekly, twice a month, monthly? How long do most clients stay?

6. What are your fees?

7. How do you see our distinct roles in a client's life?

8. Are you willing to take a consultant's role in my relationship with a client, or would you prefer to maintain a separate relationship with that client? (There's no right or wrong way to structure your collaboration. Just identify your preferences, be flexible, and trust your instincts.)

Be sure to give yourself a choice by interviewing more than one candidate. For instance, you may find a broadly credentialed therapist you'd enjoy working with in person, and a more specialized expert who can handle appropriate referrals.

Once you find a list of professionals you feel comfortable recommending to your clients, you may want to explore further ways to collaborate with them. For example, you might consider offering new clients an initial session with a money therapist as part of your introductory package. This helps identify key emotional issues right off the bat, and ultimately facilitates decision-making.

Another possibility is to invite a therapist-coach to participate in joint planner/client sessions. An Atlanta financial planning firm called GV Financial Advisors reported that this strategy made work with clients more fulfilling for all concerned.

To help your clients understand money psychology, you can also offer seminars on aspects of this important topic. I find myself increasingly involved in helping advisors educate their clients about money personality types and their strengths, preferences, and blind spots; couples polarization patterns and how to resolve them; major male–female differences around money, and so on.

If you're interested in learning more about the therapy process, there are many excellent guides for the lay reader. I would recommend Sheldon Kopp's books, such as *If You Meet the Buddha on the Road, Kill Him: The Pilgrimage of Psychotherapy Patients* (Bantam, 1988), and any of Harriet Lerner's books, especially *Fear and Other Uninvited Guests: Tackling the Anxiety, Fear, and Shame That Keep Us from Optimal Living and Loving* (HarperCollins, 2004). A fascinating book describing a wide range of therapeutic approaches to bizarre situations is *The Mummy at the Dining Room Table: Eminent Therapists Reveal Their Most Unusual Cases*, edited by Jeffrey A. Kottler and Jon Carlson (Jossey-Bass, 2003).

Helping Clients Open Up

If you would like to be more involved in helping clients share their deeper feelings about money, consider using one or more of the following self-awareness assignments.

The first exercise I often propose is for clients to list up to three things about themselves and their money that they feel good about, and up to three things that they're not so happy with. In addition to the pointers their answers provide, you can learn even more by asking your client to identify which list was harder to write. If the positive list was more difficult, you may need to focus on building up the client's self-confidence in order to make real progress together.

Another exercise, the Fantasy Autobiography, helps clients identify their deepest yearnings and clarify the goals for your work together. If clients have trouble getting specific in their autobiography, I ask them to write an ideal *New York Times* obituary for themselves in 300 words or less.

A third and more complex exercise is a Money Dialogue: an imagined conversation, written or taped, between the client and Money about how their "relationship" is going. After the dialogue winds down, the client comments on it from the different viewpoints of those who have been influential in his or her moneylife. This starts with parents and may also include other relatives, a current or former spouse, a mentor or spiritual advisor, and finally, the voice of God or inner wisdom. This powerful assignment can help you ascertain where clients stand in relation to money, where they have been, and where they need to go to reach balance.

All of these exercises are invitations to reach deep inside oneself. Though they are not dangerous in themselves, they may sometimes encourage more fragile clients to open up in ways that reveal a need for more help and support than you can provide. But in many other cases, they will merely make your work more three-dimensional.

The Payoff

A client who manages the endowment fund for a local charitable foundation confesses to you that despite his stellar track record for the charity, his own finances are in terrible shape. In discussing his background, it comes out that his stern, controlling parents considered him to be a screwup and made him answer for every penny they gave him. How would you handle this?

If your answer is something like "I'd recommend practical solutions to help him get organized, while suggesting that he get some therapy to work on his self-esteem and self-sabotage issues," well done!

Once you feel comfortable with the distinction between your perspective as a therapeutic educator and the role of counseling, coaching, and therapy, you will be better prepared to guide clients toward support for their emotional struggles around money and other issues. This will help you build trust and a stronger professional bond with them, and will pave the way for them to respond appropriately to your advice when the time is right.

CHAPTER 12

Sustainable Growth

One is the loneliest number that you'll ever do. But if you're a sole practitioner, you may think it's much simpler than expanding your business.

Financial planning often attracts men and women who consider themselves primarily as caretakers of their clients' well-being, and only secondarily as businesspeople. Many of them believe that working independently is the best way to provide excellent service to their clients.

This mindset can make a sole practitioner reluctant to hire more staff, join forces with other planners, or partner with experts in other specialties. Yet growth can pay off in quality colleagues and staff, larger referral networks, and more opportunities for strategic referral alliances, all of which help bring in more clients and enhance your revenue stream. Down the road, expansion may also help ensure that your business will continue serving your clients and generating income for you after you retire. Moreover, in today's regulatory environment, new compliance rules make it harder and harder to keep wearing all the hats yourself.

Some planners, like Chris Dowley of Dowley & Co. in Marblehead, Massachusetts, believe that taking on partners or building up staff is "too much trouble, and not worth the hassle." Chris has developed a solo practice that now lavishes attention on 52 clients. He works with their CPAs, estate planners, and other professionals when needed, but says his philosophy is "KISS — Keep It Simple, Stupid. I want control and simplicity. I am a great financial advisor, but a lousy manager of people."

If a solo practice is working fine for you and you see a way to achieve your goals without expanding your business, by all means hold your course. But if you've decided that adding capability could help you get where you want to go, be sure you know the challenges you're apt to face. Money issues aside, are you prepared for the personal changes — the "trouble" and "hassle" that expansion would entail?

If you're dedicated to giving your clients personal, hands-on attention, the idea of sharing or delegating this responsibility may make you very uncomfortable. Most likely, a good part of your self-worth is tied to the quality of what you do for your clients. You're concerned about risking the relationship you've developed with them and the trust they've developed in you. Maybe previous experiences with work partners who shirked their responsibilities have soured you on collaboration. How can you give control to others who might screw up what you've so painstakingly built?

O Solo Me?

If you're not sure whether to grow beyond a solo practice, it may help to go back to basics. Give some thought to what you want your business to be, what you want to give and accomplish, and how you can use your talents, experience, and energy most effectively. Once you define the worklife that suits you best, it may be easier to see if there's anything you'd like to do differently.

Bob Clark suggested some excellent questions to ask yourself in his column "Is Bigger Really Better?" (*Investment Advisor,* April 2006). With Bob's permission, I'd like to expand on his list:

* Why are you a financial advisor? Rank the following answers in order of importance:

  (a) To serve clients

  (b) To make money

  (c) To be your own boss

* What makes you want to go to work in the morning?

* What part of your work would you gladly give up?

* Have you ever worked with peer partners? What did you learn from the experience?

* Have you ever managed other people? What did you learn from it?

* How much control of your work environment do you need to have?

* If you could change anything about your worklife, environment, etc., what would it be?

* What would an ideal work day look like and feel like?

* How much money do you really need to be happy? How much do you already have?

* If you could choose to live more simply and work less (or not at all), would you do it?

* How would you feel if your business stayed the size it is now?

If it's still difficult to decide whether to change the way you do business, try an exercise I call Fantasy Obituary. Pretend that an obituary writer is summarizing your life. What did you accomplish between now and your much-lamented demise? If you find you're torn between a couple of different scenarios (for example, building a nationally known business or an early retirement followed by joining the Peace Corps), write an obituary with each script and see which feels better to you. This should help you get clearer on your personal, professional, and financial goals. Follow through by writing down these goals—near-, middle-, and long-term. If you go through the process several times, you'll see which desires crop up consistently. You can be confident then that these are not just momentary impulses, but goals you can trust. Whichever path you choose—growing your business, or keeping it just as it is and using your energy elsewhere—you'll feel the peace of knowing you've considered your options wisely and well.

I think the first step in letting go is to determine what parts of your business you insist on being totally responsible for. Typically, these would be the areas that are most important for client satisfaction and profitability. Make a second list of services, tasks, or competencies you want to stay closely involved in. Last, what aspects of your work would you be willing (or even delighted) to give to an assistant or a specialist? This final list could include anything from recordkeeping to tax preparation. If you are realistic about your skills and time management, these lists will help you see where you need support.

Learning to Share Control

Let's say you would like to hand off preparing your clients' tax returns to a knowledgeable expert. Although there are some excellent accounting firms in your area, you hesitate to give any of these pros access to your client relationships. Somehow, you feel it would make you appear inadequate as an advisor. Less valuable. Less unique. What if your clients actually preferred working with those CPAs to working with you?

When your self-esteem is bound up in controlling every aspect of your work, there are two exercises I would recommend. First, take some time to write down what drives you — your joys, gifts, strengths, passions, even your mission in life. How and where are you making use of these energies and abilities? In what other ways outside of work could you exercise them? For example, suppose you love receiving clients' praise when you personally present a plan to them. Would you be more willing to cede this role to a junior planner if you were enjoying audience applause in a community theater group?

Second, generate a list of your clients and highlight the ones you would be willing to gradually pass along to an affiliated planner. What characteristics should this partner have? Instead of trying to find someone just like yourself (who may not even exist), look for an individual who shares your values and integrity and who has strengths where you are weak. It's not essential that a potential partner have exactly the same goals, as long as they are compatible with yours.

If you find a suitable partner whose views jibe with your own, I would approach this person like a potential spouse. In other words, live together for a while. Structure a trial period for your relationship that lets both of you practice co-consulting skills without being locked into the new arrangement.

This may not be easy. Learning to share decision-making means switching from a "me" mentality to "we." You'll need to let go of the total control of your business that you used to have and surrender to a joint vision that you and your partner hold.

Here's where good listening skills can really pay off. Practice listening to each other openly and empathetically. I suggest following the Harville Hendrix mirroring method, which begins with each of you playing back exactly what the other said. Then validate the other person's comment, noting what makes sense about it from his or her perspective. Last, empathize ("I imagine you might also be feeling..."). If you both become familiar with this process and learn to enter deeply into each other's world, you'll be able to negotiate more effectively when you and your partner have different ideas about a decision or direction for the firm. The result should be a solution that works for you both.

The Right Staff

For a sole practitioner, sharing control with a peer may seem far easier than being responsible for the productivity, development, and compensation of employees. How can you maximize your strengths and minimize your flaws as a boss?

The first step is to manage expectations. In other words, know precisely what you want the prospective employee to do. Handle recordkeeping and compliance? Respond to client questions and concerns? Initiate contact with clients? Find new clients? How will his or her responsibilities intersect with yours (and those of anyone else in the firm)? What professional skills will be required?

When you find a candidate with an appropriate skill set, the second step is to make sure he or she has the qualities you want in a member of your "work family." If you've developed a mission statement and goals for your business, share them with people you are thinking seriously of hiring. Talk about your company's values and ask about their own. You want to be clear on what motivates them, what they feel committed to, and whether they can get on board with your mission.

The importance of this preliminary research can't be overstated. If you enjoy your business, clearly you've created a culture that works for you.

Hiring the right people will help you sustain the elements of it that you value most.

Managing for Results

The most important part of managing is setting clear, realistic objectives for your employees and providing the guidance they need to reach these objectives. Frequent meetings may be necessary, at least until you both know what to expect of each other. Probe for any concerns or questions and answer them honestly.

As a longtime fan of *The One Minute Manager* by Ken Blanchard and Spencer Johnson, I would suggest it or *Putting the One Minute Manager to Work* (William Morrow, 2006), for advice to help bosses become better managers. These books point out the importance of making your expectations clear and giving frequent feedback. Don't hesitate to deliver a "one-minute reprimand" (ideally in private) for something an employee needs to change. But positive reinforcement is an even stronger motivator, so remind yourself to share your appreciation (ideally in public) for things that were done well. (I'd take more than a minute for this, if possible!)

By being a good leader as well as a good manager, you can inspire employees to put more creative energy and talent into their work. Remember, though, that it's not enough just to say what your company stands for; you have to walk the talk. For example, if you want employees to believe that honesty is part of your firm's DNA, don't even think of fibbing to a client that "a conference" kept you from delivering a plan on time. If you're interested in learning how values-based leadership can help you create the kind of company people want to work for, I recommend an interesting guide: *Making Your Company Human: Inspiring Others to Reach Their Potential* (LSK Books, 2006) by Le Herron, a former CEO, with Sherry Christie.

The Joys of Mentoring

Once you reach a certain level of success, one of the most important and satisfying ways you can give back is to mentor a younger planner. The more secure you are in your own unique voice and skills, the more comfortable you will be with passing along your wisdom to newcomers in the field. Many planners find mentoring as fulfilling as providing advice to clients.

If you feel uneasy about giving these younger folks meaningful work that can help them grow in their career, consider trying the self-esteem exercise I mentioned earlier. Good planners who are effective leaders are unlikely to suffer much from sharing their knowhow. I'm reminded of a time when I sought out experts in a field I wanted to learn more about. One of the two practitioners I talked to was negative, self-serving, and stingy with information; the second was positive, generous, and open-hearted. It doesn't surprise me at all that Ms. Miser's business eventually foundered, while Ms. Generous' practice still thrives.

There's enough business to go around for everybody. Moreover, how will tomorrow's planners learn excellence, if not from people like you? Sharing your knowledge to help a younger person succeed is like planting an acorn so your grandchildren will have shade.

You Don't Have to Do It Alone

If the idea of partnering with other pros or hiring employees still makes you think of all the things that can go wrong, you may need to reframe your negative mindset. Talk to colleagues who have successfully grown their businesses so you can cultivate a more positive vision of what expansion can do for you.

If you undertake the due diligence I have suggested, I believe you'll be rewarded with productive and satisfying business relationships. Tuning in to your employees' or partners' passions in work (and away from work), learning what their gifts are, and positioning yourself as a mentor to help them take advantage of these gifts will create a winning situation for everyone.

While you're getting accustomed to this new way of working, I would recommend consulting in person or by phone with a business coach who can help you fine-tune your managerial or partnering skills. An alternative would be to hire an organizational consultant, who can facilitate monthly meetings that help you and your staff learn to work together more effectively.

Even when your business arrangement is no longer new, an outside consultant may be well worth the expense. Work cultures tend to become closed systems in which the inhabitants can't see themselves and each other clearly. Bringing in a trained, objective observer helps "breathe air into the system" and keep it fresh and growing.

Keeping Your Personal Voice

Once you are clear on your goals, skills, passions, vision, strengths and weaknesses, there's no limit to how creative you can be in designing your ideal practice.

In Watertown, Connecticut, for example, George Taylor has created a virtual office that allows him and his two staff members to work out of their homes. Client meetings are held at his house, at the client's office, or at a conference room made available by an accounting firm. Technology has made his business, Temenos, Inc., so efficient that he works only about 30 hours a week, with breaks for gardening or volunteering as a money management teacher at the local high school.

George told me he has consciously positioned his business as an income source, not a capital asset to be put on the market one day. Passionate and energized about his work, he feels that the way he runs his business lets him devote much more attention to clients.

If you go through the exercises I've suggested, you may experience a freeing-up of your own mind and a fuller understanding and appreciation of your unique gifts and qualities. These exercises helped me more fully appreciate my love of color and sense of humor, which manifest themselves in jewelry-making and spoof songwriting. When I express these gifts in ways I can share with others, it energizes and nourishes me.

Think of changes in your practice as a way not just to increase your income, but also to share your gifts with those around you. In the end, growing your business could offer you a priceless opportunity to grow your own spirit.

PART IV

Managing Stress

As a species whose ancestors hunted saber-toothed tigers and survived being pursued by hungry cave bears, we have a remarkable tolerance for stress. Many of us live among thousands or millions of others, work six or seven days a week, compete with 36-ton semis on the highway, and relax with news media whose motto is "If it bleeds, it leads."

But nothing in our DNA has prepared us to cope with stresses like 9/11, which destroyed our sense of security and safety in a single morning, or an economic meltdown that in a few weeks nearly halved the wealth that many investors had spent decades accumulating.

For some time, many advisors around the country have been going through the stages of mourning and loss: denial, anger, bargaining, sadness, and—the last and most difficult phase—trying to arrive at some semblance of peace and balance. How can you cope more successfully with the inordinate pressures you experience every day?

Everyone has the inner wisdom to know what they need to heal and thrive. So first, learn to recognize your stress patterns. How do you feel, act, and react when you're facing undue stress? Whenever this occurs, you will revert to your primitive survival pattern, which is always somewhat dysfunctional.

Once you recognize this, you can ask yourself what has worked in the past to help you return to better functioning, emotionally and professionally. The answer may be spending more time with family or friends, practicing a hobby you enjoy, exercising, meditating, or learning something new. Reminding yourself of the things you feel grateful for in a daily "gratitude journal" is another powerful way to escape feeling overwhelmed, depressed, or hopeless. We all have different toolkits for self-restoration, which we need to keep expanding and refining to give ourselves more ways to recover. But the first step in getting "back to one" is to ask yourself the right questions, so you can come up with answers that will steer you back to your adult, rational mode.

When clients are similarly stressed-out, ask them the same questions. How do they behave when they're under pressure? What tools have they used before to get out of the doldrums and restore their more productive and more positive selves? By helping them explore these patterns, you may be able to hasten the healing of another overstressed or traumatized spirit.

CHAPTER 13

The Present, Tense

It may not be possible to reduce the stress in your life. But there are ways to keep it from slowing you down.

Helping professions are notoriously stressful. As a financial advisor, you have to help your clients deal with highly charged and taboo areas such as control, money, love, and death—subjects you may not feel completely comfortable with. Adding insult to discomfort, once you are able to develop a plan that deals with these touchy areas, the feedback you often hear most loudly is about what doesn't work.

Add more competition, more regulation, and other changes in financial services to the mix, toss in the tensions of the wider world, like terrorism and war, and you're careening off the stress scale. That's without factoring in your personal pressures regarding children, intimate partners, parents, and friends. Remember, stress-related symptoms can also be caused by "good" changes like a new marriage, a new house, or even taking a long vacation.

By now you may be tempted to lie down and pull the covers over your head. The fact is, however, that stress is as unavoidable in the business of financial advice as it is in coaching and therapy. After years of helping people avoid "stress fractures" of both personal and professional origin, I've learned a few things I'd like to share with you.

Most of us need a certain amount of healthy challenge in our lives. Without opportunities to struggle and succeed, we grow dissatisfied and bored. By my definition, stress is the unhealthy result of living with challenges that we cannot hope to control, such as random terrorist attacks or an unrealistically demanding boss.

The negative effects of too much stress are everywhere. Obesity, hypertension, depression, reliance on alcohol or drugs, and anxiety affect our physical and mental health, and ultimately can shorten our lives. Home and work relationships suffer when we operate in a stressed-out mode. Compounding the problem is our cultural tendency to always do-do-do, instead of just to be.

Basically, if the challenges you face are making you feel helpless or even sick, you're overstressed. It's critical to understand the seriousness of this problem, and find ways to manage stress in your life.

How Do You Handle Stress?

Does stress affect you physically, with headaches, backaches, stomach problems, insomnia? Does it make you error-prone or unable to concentrate? How do you act when you're stressed—highly emotional, irritable, or explosive? Or do you withdraw from everything around you?

An evaluation of personal coping patterns can be very helpful in developing a stress management repertoire. I firmly believe in the power and virtue of "practicing the nonhabitual." For example, if you tend to isolate yourself when stressed, you may be able to escape this pattern—and some of your stress—by reaching out to a friend, a loved one, or a counselor. If you're more likely to become overemotional or even frantic, it may help to talk calmly with someone you trust, in a safe place.

To minimize physical or mental reactions to stress, learn to step back, take a few deep breaths, and re-center yourself with a thought, a place, or an activity that grounds you. In so doing, you may have to unlearn patterns that are actually contributing to the stress you feel today.

Developing a Personal Anti-Stress Strategy

There's a lot you can do to manage stress better. First of all, identify some on-the-spot stress-busters that work for you. When you are really tense, what's the very first thing you need to do to get back to connection, self-nurturing, and a sense of hope and healing? (Author Sheldon Kopp calls this "back to one.") Is it five minutes of deep, slow breathing? A call to your partner or best friend? Praying? Meditating? Whatever it is, commit to doing it, no matter how busy you are, as the first step in digging yourself out of a stress hole.

It's just as important to work on shoring up your reserves so that when stress hits, you are better able to take it in stride. Some of the activities that fall into this category include regular exercise, meditation, keeping a journal, maintaining a gratitude list, writing down daily successes, and volunteering. Here's how these anti-stress strategies can help:

Activity No. 1: Move

There are two kinds of people in the world: those who love to sweat, and everybody else. If you're the type who cringes while others rhapsodize about the thrill of a pumping pulse and rampaging endorphins, the secret is to search for your own best form of exercise. In my case, I realized that the terrific workout videos I bought always ended up gathering dust in my basement. A weekly meeting with a personal trainer is perfect to keep me motivated. Tap dancing and ballroom dancing twice a week add to my "bliss." Do what works for you.

Activity No. 2: Meditate

Before you start shaking your head or muttering, "Uh-uh, not for me," let me reassure you that you don't need to sit still in order to meditate, and you can do it anywhere. Many people listen to relaxation tapes; some join a group or meet with a friend to sit and breathe deeply; others practice walking meditation.

A recommended way to begin (or end) meditation is with an exercise in which you imagine being in some extremely peaceful place where you can drink in the warmth and restfulness. My own visualization exercise usually starts at my own private beach and moves on to a meadow. There, one or two animals (a different one each time) come to me and walk me from the meadow into the woods. We cross over a stream to a wise woman who answers a question that's troubling me, or gives me a bit of wisdom that helps guide me through the day.

This restorative exercise doesn't have to take lots of time. Fifteen minutes or so in the morning suits me best. For others, meditating after a long day may feel more relaxing. The key is figuring out what works for you, and committing yourself to do it regularly.

Activity No. 3: Write

Many kinds of daily writing help relieve stress. In her book *The Artist's Way: A Spiritual Path to Higher Creativity* (Tarcher, 2002), which is not just for artists, Julia Cameron recommends writing three journal pages first thing in the morning to clear your mind and heart for the day. Don't worry about subject matter, grammar, or style; just write. I find writing these "morning pages" to be very refreshing.

Another early-morning suggestion is to jot down the positive qualities about yourself that come to mind. This can re-center you in an upbeat mental state and color the rest of your day.

If you often feel that nothing is working out for you, set your office alarm for the same time every day to keep a gratitude journal. By taking five minutes to write down things you are currently grateful for, you will find it easier to reconnect to the blessings in your life at times of tension, loss, disillusionment, disappointment, or heartache.

Another de-stressing exercise if you feel unappreciated is to write down every day's small and large successes. If you do this at night, I can almost guarantee it will improve the quality of your sleep.

Activity No. 4: Connect

Connect: 12 Vital Ties That Open Your Heart, Lengthen Your Life, and Deepen Your Soul (Pantheon, 1999), by my friend and colleague Edward (Ned) Hallowell, is a wonderful primer for stress relief. In it, Ned outlines various ways that people need to connect with the world and with themselves in order to nurture themselves fully. He mentions family, friends, work, beauty, nature and special places, pets and other animals, spiritual belief, and creative activity as some of the connections that can help dissolve stress.

Spending quality time with the people who are closest to you often helps ease stress. In many cases, of course, these relationships are also the ones that cause intense stress in the first place, so be sure to choose your companions carefully when you feel uptight.

Sometimes a rather stressful relationship can be transformed by making small but powerful changes. For example, instead of retreating after dinner to nurse the day's tensions, a close friend of mine began to play cribbage, backgammon, and dominos with her husband. They've had a huge amount of fun and have been able to reconnect on many levels.

In the workplace, finding or creating a support group can go a long way toward making your job more satisfying. I can testify to this from my own experience: despite an incredible variety of interests, styles, and personalities, the group of therapists I trained with in the 1970s has managed to stay connected for 30 years. We meet once or twice a month with a facilitator to share feelings about our lives and our work, hold three-hour retreats several times a year, and host quarterly potluck dinners for ourselves and our families.

If a peer group like this doesn't exist where you work, or you are a sole practitioner, consider forming one with supportive colleagues. Don't look for people who always agree with you, but those who make you feel good about yourself and have opinions you value. Truly supportive people can disagree with you without putting you down, soothe you when you are upset, and confront you, if need be, with gentleness, care, and concern.

I also firmly believe that every workplace should consider facilitated retreats or staff meetings so someone from the outside can "blow air into the system" and keep problems from building up. These facilitated meetings can be real stress-reducers.

Activity No. 5: Give

Community connections are important in warding off stress and isolation. Volunteering your time in a good cause can help reverse feelings of hopelessness in the face of distressing events and trends. The many volunteer-supported organizations in every community are a reminder that there are good and worthwhile people everywhere and that you, too, can contribute to making the world a better place.

Charitable giving is another way to connect with positive energy. You're not only supporting an organization you believe in, but also passing on a legacy while you are still around to enjoy it. This can foster self-love and recharge your spirit.

Activity No. 6: Be With Beauty

Spending time in beautiful places is a wonderful way to combat tensions. This doesn't necessarily mean hiking through the wilderness or kayaking to Campobello. I'm sure I'm not the only nature wimp who gets stressed out just thinking about snakes, sharks, rip tides, and poison ivy. Brought up in and near New York City, I find my relaxation in beautiful gardens. The greenhouse orchids and Japanese rock garden at Hillwood, the former home of Marjorie Merriweather Post, make me feel totally safe and nurtured.

What kind of beauty turns you on? If it's music or art, these can be wonderful connections to pursue. Just don't let yourself be forced into "culturally correct" genres that do nothing for you. In other words, if you prefer Travis Tritt to Bach or Thomas Kinkade to Picasso, follow your bliss. In my case, bliss is sitting in a theater listening to the overture of a Broadway musical. Who cares if some people say show tunes are less "valuable" or "important" than classical music or opera? Find what you really like, buy season tickets, and treat yourself regularly to the kind of beauty, pleasure, and healing that works for you.

Activity No. 7: Create

One of the most effective ways to relieve stress is to nurture your own creativity. In fact, another important insight I've practiced from *The Artist's Way* is to take myself on a weekly "artist's date."

Depending on your interests, this might involve any kind of creative activity: writing a poem, restoring a garden, composing music, drawing in the park, or just walking and observing in a peaceful place. I enjoy going to Hillwood and painting flowers in the greenhouse or on the grounds. When I take myself on an "artist's date," everything feels easier that week, and I'm much more at peace with myself and the world.

Why Is Managing Stress So Hard?

No matter how much therapy or personal growth work you've had, stress will always make you revert to your primitive survival mode. You'll need to work your way back to the rational adult thriving mode where you are functioning and working at your best. Daily rituals like keeping a journal, exercising, or volunteering can help you re-anchor in a place where you like yourself, recall your blessings and your strengths, and recharge yourself with positive energy.

Some people have more trouble than others in struggling back to this positive mindset. In fact, it's not unusual to prefer living with old pain rather than to make changes in hope of experiencing new pleasure. Stress is something we're familiar with, whereas being stress-free may take us to a place we've never been before.

In addition, some of us are programmed with old messages that run counter to self-support and self-love. Unfortunately, my mother was like this. She never knew how to relax and do nothing. When I came in from playing, she would say to my six-year-old self, "How can you be so happy when children are starving in Europe?" Although it may be hard to imagine her intense disapproval of people who "liked to play all the time," the fact remains that I have to consciously give myself permission before I can relax and have fun.

I'm sure that much of this won't be new to you. You may well have tried exercise, meditation, keeping a journal, or one of the other approaches I've suggested. Maybe you felt it did you good. But somehow, you just couldn't find the stick-to-itiveness to keep going.

Finding Time to Manage Stress

When you can barely juggle all your current responsibilities, how can you possibly squeeze out time to de-stress yourself? It may sound counterintuitive, but readjusting your priorities to include stress-busting activities can actually increase your positive energy and efficiency, so you end up taking less time to accomplish the other tasks on your agenda.

Trust me, and take a leap of faith. For a month, or at least a couple of weeks, try something that helps you relax: maybe deep breathing exercises, stretching at your desk, or a walk at lunchtime. Make a note of what feels different about your life afterward. If you're still not sure whether to make time for this activity, you'll have the wherewithal for a cost-benefit analysis that tells you whether the results were worth it.

I empathize. Our society is oriented toward 15-second product solutions, 22-minute room makeovers, and seven-day weight-loss programs. More seriously, we tend to reward such addictive pseudo-solutions as overwork ("It's only five o'clock. What do you mean, you're going home?"), overeating ("Can I super-size that for you?"), and overspending ("You are pre-approved for a personal loan of up to $10,000"). These patterns of overindulgence never really satisfy our deepest needs for self-love, self-respect, and self-worth, which continue to grow as we mature.

In order to train yourself to do what's ultimately in your best interest, you may need to practice some behavior modification and reinforcement. For instance, suppose you set a goal of meditating or writing in a journal for 20 minutes three mornings a week. As the first step, put it on your calendar. Second, give yourself a reward (one that doesn't undermine your progress) to celebrate when you do it. Third, write down how it feels to take on this commitment and practice this new behavior. By allowing you to monitor your resistance and your progress, this technique can help combat a lack of discipline that may have sabotaged you in the past.

In a September 12, 2004, article, *The New York Times* noted a survey showing that Wall Street brokers and traders had a rate of clinical depression more than three times the national average. However, this research was done in 2000, while the market was booming, cab drivers were day-trading, and investors checked their daily balances with glee. What in the world was there for investment professionals to be so stressed about? The *Times* concluded it was the feeling of being helpless amid "the grinding pressures of a rapidly changing industry."

These pressures haven't changed. By putting yourself first, however, I believe you can learn to manage stress. In the process, you will become more productive at work, experience more efficiency at home, and ultimately add years—happier years—to your life.

CHAPTER 14
After Shock

Maybe it's time to revisit the life changes you thought about while the smoke was rising from Ground Zero.

It's hard to believe that so much time has passed since the horrific events of September 11, 2001, unfolded before our eyes. Even if we didn't lose friends or family on that day, many of us developed a personal version of post-traumatic stress disorder from gazing at the cratered field in Pennsylvania and the smoking gouge in the Pentagon, and most of all from watching those towers fall again and again. Shaken to the core, we lost a sense of security, calm, and optimism that has been hard to recapture in the years since.

After that calamitous day, many of us worried about how our nation could avoid being a target of aggression. Some people panicked about the difficulty of keeping their loved ones safe from terrorists. Our defenses went up at home, at school, at work, and on the road.

On a visceral level, 9/11 made a lot of people wonder what was really important in their lives. Knowing that on any given day you or those you love might not come home again, even while living or working in a "safe" town or profession, you may have weighed how to enjoy more fully the relationships and activities that meant a lot to you.

Perhaps you vowed to change your life by working smarter, adopting healthier habits, spending more time with loved ones, or pursuing a longtime dream. At the very least, you may have resolved to develop an estate plan, a succession plan, or both.

Years after the shattering events of 2001, what has happened to those vows?

If you're still living and working the same old way, you're not alone. Many of us remain stuck in our former patterns. We may have tried to do too much too fast or didn't have a plan to make change happen. But in many cases, the trauma of what we witnessed simply locked us in a deep freeze. Disturbed by the cataclysmic shift in our view of the world, we retreated to the familiarity of our old comfort zone.

Today, the world is not any safer. If anything, it seems more dangers have arisen: global economic crises, killer hurricanes, train bombers, North Korean nukes, bird flu, and widespread violence in the Middle East and elsewhere. Such unrelenting pressure exacts a toll on many of us in higher rates of anxiety, depression, hypertension, and other manifestations of stress.

Although it's impossible to avoid the worry and trauma produced by these perils, you may be able to use your fears in a good way to improve the future for yourself, your loved ones, your clients, and generations to come.

Getting Over the Past

The events of September 11, coupled with recurring images of death and destruction in Baghdad, Beirut, Darfur, Haifa, and Mumbai, to name just a few, have left many of us "traumatized and dissociated," in the words of neurologist and author Robert Scaer.

Coping With Tragedy

Earth-shattering events like the 9/11 terrorist attacks plunge many people into shock and overwhelming feelings of fear, rage, anxiety, and despair. How can you help your clients get back to some emotional balance and facilitate healing in the midst of unspeakable loss?

First, get in touch with clients and their families and express your concern. Listen and empathize without jumping in too quickly to try to solve their dilemmas. But when they are ready for caring advice, remember that there are several ways people can be helped to heal:

1. Urge them to seek out and embrace the things in their lives that help them reconnect to hope and healing.

2. Suggest that they take some meaningful action against the scourge of events.

3. Encourage them to reach out to family, friends, and even strangers, to give and to receive comfort and solidarity.

4. Help those who are spiritually oriented to seek comfort and connection in this way.

Finally, offer practical help (like revisiting financial goals) only when the client's emotional state is balanced enough to know what he or she really wants.

In an article by Joseph Hart in July/August 2006 *Utne* magazine, Scaer points out that despite our society's abundance, many of us labor under punishing life stresses on a daily basis. We spend volumes of energy on our work, children, parents, and homes. We coach, chauffeur, raise funds for deserving causes, and for relaxation we run on treadmills. No wonder so many of us feel drained!

If you feel paralyzed by the idea of shaping the future, this cumulative anxiety, uncertainty, and pressure may well be the reason why. But dealing with trauma can actually be a way to energize and transform ourselves. We're called on to repair what was broken, in ourselves or in the larger world. This can be much more empowering than living a life where adversity never happens. Remember Nietzsche's dictum: "Whatever does not kill me makes me stronger."

Roughly half the people who have faced adversity say that the experience improved their lives, according to an article by Kathleen McGowan in the March/April 2006 issue of *Psychology Today*. "Those who weather adversity well are living proof of one of the paradoxes of happiness: we need more than pleasure to live the best possible life," says McGowan. Psychologists call the process "post-traumatic growth."

In fact, the only way we grow wiser, more insightful, compassionate, altruistic, and creative may be by coping with hard times, because it takes these traumatic conditions to break through our normal ego-protecting armor and force us to change. Western societies' emphasis on sparing people any adversity, pain, or anxiety may paradoxically cause us to miss out on "the rich, full joy that comes from a meaningful life," McGowan says.

This can include a spiritual dimension that may have been lacking before. *Utne*'s Hart quotes Gina Ross, author of *Beyond the Trauma Vortex: The Media's Role in Healing Fear, Terror, and Violence* (North Atlantic Books, 2003), to the effect that trauma is one of the four paths to spirituality, along with prayer, meditation, and sexuality. (That last one's something to think about!)

American culture preaches the virtues of picking yourself up after a hard knock, dusting yourself off, and starting all over again. Of course, this is not as easy as it sounds, but if and when you can move forward past the fear, anxiety, and sadness of a past trauma, growth can occur.

The Value of Adversity

I would suggest asking yourself some searching questions about how 9/11 and its aftermath affected you. Encourage your clients to do the same.

It may be that your initial reaction was hasty and incomplete. For example, some clients ran out and bought a lot of life insurance instead of drawing up or updating their wills. When people are panicked, they often take any quick action to quiet their fears. If you (or your clients) have been in the grip of post-traumatic stress, can you let go of it now to reassess your beliefs, your values, and your deepest desires for the future, in order to make a plan that will move you toward your higher goals?

For many of us, letting go isn't easy. Personally, I tend to be a high-anxiety type, prone to fretting about real problems or potential threats. Years ago, I took a firewalking workshop where I actually walked barefoot on hot coals without getting burned. To my surprise, this achievement helped reduce my general level of anxiety a great deal.

Overcoming adversity often makes people less fearful, McGowan points out, in spite of the horrific experiences they may have endured. "They are surprised by their own strength, confident that they can handle whatever else life throws at them," she says.

You may not necessarily want to take up firewalking to master your fears, much less swing on a flying trapeze as philosopher Sam Keen advocates ("What was terror becomes joy," says Keen, author of *Fire In the Belly: On Being a Man* [Bantam, 1992]). But learning to accept and overcome fear, rather than being paralyzed by it, can transform the fearful experience into a source of strength and power. U.S. Senator John McCain, a former Navy flier who spent five hellish years as a prisoner of war after being shot down over North Vietnam, says, "I now know the difference between what's important and what isn't."

However, "letting go" doesn't mean avoiding larger issues that disturb you as you contemplate the state of the world today. Volunteering to help other people here or abroad, becoming more politically active, or mentoring younger people may be just what you need to transform feelings of powerlessness into personal fulfillment. Engaging with a spiritual or community network of like-minded individuals can also help you and your clients feel less stressed and alone, more connected and invigorated.

Shaping the Future

If you're able to step back and look at the bigger picture now, consider whether September 11 changed you. What was most traumatic and earthshaking about it? Did it affect the way you live your life? Your relationships? Your work? Your interests? Your vision of the future? If you set goals for yourself back then, to what extent did you achieve them?

If you reached those goals, there may be some conclusions you can draw from examining your success:

- How did you do it? Was it alone, or with support? With a plan, or just ad lib?

- Did you get as far as you wanted to go? Should you consider a "stretch" goal to suit your present-day needs?

- Is there something more you want or need to achieve? Maybe now is an appropriate time to honor the lessons of 9/11 by learning how to become a better person or a more effective advisor. Should you move toward a better balance between work and leisure? Or should you do more to leave "footprints" in your community and beyond? For example, Warren Buffett's business success may not change the world, but his philanthropy almost certainly will.

On the other hand, if you didn't get anywhere on a goal you set, think about why it didn't happen:

- What got in the way?

- Is it still worth achieving? If so, are you ready to work on overcoming what held you back before?

- Have other goals become more important?

Once you've identified changes you'd like to make in your life, consider how to improve the odds of succeeding.

Making Change Happen

To overcome physical obstacles in the way of reaching a goal, a plan is essential. For example, if you've set a goal of cutting back on your workload, your plan might include investing in time-saving technology; hiring an assistant, a paraplanner, or another planner; outsourcing chores that don't add much value to client relationships, or referring out time-intensive clients who are unprofitable or outside your preferred area of expertise.

Overcoming psychological obstacles can be more difficult. People don't develop new habits all at once; it's a process that involves as many as six steps, according to psychologist and author James Prochaska. (See Chapter 9, "Change of Heart," for more details.) If you've established a goal that requires unfamiliar new behavior, be prepared to work through most or all of the stages he has identified:

1. In Precontemplation, you're still in denial that you need to change. (You're probably past this stage already.)

2. In the Contemplation phase, you're aware of a problem but rationalize that it's not serious enough to force you to change. To move out of this phase, explore whether your current behavior really serves you well. A trauma can also shock you into willingness to change.

3. In the Preparation stage, you make a commitment to taking a specific course of action and rehearse in your mind how you will follow through.

4. In the Action stage, you actually start a new pattern of behavior, incorporating strategies to reward progress and avoid backsliding. Support from family, friends, or fellow strugglers can be very helpful.

5. In Maintenance, you establish habits to reinforce your new behavior.

6. In the Termination stage, the new habit has become so ingrained that you don't need any special effort to keep it up.

Beginning a new behavior or eliminating an old habit is often a bumpy trip, fraught with anxiety. But the rewards at the end of the journey can be tremendously satisfying.

After 9/11: A Change of Life

On September 11, 2001, Kathryn Nusbaum, now managing director of the financial planning firm Middle America Planning in Mt. Lebanon, Pennsylvania, had just gone back to work at Morgan Stanley in midtown Manhattan, leaving her new baby with a nanny. When she heard of the attack, her agonized fear for her husband, Robert, who worked in the World Financial Center next door to the World Trade Center, paralleled his horror at seeing the twin towers collapse as people jumped to their death.

With no phones working, it took Kathryn and Robert endless hours to walk home to their small apartment in midtown Manhattan near the United Nations and make sure that each other, and their baby, were all right. That night, they took in 15 people who had nowhere else to go.

In the next few days, Kathryn says, they went to several funerals for people they knew who had been killed in the attack. Nonetheless, they recall, it was an inspirational time. New Yorkers opened their doors to each other and pulled together in other amazing ways. Through the Financial Planning Association, Robert, then a senior financial analyst in Merrill Lynch's Investment Management Group, volunteered financial advice to families of the 9/11 victims.

Where Will You Go From Here?

Here's a practical yet respectful way to honor those who died on 9/11, while recalling and perhaps reviving the resolutions you may have made then:

Every September 11, consider taking some time to reflect on what you've done with your life over the intervening years, and how you would like to change it from now on. The questions below may help you get started:

- If you made resolutions or set goals for yourself after 9/11/01, did you achieve them to your satisfaction?

- What did you want to accomplish but couldn't?

- Five years from now, what changes do you hope to see in yourself, in your relationship with your family or your circle of friends, and in your practice? What changes would you like to see in society?

- Step by step, how can you make this happen? How long will it take? Using a timeline can help you stay focused, but be gentle with yourself if you need to amend the timeline as you go along.

- Finally, how will you measure your progress?

Although dealing with the aftermath of this tragedy was difficult at times, the Nusbaums embarked on a deeply soul-searching process about what was important to them and what kind of life they wanted to have. After carefully researching the best place to live, they moved to Pittsburgh and started their own financial planning firm.

In retrospect, Kathryn believes the traumatic experience was immensely valuable. "I certainly got to a much better place in my life," she says. "I feel a much greater appreciation of all the good things in life."

While September 11 was a horrific, life-changing event for most of us, it's important not to remain frozen in shock. Instead, we need to grasp this opportunity to will ourselves into growth and renewal.

There is much truth in the Serenity Prayer attributed to theologian Reinhold Niebuhr: "God grant me the serenity to accept the things I cannot change; courage to change the things I can; and wisdom to know the difference."

We can't guarantee ourselves a safe future, but to some extent we can control what we do with the time given to us. In memory of a catastrophe that brought out the best in so many people, let's take stock of what really matters to us and what legacy we want to leave to our families, our clients, and our communities.

CHAPTER 15

Thank Goodness

Why isn't it easier for us to appreciate what we've got?

Each year, a special time occurs when Americans sit down together to give heartfelt thanks for the many good things in our lives. It's a day we call. . . Turkey Day.

I mean Thanksgiving, of course. But its popular nickname suggests a curious discomfort with the idea of gratitude. Shouldn't we be glad to have a holiday dedicated to celebrating blessings instead of memorializing old sources of pain? In a world so fraught with conflict and trauma, fear and negativity, time spent savoring the positive aspects of our lives can be truly life-affirming and possibly life-saving.

So why is it hard for us to let in the good stuff? One reason, I believe, is that many of us prefer the familiarity of old pain and anxiety to the uncertainty of new feelings. New pleasure, in particular, can seem scary and destabilizing, threatening to sweep us away to places we've never been before. We'd rather keep seeing the glass as half-empty, because doing otherwise would mean altering the way we view everything else.

Another reason, strange as it sounds, is superstition. Knowingly or unknowingly, we often believe that if we openly acknowledge our blessings, spiteful fate may decide to take them away. By focusing instead on the bad things in our lives—in essence, trying to protect ourselves with our fears and stresses—we hope to avert fate's jealousy. This "superstition of pessimism" is as old as the hills, and to some degree it's self-fulfilling. After all, negative thinkers are more likely to feel thwarted and frustrated in pursuing their goals—a clear case of divine disfavor, right?

Pressure to do more, earn more, and display our success with a bigger house or more expensive car also keeps many of us dissatisfied with what we are and have achieved. So we spend our lives continually yearning, and feel bitter disappointment when we don't get that promotion or our children don't turn out the way we wanted.

It's no wonder, then, that so many of us have difficulty admitting when things are going well. Or why the beautiful word "thanksgiving" is often replaced by the name of a bird that's a synonym for a big letdown.

Why Be Grateful?

By encouraging your clients to more deeply savor the blessings they experience, you can help them revitalize their lives. The same is true for you.

Julia Cameron in *The Artist's Way: A Spiritual Path to Higher Creativity* (Tarcher, 2002) and Sarah Ban Breathnach in *Simple Abundance: A Daybook of Comfort and Joy* (Warner Books, 1998) both praise the power of gratitude. Citing a French proverb, "Gratitude is the heart's memory," Ban Breathnach suggests that being thankful "sets in motion an ancient spiritual law: the more you have and are grateful for, the more will be given you."

Don Montagna, former head of the Washington Ethical Society, also espoused this view in a course on relationship-building that I took a few years ago. "When you focus on the negative, it will grow," he told us. "When you focus on the positive, it will expand accordingly."

I'm also reminded that John Gray, author of the epochal *Men Are from Mars, Women Are from Venus: The Classic Guide to Understanding the Opposite Sex* (Harper Paperbacks, 2004) advises women to concentrate on what men do right instead of what they do wrong. Anxious not to replicate my mother's habitual fault-finding, I tried this early in my relationship with a boyfriend I really liked. My focus on the glass being more than half full, instead of slightly empty, contributed to a honeymoon period that has led to a marriage of more than 20 years.

From Guilt to Gratitude

We all know discontented clients and colleagues who gripe about what they want instead of being grateful for what they have. Some time ago, I worked with a client who was in the process of receiving a great deal of money from her wealthy father, but felt angry that she was not being given even more. To help her let go of the resentment, I led her in exploring emotional areas where she had felt deprived in childhood—the first step in separating that old pain from the financial demands she was making to compensate for it.

Slowly, she began to accept what she didn't get and appreciate what she did receive. This led her to an understanding of how to communicate healthier attitudes about money to her children. Eventually, she may decide to use some of her wealth to affect the world in a personally meaningful way.

The perception of having too much money can be as debilitating as thinking you have too little. Rich Colman, a financial advisor and tax expert who is a principal in the Colman Knight Advisory Group in Carlisle, Massachusetts, told me about a client who was earning $18,000 a year when he unexpectedly inherited millions of dollars. First shocked, then angry about this sudden enormous windfall, he was unable to let himself buy the nice house that he could now well afford.

2, 4, 6, 8, Who Do We Appreciate?

When clients are feeling isolated, unappreciated, or depressed, consider encouraging them to organize a support group with whom they can share their successes, yearnings for positive change, and sources of gratitude. Most of us need societal support to help soothe and inspire ourselves, especially in view of all the negativity and criticism with which we are constantly bombarded by the news media.

In my years of counseling, I worked with many heirs and heiresses who felt crippling guilt and shame that, through no effort of their own, they now had much more money than so many others in the world. Once they learned to admit their repressed gratitude for the choices and freedom their wealth provided, they were able to harness this positive energy and use their money in ways that benefited them, their loved ones, and others. The transformation from neurotic guilt to healthy gratitude was inspiring to witness.

A good exercise for clients who are struggling with these issues begins with two sheets of paper. On the first sheet, urge them to write down their regrets. What do they wish they had achieved by now? How much more, or less, money do they wish they had? What roads do they regret not taking? How differently would they have handled relationships with their loved ones? When this list is done, put it through a paper shredder. (Yes, you read that right.)

On the second sheet, they should write down personal accomplishments, qualities, and life experiences that they appreciate and feel proud of. This is the list they need to keep. They might even make copies to leave in different places, so they can read and re-read it to feel more soothed, satisfied, and grateful.

Not Enough, or Too Much?

One of the most frustrating situations for a planner is when you show clients they can actually afford to do something they yearn for—and they don't do it. Instead of the satisfaction of helping them achieve the comfort and pleasure they say they want and need, you're left feeling puzzled and disappointed when they resist taking actions that would make a hugely positive difference in their life.

Rick Kahler, president of Kahler Financial Group in Rapid City, South Dakota, told me the story of a 50-ish client whose dream was to retire and pursue his love of the outdoors. Convinced that he couldn't afford to leave the rat race, he would lie awake at night worrying about his businesses.

Ironically, Rick said, if this client liquidated just 3% annually of his $15 million net worth, he would be able to retire on $450,000 a year and do whatever he pleased for the rest of his life. Instead he continues running his businesses, complaining about the stress and unable to believe that he has "enough." Some of the money messages blinding him to the potential for happiness are "Don't spend your principal"; "You've got to work hard to make money"; "You don't deserve to be wealthy"; and "Your success is a fluke." With money scripts like these, Rick points out, it's easy to see why people remain stuck in old limiting patterns instead of taking advantage of opportunities to enjoy life.

Rick's understanding of this "Scrooge" mentality led him, Ted Klontz, and Brad Klontz to write about it in *The Financial Wisdom of Ebenezer Scrooge: 5 Principles to Transform Your Relationship with Money* (HCI, 2005). Scroogey clients won't spend to benefit themselves or others because of their unhealthy beliefs about money. Though these beliefs vary, the result is the same: hurtful behaviors persist because they're familiar and support people's underlying money scripts.

Getting People to Change

How do you encourage someone trapped in old familiar pain to let go of it and appreciate the good things in their life? That, as Rick Kahler puts it, is the $64,000 question.

Sometimes clients can do this on a cognitive level. Realizing that their unconscious beliefs are erroneous, they are able to embrace a new way of thinking. For example, another of Rich Colman's clients, a doctor, was stuck in feelings of scarcity and negativity. Despite earning $400,000 a year and having $5 million in assets, he lived like a poorly paid medical student, afraid to spend money on an expensive bottle of wine. By talking to him and running the numbers in various ways, Rich helped him see how much money he actually had. With this new understanding of his true situation, the doctor was able to give himself permission to enjoy his money. According to Rich, the change when his client "let in the good stuff" was palpable and satisfying to be around.

But just as often, people are unable to change their behavior, even when they become aware of the destructive beliefs driving it. In cases like these, I've seen great success when they engage a financial counselor or therapist to help them get past their emotional blocks.

What's involved in this process? Typically, it begins by exploring self-limiting money beliefs and behaviors from childhood, past marriages, or other negative experiences. As a therapist, I then help the client challenge old constraining attitudes and actions with a variety of insight-oriented exercises, such as recurring Money Dialogues and homework assignments to "practice the nonhabitual." In ongoing sessions, clients are encouraged to begin adopting new behaviors that will lead them from a primitive survival mode to an adult "thriving" mode. A mind/body technique I've learned from trainer Pat McCallum of Eugene, Oregon, which argues that you can identify learned, limiting behaviors and change those behaviors, is especially valuable in helping people "reframe" their limiting patterns and move to an expanded, healthier view of their moneylife.

Write It Up

One of the best ways to experience the power of gratitude is to record your blessings in a daily "gratitude journal." The entries can be as simple as "Bob cooked dinner tonight—AND washed up!" or as poetic as a description of a beautiful sunset. Maintaining a gratitude journal invariably energizes me and makes my life seem richer and more pleasurable.

More methodically-minded people may prefer this variation: every night before going to bed, write down five things you feel grateful for that occurred during the day. Do this for 21 days. Why 21? Some psychologists believe that's the length of time it takes to change a habit. Once you have practiced this discipline 21 times, there's a good chance you will have adopted a new habit of acknowledging the sources of gratitude in your life, and anchored yourself in a more positive mindset. (My thanks to Marci Shimoff for this exercise, which appears in an anthology to which I also contributed: *Breaking Through: Getting Past the Stuck Points In Your Life*, edited by Barbara Stanny with Oriana Green [Powerful Woman Press, 2006]).

I invite you to share these life-enhancing exercises with your clients. Encourage them to re-read their gratitude lists throughout the day so they can more deeply savor the blessings in their lives.

Changes in Attitude

Changing people's attitudes is actually a two-pronged process. First, we have to let go of the pain and money messages from the past that are limiting us. Then we need to learn new habits that will allow us to appreciate positive experiences, letting in new pleasure.

Learning how to appreciate the good stuff is a process that Ed Jacobson has been teaching financial planners for the past several years. Ed, a psychologist, coach, business consultant, and speaker based in Madison, Wisconsin, recently published an insightful guide to savoring life in *This Appreciative Moment*, his online newsletter. The guide quoted psychologists Fred Bryant and Joe Veroff, who identify five techniques to promote appreciation and gratitude that you may want to suggest to clients (and practice yourself):

1. **Sharing the experience with others.** This includes commenting on the experience and how enjoyable it is while it's taking place, as well as telling about it later and relating how much you enjoyed it. Sharing your comments after the fact calls up memories, which may stimulate production of neurochemicals similar to those produced during the event itself. Ed Jacobson notes that when he wrote about a poignant experience that took place near the end of his father's life, the act of writing about it rekindled the experience vividly for him.

2. **Memory-building.** The building blocks here are photographs and physical mementos of an event, which serve to stimulate reminiscence. I often suggest that clients carry photos or objects to help anchor positive memories and extend their "savoring potential."

3. **Sharpening perceptions.** This is similar to meditation: you focus on a single aspect of an experience to the exclusion of all others. At a concert, for example, you might concentrate on the sound of the bass. Walking across town, you could focus your attention on the different smells you encounter. This intense tuning-in may be difficult and is impractical in some situations, but when feasible it will help you etch the experience more sharply in your memory and relive it in the future.

4. **Absorption.** This is the process of fully immersing yourself in a sensory experience, rather than thinking or talking about it. It's not as easy as it sounds. In fact, Ed Jacobson comments that many of us

find it difficult to become absorbed because we are verbally, socially, or cognitively oriented rather than tuned in to our senses. Striving to become more mindful of physical sensations may greatly extend our capacity for appreciation.

5. **Self-congratulation.** Most of us have been told it's arrogant to feel too good about ourselves. Instead, we are taught to humbly shrug off our qualities and achievements.

Maybe this is another example of fearing to tempt fate, but I think it gravely misconstrues what we humans need to survive and thrive. Self-love, self-respect, and self-validation drive us to express our creativity and fully develop our gifts. A certain amount of self-congratulation is very healthy when we receive praise or an award, or when a milestone event occurs that we've worked hard to make possible. Without it, we fail to see our place in the world and acknowledge what we have contributed.

Of course, too much self-congratulation can block appreciation of others. You probably know people who are so self-congratulatory that you hate to be around them. But many others who hesitate to claim their strengths and virtues would do well to add self-affirmation and self-appreciation to their emotional repertoire.

Letting In the Good Stuff

I'm fond of a quote from Melody Beattie, the author of several books about taking charge of one's life. "Gratitude unlocks the fullness of life," she says. "It turns what we have into enough, and more. It turns denial into acceptance, chaos to order, confusion to clarity."

This outcome is confirmed by my own experience and that of advisors who have shared their stories with me. Rich Colman, for example, tells about having helped a client identify his life dreams by probing about his goals, passions, and aspirations. The client started working less, spending less, and enjoying his life much more as he began to create the life he once merely dreamed of.

Rick Kahler told me about a client couple in their 60s whose dream was to retire and travel the U.S. When he assured them that it was possible for them to quit work immediately and pursue their dream, they didn't hesitate. "That was five years ago," Rick says. "When I spoke with them recently, they said they are having the time of their life and have no plans to stop."

Allowing ourselves to appreciate what we have can create an amazing sense of abundance and fulfillment. Let's make life all about what we love, cherish, and are thankful for in our lives, and make gratitude a daily practice.

PART V

The Right Thing to Do

Don't you feel sometimes like you're adrift on a sea of moral relativism? "I did not have sex with that woman," our country's leader prevaricates, while me-first CEOs pocket millions as their trusting employees lose their pensions, their homes, and their shirts. The self-justifying dishonesty, greed, and betrayal are egregious enough to make you long for the days when right was right and wrong was wrong. Where have you gone, Joe DiMaggio?

In many cases, Joltin' Joe hasn't really left and gone away. All it takes to restore that seemingly bygone era is some sincere self-examination to determine where you stand in terms of ethical behavior with your clients, your colleagues, and yourself.

The most important first step is to assess your beliefs and values and make a fearless inventory of the times you have breached them. When have you been dishonest with yourself or with others? Were you motivated by self-interest, or did you avoid full disclosure in order to protect someone else's feelings? To what extent are you walking your talk, morally and ethically? What can you do to raise the bar for yourself?

Of course, a fiduciary responsibility to act in your clients' best interest mandates full disclosure with them. Your training and licensing as a financial professional also dictate an ethical foundation in your work with colleagues. Most advisors follow these precepts as a matter of course—not just because they want their clients and their colleagues to succeed and their practice to prosper, but because it's the right thing to do.

But suppose a client asks you to collude in keeping secret some improper behavior of his? What do you do if your boss puts the moves on an employee in your office? What if a fellow practitioner begins an intimate relationship with a client? Where do you draw the line? At what point do you say, "No, I can't be a party to this"?

Confronting our own "lower selves" is part of a healing and clarifying process that can make this choice easier as time goes on. The goal is not to see everything as black or white (which can lead to decisions that at times are inordinately cruel), but to understand and uphold the values that define you as a unique human being.

These are tricky issues, and we are facing them in challenging times. We hope the next chapters will shed enough light to help you proceed when the moral terrain is murky, or downright dark.

CHAPTER 16

Les Liaisons Dangereuses

Hanky-panky on the job doesn't affect just two people. Here's some advice on a subject that isn't covered in the CFP ethics course.

Several years ago, a friend of mine objected to higher-ups about an ongoing affair at his company between a senior executive and a lower-level employee.

The liaison was hardly a secret in the firm, with opinion divided between those who denied that the couple's dual relationship (boss/employee and intimate partners) made any difference, and others who considered it to be unprofessional and destructive. When my friend, a man of great integrity and devotion to his work, pointed out publicly that the affair had resulted in special benefits for the department where the junior employee worked, his forthrightness cost him his job of 18 years.

In the sea of human relationships, it's not unknown for advisors, too, to sail a little close to the wind. Dating a client can compromise one's ability to think straight and do an honest, trustworthy job, not only with that person but with others. And as my friend's case demonstrates, opening this Pandora's box can lead to unforeseen consequences.

According to Linda Gadkowski, an advisor who teaches the required ethics courses for the Certified Financial Planner Board of Standards, there is no explicit reference to job-related sexual indiscretion in the CFP Board's ethics code. This strikes me as odd. Is male-female attraction in the workplace still such a taboo subject that no one wants to talk about it?

After more than 30 years as a therapist, I have some opinions on the subject that may be valuable if you yourself are in such a relationship—or are confronted with one where you work.

Imbalance of Power

If a therapist has an affair with a client, even after therapy has been terminated, it is a serious breach of ethics because the very nature of the therapeutic relationship is unequal.

It's common for clients, viewing their therapist as a professional authority figure, to transfer to him or her the attributes of a parent. This may occur in an attempt to recreate the past or forge a new and improved relationship with maternal or paternal authority. Either way, "transference" blurs the professional connection with elements of the parent/child relationship. Thus, an affair would be highly unethical, no matter who initiates it.

When it comes to life coaching, transference is diluted because a coach is generally seen as more of an equal. It's not frowned upon to have a limited social relationship. In my opinion, however, it would still be highly unprofessional for a coach to have an intimate relationship with a client. I would have less concern about an affair with someone who is no longer a client.

Many financial advisors encourage their clients to view them not as an authority figure but as a partner on the journey of financial empowerment. In so doing, they may create a relationship that is more evenly balanced and falls into the same ethical gray area inhabited by life coaching.

The outcome is complicated when powerful instances of transference occur between more authoritative advisors and their clients, or between colleagues who work together. Dual professional and personal relationships are fraught with difficulty, and should be evaluated in terms of the emotional cost to the individuals involved and those who work with them.

Transference Is All Around Us

As a therapist friend said to me, "Our relationships are awash in a sea of transference." In simple terms, we all have patterns of behavior, attitudes, and needs that begin with our earliest relationships: our parents, siblings, and other powerful figures in our lives. We transfer these early imprinted ways of acting, reacting, believing, and needing to our later relationships. When we choose a spouse, according to the renowned therapist and educator Harville Hendrix, we are attracted to someone on whom we can project the positive and negative qualities of our parents—and then we hope to get from that mate what we never received from our mother and father.

At work, we often react to authority figures just as we did to one of our parents. (And it may be a woman boss, not necessarily a man, who reminds us of Dad. Our needs and expectations have more to do with personality and approach to life than with gender.) Similarly, other colleagues may come to resemble a parent, a sibling, or another strong influence in our early lives. The longer we stay in a particular work environment, the more likely our co-workers are to become a "work family," reawakening past experiences, hurts, wounds, and even traumas.

When these relationships represent something negative, such as dashed hopes, critical judgments, or rejection, they create negative transference. When they're good, or recreate positive feelings, they constitute positive transference.

Because you are an authority whom clients approach for help, you will almost inevitably be put in the role of an authority figure from the past. Depending on your style and personality, this relationship may evolve into a strong transference, either positive or negative.

And there are two sides to the coin. Some clients may remind you of powerful relationships in your own past, such as a too-demanding parent or a sibling who worshipped you. You may also relate to work colleagues through a transferential lens. How do you know when this is happening, and what can you do about it?

Identifying and Managing Transference

When you have an immediate and intense reaction—positive or negative—to new clients or colleagues, transference is occurring. You may feel at the first meeting as though you've known them forever, because they echo earlier parental or sibling relationships. Someone who "sets you off" right away is almost surely reminding you of another person in your past with whom you've been in conflict.

In a long-established work family, you probably will be able to identify who are the "parents" and the "siblings," and which colleagues recreate your own family of origin. These issues are explored in "The Power of Transference," an article in the September 2004 *Harvard Business Review* by Michael Maccoby, a psychoanalyst, business consultant, and Harvard professor.

To responsibly manage transferential issues in an organization, Maccoby stresses the importance of knowing yourself as well as you can in order to minimize tendencies toward rationalization or denial. One way to foster honest self-evaluation is to get feedback about yourself from family, business colleagues, and outsiders.

His second recommendation is to promote mutual understanding by making sure people see you clearly and know you well. I often recommend regular work retreats that allow everyone to view workplace relationships through another set of lenses. Openly share your vulnerabilities, strengths, and weaknesses with colleagues you trust. Be open to feedback about how your relationships may be affecting them. If you are in a position of power, make your expectations as obvious as possible and try to understand as clearly as possible what others expect of you.

Affairs of the Heart

At the beginning of a sexual relationship, most people are in an altered state, variously known as being in love, being infatuated, or being in lust. In this honeymoon phase of the relationship, you are literally in a trance. A bubble separates the two of you from the rest of the world. Imagine trying to do your job properly when you are in no condition to think clearly, see clearly, view each other clearly, or see the effect of your relationship on others around you!

That's why I support setting internal boundaries that preclude advisors from dating clients and co-workers. In the first situation, you are compromising your professional relationship with the client. If you are invested in continuing the affair, the least you can do is to refer this client to a colleague (not, ideally, in your own company).

Sadly, a more common behavior is for those in this trance state to tell themselves that they can manage the situation. They continue to serve as the client's advisor, hoping news of the dual relationship won't leak out. If it does, I guarantee that other clients will feel jealous, repulsed, unsafe, creeped out, or all of the above, depending on their own transference with you as well as their personal history. Your colleagues, too, will have doubts about your competence and professionalism.

If your intimate relationship involves someone you work with, the bond you forge with this person will change your relationships with everyone else. Just as children of divorcing couples pick up on conflict even if their parents try to hide it, many sensitive colleagues will sense that "something weird" is going on, well before they discover the truth. If you do professional favors for your lover (or allow a partner superior to you to favor you), you risk arousing the resentment and anger of colleagues.

As you can tell, I strongly advise against engaging in these dangerous relationships in the first place. But if you do, it's critical to be honest with yourself and others about it. Terminate your client and refer him to another advisor. If the relationship is between co-workers, one of you should leave the organization. This may sound harsh, but I believe that anything else will create havoc for years to come.

How Much Should You Share?

What about non-sexual relationships in the workplace? How friendly can you be with clients or other colleagues without trespassing over professional boundaries?

This is a much subtler and more complicated area. Many advisors have a friendly, open style and seem to easily manage having clients as friends. In fact, I imagine there may be more advisors who juggle these dual roles than those who never mix business with friendship.

Sometimes it's easier to confront a client who is a friend. At other times, it's more difficult. If you try to intervene with a friend who is engaged in financially self-destructive behavior, you have more to lose than if your role is strictly professional.

Similarly, many advisors have close friendships with work colleagues. If there is a disparity in income or power between you, you have to deal with this. It also makes a difference whether the friendship is a secret or is openly acknowledged. And you need to be open to feedback about how it may be affecting your co-workers.

Negotiating these relationships is complicated, yet many advisors appear to handle it well. To some extent, one lives and learns.

I can testify to this from my own experience. During the 1970s, when I was trained as an experiential "feminist therapist," it was okay to share aspects of one's own journey when appropriate. I would attend my clients' weddings and concerts, but didn't socialize further. This seemed to work well.

Years later, I bent my own boundary rules by allowing myself to have a "light" friendship with a former client. I invited her to my house for a party and we had lunch together a few times. But then she referred a friend to me for therapy, and the relationship didn't take. Our friendship dissolved soon afterward. In retrospect, I wish I had held the line I created for myself and not allowed my "mushy boundary" tendencies to take over.

I certainly don't endorse excluding clients from all aspects of your personal life. But along with the danger of sexual intimacy, I do caution against obliviousness to the effects of closeness and bonding, between advisor and client or advisor and co-worker.

There is no perfect way to negotiate all the complexities of closeness and distance in the workplace. But if you try to stay aware of your own transferential relationships, you will evolve toward seeing the people you work with as themselves, not as revenants from your past. By cultivating an open, curious attitude about the effect of your relationships on others and on the overall firm's morale, you will know how to keep the right professional balance between yourself, your clients, and your colleagues.

This challenging task reminds me of the advice that therapist and author Sheldon Kopp once gave his sons. "When you hurt someone," he counseled, "I hope you do it consciously." He didn't counsel his sons to never take the risk of hurting anybody. He was telling them to be mindful of the results of their actions.

I agree completely. Be conscious of what you do and how it affects others. That may not be the Golden Rule, but I think it is one of the best ways to become a better advisor.

If You Have an Intimate Relationship	
with a client . . .	
DO:	DON'T:
▸ Be open to evaluating its effect on your work performance ▸ Be sensitive to its impact on your relationships with others at work ▸ Be willing to talk about it with a trusted professional or friend ▸ Refer your client to another advisor, preferably not in your firm	▸ Assume that your ability to think clearly is intact ▸ Insist that this is your own private business with no effect on anyone else ▸ Sneak around and try to keep it a secret (you won't succeed) ▸ Make yourself a beneficiary in their will (don't even think about it!)
with a colleague . . .	
DO:	DON'T:
▸ Be super-vigilant about treating all your co-workers equally and fairly ▸ Try to minimize contact at work ▸ Be open to feedback from trusted colleagues about your work performance and the effect on co-workers ▸ Be prepared to seriously contemplate one of you leaving the organization	▸ Accept or give special favors because of your relationship ▸ Make excuses to get together ▸ Assume that your relationship is not affecting the climate at work ▸ Assume that you can keep your client's best interests in the forefront

CHAPTER 17

Pants on Fire

It's not always easy, but the truth can set you free.

The news is full of senior government officials involved in sex scandals, highly paid CEOs charged with options backdating, reputable writers and journalists caught in literary fraud and plagiarism, and well-known attorneys convicted of racketeering. Why does there seem to be so much more lying, cheating, and stealing going on lately? Is our society in the midst of a moral meltdown?

The issue of honesty in independent advisory practices has risen to the surface with the recent hullabaloo about whether RIAs should be regulated more strictly. As Mark Tibergien (now managing director of Pershing Advisor Solutions in Jersey City) mused to me lately, "Just because someone is a fiduciary, does that make them operate with integrity?"

Most of the advisors I've encountered through the years try their utmost to practice with honesty and integrity. Nonetheless, we have all been guilty at one time or another of "little white lies" to spare people's feelings, or sins of omission to protect our own self-interest.

The majority of your clients, I wager, keep money secrets (and other secrets that may be relevant to your work together) from you, from their spouses, and sometimes from themselves. Because a lack of truthfulness can sabotage their financial plans, as well as their relationships with each other and with you, it's worth examining why people lie and how you can foster more honesty in your practice.

Lying Is All Around Us

Gail Saltz, a psychiatrist and author of *Anatomy of a Secret Life: The Psychology of Living a Lie* (Broadway, 2006), notes that children usually start lying to manipulate their environment at around age 4 or 5, when they gain an awareness of the use and power of language. They may lie to get out of a sticky situation, to avoid being punished for some transgression, or to get what they want. If you had siblings, I'm sure you remember their duplicity in pursuit of self-serving ends. It may be more difficult to recall, but you probably did the same.

"I believe that lying and cheating has its roots in low self-esteem, often originating in some type of earlier trauma or events experienced as trauma," says Larry Moskat, a former psychotherapist turned financial planner in Scottsdale, Arizona. "When we are very unhappy being who we perceive we are, we tend to 'become someone else.'"

Neglect or abuse can damage people's self-esteem to the point where they manufacture new "truths" about themselves, remaking themselves as someone different. In some cases, lying may be about hating who we are and what we think people believe about us. After a while lying can become an entrenched way of life for some people, allowing them to slip into another, more palatable "reality."

What We Say and What We Do

With some help from Wikipedia, I've identified 12 kinds of lies. Eight of them are on the milder, more innocuous side:

- **Bluffing:** Deception in the context of a game, not usually seen as immoral.

- **Emergency lie:** A white lie used when the truth might harm a third party, such as a neighbor lying to an angry abusive husband about the whereabouts of his wife.

- **Exaggerating:** Magnifying or embroidering on a truth until it becomes false. ("When I attended Yale, I got straight A's and roomed with Hillary Clinton.")

- **Jocose lie:** A lie that everyone knows is meant in jest.

- **Lie to children:** For instance, "The stork brought you."

- **Lie by omission:** Deliberately not speaking up about the truth in order to leave others with a misconception.

- **Misleading:** Saying something that isn't an outright lie, but has as its purpose making another person believe an untruth.

- **White lie:** A small lie offering some benefit to the liar, hearer, or both that would cause no discord if uncovered.

The remaining four kinds of lying are usually considered more reprehensible:

- **Bald-faced lie:** Everyone concerned knows it's a lie.

- **Hypocrisy:** Practicing one thing but professing the opposite.

- **Noble lie:** A lie that offers some benefit to the liar, perhaps helps maintain order in society, and would cause discord if uncovered— often the refuge of politicians and other scoundrels.

- **Perjury:** Lying under oath or in a court of law.

In surveys about lying, we Americans tend to be hypocritical ourselves. For example, the Pew Research Center found in a 2006 study that 43% of interviewees believed lying to spare someone's feelings was morally wrong. I can't believe that four out of 10 people in this country think it's immoral to say something nice instead of blurting out, "Honey, that hairdo makes you look like Bozo the Clown."

In the same Pew study, 79% of respondents said that failing to fully report one's income on a tax return was morally wrong. Yet according to the IRS, individual taxpayers failed to include nearly $200 billion on their 2001 returns (the most recent year analyzed). I believe many of us have fudged the numbers when filing taxes, or at least know others who have done so. Yet we have tremendous moral judgments about this behavior.

Ted Klontz, Ph.D., a psychologist and president of Klontz Coaching and Consulting in Nashville, Tennessee, believes that "absolute truth is actually the most taboo subject matter in our culture." In his view, lying is a behavior we learn because it is rewarded most of the time, unlike telling the truth.

Klontz agrees that denial runs rampant in our psyches. "We like to pretend that lying isn't as pervasive as it really is," he notes, "but we really expect everybody to lie, at least up to a point (that point being rather arbitrary). It serves as a social lubricant. We teach our children that it should be done, and how to do it."

We all want to think of ourselves as moral, honest, and good people. And in general, most of us are. As one of our favorite national myths about George Washington and the cherry tree illustrates, we also want to think of our leaders as honest and ethical people. In fact, we often expect them to have a more noble character and loftier ideals than we do ourselves. That's why it's so disheartening when someone who has worked hard to get to the top, such as Governor Eliot Spitzer or Senator Larry Craig, is revealed to have feet of clay.

How Honest Are You?

Mark Tibergien (CEO of Pershing Advisor Solutions and a fellow *IA* columnist) has devised a terrific list of questions you can ask yourself to clarify just how honest and open you are. The answers may be especially informative if you've persuaded yourself that you're always truthful and transparent with clients and colleagues:

1. Have you ever told a client that you didn't get his message when in fact you knew he called you days ago? You may have told yourself it was just a little white lie—"and I'm talking to him now, so what's the harm?"

2. Have you ever become aware of a compliance violation committed by an associate that could hurt your firm, but you chose not to refer it to authorities? I would add: Would you act quickly to remedy the situation, even if it was difficult or uncomfortable to do so?

3. Have you ever taken credit for bringing in a new client, even though a younger associate created the opportunity? Your rationalization might have been "Well, they have years to make a name for themselves..."

4. Have you ever accepted a new client who chose you on the basis of a strong referral, but you knew you did not have the depth of experience to serve them properly? Were you able to offer top-notch service? Or did you have twinges of guilt and maybe think about calling in a consultant to make up for your lack of expertise?

5. Have you ever had a client tell you he refuses to work with someone else in your business because the person is a woman (or a man, or African-American, or Hispanic, or too old, or too young) and you made the change so as not to lose the business? How do you feel about that?

Why Take the Risk?

What prompts respected individuals to take outrageous risks in their private life and lie about it? Is it contempt for public values? Perhaps it's hubris—the assumption that they are powerful enough to get away with anything.

Dave Drucker, an Albuquerque financial advisor and founder of Drucker Knowledge Systems, reminds me that compartmentalization—the ability to keep separate two contrary sets of attitudes and behaviors—may help explain why powerful people can maintain a high level of moral and ethical behavior in public and simultaneously abandon morality and common sense in areas of their private life.

Interestingly, neurologists are uncovering evidence that power, sex, and risk are hard-wired together, at least in men. The area at the base of the brain that reacts to erotic stimulation also lights up when men take financial risks, according to a recent research by Camelia Kuhnen, a Northwestern University finance professor, and Brian Knutson, a Stanford University psychologist. When this pleasure center was activated with erotic images, male subjects risked even more money. (Professor Kuhnen said her study didn't use female subjects because it was more difficult finding an erotic image that would appeal to a wide range of women.) In another new study, Cambridge University researchers have found a link between higher testosterone levels and more aggressive stock trading. One of the researchers hypothesized in an interview, "If more women and older men were trading, the markets would be more stable."

But let's get back to financial planning. In order to understand how to handle clients and colleagues who speak or act dishonestly, I think it's useful to start by looking inward at our own attitudes, behaviors, and moral judgments about lying, cheating, and stealing.

My Own Misleading

An experience I had many years ago helped shape my own attitude toward truth-telling. It makes me wince a bit to relate it, but it taught me a painful lesson that you may find of value as well.

I have always loved being interviewed on radio and television, and thought it would be wonderful to be paid for this "work" that I enjoyed so much. So when a company arranged for me to be on a TV talk show, I jumped at the chance to be paid as a representative for their products, which I honestly believed in and used myself. Of course, the fact that I was being sponsored was not to be mentioned. The interview went so well that it turned into a second appearance on the show. Both times I mentioned the name of my sponsor. Alas, I overdid it: the host commented on my enthusiasm and asked if I owned stock in the company.

Hot with humiliation, I answered, "No, it's just enhanced my life and the lives of my clients," a literal truth that didn't address the spirit of the question. Two weeks of emotional and moral agony ensued, while I waited to see if this confrontation would be edited out of my appearance on the show. Horrors! The segment aired with my moment of discomfiture kept in. My sponsor was delighted that its name was repeated so often, but I vowed that I would never again let myself sail under false colors. The deeper lesson I learned, with a fair amount of shame, was that I—who considered myself someone who would never sell out for money—had done precisely that. As a result, I gained more compassion for others in the same boat. I no longer consider myself to be above them. And as far as I am aware, I have never sold out like that again.

Taking Your Moral Inventory

Spend a few minutes thinking about your own life experiences. Do you have any memories of lying, cheating, or stealing? Adolescent shoplifting? Cheating on a test? Lying and getting caught—or getting away with it?

If you're beating yourself up for having been dishonest, rest assured that you're far from alone. That doesn't make it okay, of course, but it doesn't make you an ax murderer either. What's important is being honest with yourself about what you do or have done. If you haven't acted in accordance with your values and your integrity, be aware of what you've been telling yourself to justify it. This greater self-awareness may help you listen to others who have similarly lapsed without either condemning them or making light of their transgression.

Once you've completed this moral inventory, ask yourself if there are certain kinds of clients and behaviors that you just won't tolerate in your practice. Where do you draw the line, and why?

Rich Colman, a financial advisor and partner at Colman Knight Advisory Group, Carlisle, Massachusetts, told me about a client who had taken what he should have paid in estimated tax and squirreled it away to pay for a potentially costly divorce. To evade the tax issue, he lied about his actual income for the quarter. Just as Rich's firm was about to file his tax return, he came clean with the real amount. When Rich asked why he hadn't told the truth sooner, the client confessed, "I was scared to tell you." Had Rich reacted with disapproval or condemnation, the client said, it would have made him too ashamed to continue the relationship. By being receptive and not judgmental, Rich was able to not only preserve but even strengthen the client connection.

When Clients Lie to Each Other

Sometime clients will go to great lengths to keep the truth from a spouse or partner. At Colman's previous firm, he heard that a client had taken it upon himself to put all his retirement assets in an annuity. When the client's advisor pointed out that the annuity fees would add up to hundreds of thousands of dollars, the client fired the firm so his wife wouldn't find out what he had done.

The advisor couldn't keep mum, however, because of a fiduciary responsibility to the wife. The husband ended up hiring a lawyer to order the advisor not to talk to the wife. As Sir Walter Scott wrote, "Oh, what a tangled web we weave, when first we practice to deceive!"

Debra L. Morrison, a wealth manager with Capital Financial Advisors in Lincoln Park, New Jersey, had an opportunity to help rescue a marriage from a similarly devastating revelation. When she asked a client couple to bring in all their financial account information, the husband's documents included a business credit card statement with a balance of more than $45,000. When this was brought out, the wife said, thunderstruck, "We have WHAT amount of debt?" She had never known he had this card, since the billing went to his office.

After hearing both of them out, Morrison was quick to explain to the couple that this was more of a marriage and trust issue than a financial problem. She assured them that with the healthy cash flow from the husband's medical practice, they could eradicate the credit card balance with regular monthly payments. However, she added, the husband needed to own up to his money avoidance tendencies and his readiness to use this card for lunches with his associates and dinners with his wife. He agreed to cut up the card and have financial statements sent to his home address from then on. In addition, Morrison strongly recommended that the couple seek professional help to deal with this breach of confidence.

"As I locked the office door that night," she says, "I recall lamenting that I didn't have a psychology degree, but absent that, I did have empathy and keen communication and negotiation skills. So I did the best I could, and they were able to drive away in the same car." Both spouses were badly shaken, but Morrison felt hopeful that their marriage would be able to sustain the blow.

From then on, the two clients met with her quarterly to update her on their progress in regaining their financial and emotional footing. The husband developed a business plan specifying the monthly caseload he needed in order to support their lifestyle and save for retirement. As the couple talked through their past limitations around money, he was relieved to shed his avoider mantle. In the meantime, his wife was able to get past her shock and humiliation to empathize with his plight and become a fuller partner in tracking their money.

"It could have turned out to be a marriage-killer with people less determined," Morrison told me, "but it was merely a stern warning in this case. They ultimately were able to trust their mutual love, and understand the deep consequences of one partner's avoidance and the other's lack of involvement around money issues." With her expert and compassionate help, they succeeded in weathering the crisis. Today, she says, they are far stronger as a couple, and far wealthier because of the partnership that developed after this crisis of information withholding.

Persuading clients like these of your honesty and true dedication to their interests is a difficult but crucial part of building a relationship. If you hear them deeply and try sincerely to understand their fears and concerns, they will be more inclined to open up and trust you with their inmost secrets. Then you can help them create a better foundation to share power and information with one another.

How Can You Spot a Liar?

I'm such a gullible and trusting sort, I shouldn't even try to answer this question. People have attempted to devise ways to spot liars ever since humans learned to communicate, but as far as I know, no system is foolproof. As an article in *The Wall Street Journal* recently noted, people can even fool polygraph machines if they're cold-blooded enough.

It's true that body language can give you clues to a person's directness and honesty, but there are plenty of folks as honest as the day is long who find it hard to make eye contact. And, of course, lots of con artists are able to look you straight in the eye. All you can do is listen to a person's facts and their feelings, and try to make the most intelligent judgment possible about whether you're getting the whole story. If you're wrong and you've somehow been taken in, be exceedingly gentle and forgiving toward yourself.

Remember that virtually everyone has money secrets, along with feelings of guilt, shame, anxiety, and remorse about money actions that they have or haven't taken. Though I advocate being accepting and nonjudgmental with the normal range of human foibles, it's important to create clear limits on the degree of lying, manipulation, cheating (or any kind of stealing, I think) that you will tolerate in your clients or colleagues.

My Guiding Principles

While I think we each need to clarify our own views on the subject of lying, I have developed some guidelines for myself that may help you decide what you do or don't want to practice.

1. **Be humble.** Understand your own values, limits, and imperfections regarding lies by commission or omission. Avoid a "holier than thou" attitude when dealing with the sort of untruthfulness that you yourself may have been guilty of in the past.

2. **Be compassionate.** Empathize with people's tendency to show themselves in the best light, hide from conflict, avoid responsibility for their faults, and conceal money secrets, even from themselves. Help clients face the truth, but with gentleness and compassion.

3. **Weigh in on the side of kindness.** Little white lies are in many cases not only fine, but preferable to hurtful truth-telling. If an acquaintance you don't care for asks, "Do you dislike me?" I don't think you're morally obligated to tell the truth. On the other hand, if something is jeopardizing a friendship that deeply matters to you, I would risk creating temporary distress by speaking up in a sensitive but honest way.

4. **Let clients know you expect honesty.** In one of the first few sessions with a new client, consider asking, "Most of us keep some money secrets, even from ourselves. Is there anything you might be afraid to tell me that would help me understand your complete financial situation, or what you want to achieve?"

5. **Create a safe place where people can open up.** When otherwise decent clients lie to you or hide important information, find out why they felt it wasn't safe to discuss the truth with you. If something in your approach made them wary of being honest, make every effort to change that attitude or behavior to encourage more self-revelation. However, if you sense that you're dealing with someone who can't or won't stop lying, terminate the relationship for your own good.

6. **Don't let greed corrupt your integrity.** If you ever find yourself fudging the truth or withholding information to protect your own interest, bite the bullet and 'fess up. Anytime I feel out of my depth with clients who consult me for coaching or therapy, I admit it right off the bat and try to steer them to someone who will serve them better.

7. **Don't turn a blind eye to wrongdoing.** If someone at your workplace is breaking the law or violating compliance regulations,

you are legally and morally bound to try to stop it. No truly ethical person should ignore this just to avoid the stress of making waves.

Dealing with an Inveterate Liar

Thankfully, there aren't many people in our midst who are able to act dishonestly and destructively without guilt or remorse. Research on these truly disturbed individuals shows that traditional therapy methods fail with them.

As a former psychotherapist, Larry Moskat has a view of persistent liars that is more optimistic than most. Now a Scottsdale, Arizona, financial planner, he writes: "Dealing with the chronic liar/cheater, I believe, requires a more gentle touch and an acceptance of the person as they are—troubled and insecure—while gently but firmly beginning the process of dislodging their alter-selves and supporting the person underneath whom they loathe. Once trust is established, these people will begin to feel free to talk the truth as they come to learn they will not be penalized for truthfulness and honest self-expression. Self-loathing will eventually give way to a renaissance of self-assurance and self-confidence, rendering the lies unnecessary, undesired, and ultimately extinguished."

I would add the caveat that a good outcome probably depends on the degree of dishonesty, as well as the person's ability to experience true remorse and regret for his or her actions and their effect on others.

Advisors without the training or inclination to deal with such a troubled personality may do better to back away, as Keith Newcomb suggests. Newcomb, a financial planner and wealth manager at Full Life Financial in Nashville, Tennessee, told me, "One thing I've learned as I've gotten older is that, for me anyway, the key to dealing with a chronic liar or habitual cheat is simply don't deal with them. One certainly cannot change them. If you must deal with them, plan for all the contingencies 'cause you never know what they're going to come up with."

This may be the wisest course of action when you encounter clients or colleagues who lie as a way of life. New brain studies offer hope that science can actually begin to alter the brain function and chemistry of psychopathic liars. But until research identifies a successful avenue of treatment for people who lack an appropriate sense of remorse and responsibility, it may be too dangerous for you to deal with them at all.

---

8. **Truth can be a weapon; use it with care.** If a client's financial situation has worsened significantly, of course you have a responsibility to tell the truth. But when there's a good chance that hitting them with it all at once will cause them to panic, I believe it's better to unveil the truth gradually (during two or three closely timed visits, for example), determining action steps along the way, so they can integrate the information and respond more sensibly.

In summary, if I lie to myself, I believe I have a responsibility to confront this behavior for the sake of continued self-awareness and growth. If I lie to others, I need to look honestly at my motivations and what they cost, and seek the courage to tell the truth, not harshly or cruelly but in a humane way.

Michael Shapiro, a Washington, D.C., business law professor (and my husband), tells me that the Buddha is said to have broken all moral precepts except one: he always told the truth. An interesting and complicated business, isn't it?

PART VI

Who're You Calling 'Old'?

No matter how much or how little we resist, aging moves us inch by inch into a totally unfamiliar landscape. The careers we're devoted to, the parents we love, the friends we cherish—one day they're here, the next day they're gone. Other losses begin to mount up: physical, emotional, mental. With greater urgency and poignancy, we begin to think about the meaning of our lives and our inescapable mortality.

Rejecting old models from the past, baby boomers have reinvented every stage of life they go through. Blessed until recently with a cooperative stock market, they have looked forward to choosing whether to retire and, if so, when; whether to begin a whole new career path or pursue a long-deferred passion; where to live, how to live, and how to make their mark on the world as long as their stamina lasts. Although new financial constraints may narrow some of these options, they will continue to redefine their 60s and beyond in new terms: the Third Age, rewiring, renewment.

A challenging economic climate makes your work with older clients like these even more complex. It's not just the quantitative issues—do they need to keep earning money? How much? For how long?—but the qualitative ones. What drives their sense of purpose and passion for living? How can they create a life that expresses these deeper longings? As their physical capabilities weaken and sources of emotional support fall away, how can you help them deal with these losses?

Recent research has greatly increased our understanding of how the brain works, showing us that people can train themselves to maximize their mental potential and deepen the wisdom gained in decades of experience. If your clients stay involved in life and learn new things (such as a language, a musical instrument, or another culture), their minds can continue to be vigorous and agile in ways they never imagined. By helping them stay connected on every level—to themselves, the people they love, their life's work, their community, and their spiritual beliefs—you can strengthen relationships as your clients move from years of achievement to years of fulfillment and legacy.

CHAPTER 18

Retiring Minds

"Old people are no longer educable," opined Sigmund Freud in 1907. Since then, advances in brain research prove that people over 50 still have a lot to learn.

As a baby boomer, I grew up believing that most people would work until age 65, then retire to a life of rest, play, and living out their favorite fantasies. Today I have friends who retired at 40 and 55. Others are still working in their 80s. Colleagues who shut down their careers at 60 or 65 have gone back to work out of boredom or financial need. I saw my aging mother end up in a wheelchair after a series of mini-strokes, unable to speak or make meaningful emotional contact for the rest of her life. I watched my father, a retired judge, continue trying to make a difference in the world until he died at the age of 87.

As I get older, my thoughts and emotions careen from one view of aging to its opposite. In the anxiety mode, I notice how much more often I struggle to find the right word for something, or that I reverse letters and numbers when typing quickly. Then the specter of my mom's strokes, and the possibility of Alzheimer's, grip me with fear that sometimes expands into panic.

At other times, I feel good about being older. I love feeling that my years of experience have given me a sense of wisdom and calm that I didn't have before. The idea of sharing this with others in my work and in my life makes me happy.

Some of the strengths and shortcomings of aging may be new territory for you personally, as well as many of your clients. You're probably familiar with the main financial issues: income generation, "decumulation" strategies, Social Security benefit maximization, and so on. But what about the mental and emotional aspects of growing older, and how these changes may affect your own life as well as the way you work with people of retirement age?

You can expect to see more and more boomer clients struggling with issues of loss, life transition, financial insecurity, and fear of declining capacities. Aging always involves letting go, which has aspects of mourning and sadness in it. Don't try to jolly clients out of feeling this loss. But after giving them a little space to vent, you may be able to help them return to sources of hope and healing, thanks to new research that shines light on how they can keep learning, revitalizing themselves, and deepening their sense of wisdom and mastery.

How the Brain Changes

Brains are unbelievably complex. Within about three pounds of tissue, there are 100 billion or more nerve cells, each one able to make thousands of connections with others. As we age, the brain's physical makeup becomes a little less robust, just like other parts of the body. And like muscle strength, brain capacity operates on a "use it or lose it" principle.

As we age, observed neurobiologist James L. McGaugh of the University of California–Irvine in 2004 in an article for the AARP division NRTA and The Dana Alliance for Brain Initiatives, "We can make the brain work better simply by accumulating more knowledge, which builds more networks of connections in the brain. The wisdom that we acquire can compensate for the decline that may be gradually occurring."

"The brain wants to learn; it wants to be engaged as a learning machine," wrote neurobiologist Michael Merzenich of the University of California–San Francisco in the same NRTA-Dana Alliance series. But that doesn't mean rehashing the same old stuff learned in high school. The brain wants new ideas, new experiences.

"Recent discoveries in neuroscience show us that the aging brain is more flexible and adaptable than we previously thought," agrees Dr. Gene Cohen, director of the Center on Aging, Health & Humanities at George Washington University Medical Center and author of *The Mature Mind: The Positive Power of the Aging Brain* (Basic Books, 2006). According to Dr. Cohen, these studies suggest that our brain's "logical" left and "creative" right hemispheres become better integrated as we age, leading to greater creativity.

This integration also makes it easier for older people to reconcile thoughts with feelings. Personally and professionally, I've known people in their 20s who agonize over each decision, large or small, and whose emotional perfectionism creates tremendous psychic stress. Older clients and friends seem to trust their own instincts more. They appear to be more comfortable with their decisions and are able to make them more quickly and with less effort.

Learning and Communicating

Like it or not, some faculties do decline with age. But it's not as though we fall off a mental cliff at age 65; these declines actually start as far back as age 20. According to research from NRTA-Dana, these are some of the changes you may notice in clients or in yourself:

1. Taking longer to learn. Processing speed slows down with age, so you may need to factor in more time to perform tasks and learn new things. Be prepared to educate your clients about this normal fact of life, and help them take the time to work on what they want to master.

2. Difficulty in multitasking. Executive functions such as planning and reasoning become more difficult with age, as do tasks that require keeping many things in mind simultaneously. You've experienced this parallel processing glitch if you've ever gone into the next room for something, only to forget why you went there. (Here's a tip: Name the item out loud before you go.)

If clients seem confused or uncertain when asked to consider a number of options at the same time, slow things down. Try to break the decisions into simpler yes-no, either-or choices, in such a way that you still cover all the important considerations.

3. Inability to remember random facts and sources. Now where did I see that really interesting article? And what did it say that I wanted to tell my friends?

Being able to store and retrieve new information easily, a function called "strategic memory," is one of those faculties that starts to decline after the teenage years. (My 24-year-old son obviously wasn't making it up when he complained to me about "getting stupider.") To combat this decline in your own strategic memory, learn to tell yourself, "I need to remember this." Underline it mentally by repeating the information out loud or making verbal or visual associations with it. If clients complain of this problem, these solutions may help them cope.

4. Plain old forgetfulness. My contemporaries and I now find we're much more understanding when one of us forgets an appointment, fails to return a phone call, doesn't deliver a message, or neglects an errand that used to be routine. This is another normal consequence of brain aging.

Suggest to forgetful clients that the best remedy is to write things down. They can create agendas for meetings, make lists for multi-errand trips, and put notes on the dashboard or computer monitor. If they lapse, remind them to be gentle with themselves. After all, they're only human!

Retirement (Over)Spending

Many older clients lead creative, active lives, pursuing career or charitable missions, and generally enjoying their older years to the hilt. In fact, some may be enjoying life so much that overspending their limited resources becomes a concern to their families—and to you.

Spending is already a concern with the Silent Generation (ages 59-71). Many people in this age group give little thought to longevity risk, according to a June 2005 MetLife Retirement Income Decisions Study. Most of the study participants felt confident of having enough money to live comfortably to at least age 85. However, their retirement planning tended to focus on asset accumulation instead of the possibility of outliving their savings or having to care for an incapacitated spouse or parent.

It's difficult enough to urge restraint on overspending clients when they're young. With retirees, you may face a number of deep-seated motives and behaviors:

Wanting to live large despite their now-lower income.

Spending to fill up the time that their job used to fill.

Feeding an ego starved by lack of daily reinforcement. Instead of enjoying the time with loved ones or living out their dreams, these people derive their main pleasure from various kinds of overindulgence: gambling, dining out, expensive travel, and so on.

Retirees and Their Children

If your retired clients are parents, you'll probably need to address their plans for gifts and legacies to their children. You'll want to proceed gingerly, of course, since many people have deeply-held beliefs about what they're expected to do for their kids. Without ever telling them how to act, you may want to let in some fresh air by relating stories of parents who disempowered their children by overindulging them. If they're concerned about leaving an inheritance, tell them about other retired parents who weighed how much money to use for their own needs and how much to leave the kids, and how this turned out.

Above all, encourage older clients to talk financial matters over with their children. (For ideas, see "The Silent Generations" on page 195.) It's crucial to communicate while everyone is still around to discuss the pros and cons.

Bailing out their children, or giving lavishly to the kids despite their own struggle to make ends meet, sometimes out of guilt about past neglect or a need to feel needed.

How You Can Help

In these cases, you can gently and empathetically help clients look at their life choices. Give them the support they need to take better care of themselves and their future.

One of the most useful things you can do is assist them in mentally transitioning from "having it all" to "making the most of what you've got." For example, NRTA-Dana Alliance research found that 39% of retirees aged 65 to 75 are still making mortgage payments, compared with only 28% in 1989. Carrying a mortgage is normal during one's working years, but this sizable long-term liability can become a financial straitjacket for people with limited retirement resources.

In fact, many people who thought they'd pocketed their last paycheck will be forced back to work by financial pressures. If you have clients in this situation, review their spending patterns to see whether lifestyle changes could allow them to stay retired (for example, moving to a less expensive home or a location with a lower cost of living). If a return to work is inevitable, you can help them identify jobs that turn them on, challenge their skills, or give them more social contact while improving their life financially.

Aided by your skill and perspective, your older clients will be able to see that they are not locked into an undesirable course of action. In fact, this financial crisis could lead them to exciting new opportunities. They still have many choices that can help stave off boredom, assuage feelings of meaninglessness, and relieve financial stress.

Maximizing the Mind

The discovery that the brain is more plastic than previously thought is tremendously exciting. When people learn new skills or take on new challenges, the brain creates new neural connections, expanding and improving its thinking power and reservoir of wisdom.

What does this have to do with your money management role? A great deal, if you hope to stay vigorously in control of your own life and help clients do the same. Experts say activities like these can maximize vibrancy and creativity as people age:

Achieving mastery. It's been documented that feeling a sense of control and mastery helps people stay physically and mentally healthier. Learning a new language or musical instrument, taking up a new sport, or learning a new artistic or creative skill can not only make people feel good about themselves but may well strengthen the immune system.

Making friends. Many studies link social connection to lower blood pressure, a reduced risk of stroke and ensuing mental effects, a lessening of anxiety and depression, and lower death rates. Losing a life partner to death or divorce often ruptures this connection, leaving older people isolated as well as bereaved. You may be able to help these clients strengthen their relationships with family members and old friends, while encouraging them to make new acquaintances who share their interests.

Exercising the brain. Trying to outguess the contestants on *Jeopardy* or *Wheel of Fortune*, doing crossword puzzles or sudoku, reading, playing bridge, poker, or board games—frequent mental exercises like these help keep neural pathways active. For instance, NRTA–Dana Alliance researchers discovered that people who did crosswords four days a week had a risk of dementia 47% lower than others who did puzzles only once a week. My own bliss is competitive Scrabble (that counts as a crossword puzzle, right?). Ask your clients if they do something most days to stay mentally limber.

Being creative. Playing a musical instrument is another one of the top ways to reduce the risk of dementia and cognitive decline. I don't know if such comparable activities as painting, sculpting, or writing memoirs, poetry, or fiction have been studied, but I'd have to believe they are equally valuable as mental rust-busters.

Exercising the muscles. The best physical exercise to increase brainpower, according to research, is an aerobic workout involving large muscle groups. I'm happy to see dancing at the top of the list, since ballroom and tap dancing are passions of mine. Brisk walking is a good alternative. If older clients confess to a lack of zest for life, one of the questions you might ask is whether they exercise regularly. If not, there may be an activity they would enjoy incorporating into their lives, such as swimming, walking with a friend, or taking fencing lessons. Whatever works!

Eight Practical Tips for Older Clients

A phenomenal amount of information is pouring out of research labs about how the brain works, how its processes change as time goes on, and how to stimulate learning at any age. Some of the key implications for advisors:

- **Take advantage of the differences in men's and women's learning styles.** (See Chapter 6, "Gender Matters.") A planner I know makes sure she has charts and numbers to show male clients. She rarely takes this approach with women, who are more likely to feel stressed when information is presented this way. Women tend to learn better in a slightly warmer, quieter environment, sitting across from you with good eye contact. Men generally learn better at somewhat cooler temperatures, either on the move (walking and talking) or sitting beside you with information in front of them. Find out your clients' most comfortable learning style and cultivate that way of informing and educating them.

- **Minimize distractions.** To help older clients be as fully present and focused as possible, meet in a quiet room without phones ringing or keyboards chattering. Ask them to turn off cell phones so they can give you their full attention.

- **Repeat key information.** To reinforce connections in the brain, be sure to summarize the key decisions and conclusions at the end of a client meeting. You might also ask clients to tell you what they got out of the discussion, to help them mentally record what they learned as well as to show you what they may have missed.

- **Write down the important points.** This suggests that clients may learn better from an active "chalk talk" than from passively watching a bunch of PowerPoint slides. Watching another person write down an important thought helps viewers "write it" in their own memory banks. Seeing this written information again after the meeting fixes it more firmly in their minds. (You do send follow-up memos reiterating what was decided, don't you?)

- **Encourage visualization.** This gives the brain another way to access the information. You can add humor and life to your session by encouraging clients to visualize something about the material that will help them retain it. For example, when you're discussing how adding income-producing investments can reduce risk to their portfolio in a stock market downturn, you might suggest that they visualize a bear at the controls of an elevator.

- **Build on what they already know.** Associating new information with familiar ideas allows people to expand existing synaptic connections. A home equity credit line is like a mortgage with a checkbook. Long-term care insurance is like a lifeguard on the retirement beach.

- **Help them stay organized.** Encourage your clients to keep important papers in a specific place and always return them to that place. This is particularly important for messy clutterbug clients. If they fail, gently nudge them back toward the goal by helping them choose some simple categories that they can organize and locate when needed.

- **Stick to priorities.** When multitasking becomes difficult, work with your clients to create a prioritized list of tasks they can achieve in a realistic time period. Help them accept that they can't do everything, and urge them not to beat themselves up because they're not perfect. After all, growing old is still better than the alternative.

A Terrible Thing to Waste

When you use these findings from brain research to help older clients envision a more invigorating future, it can nurture their sense of self and strengthen their self-esteem. This in turn may lessen the stranglehold of overspending and overgiving behaviors.

The benefits can go way beyond their own happiness to affect others with whom they interact. If they are parents, they will be modeling for their children ways to grow old gracefully without becoming an emotional or financial burden.

As older clients increasingly call on your help, you can benefit from becoming more of an expert in aging wisely and well. Build up a resource list of local places to exercise or learn new skills, community organizations that need volunteers, therapeutic counselors for depressed or anxious clients, centers for meditation, yoga, or biofeedback, ElderHostel-type organizations for travel and learning, educational institutions that cater to the older student, and ways and places to make friends or begin dating again. These resources will heighten your value to your clients, so that you become an even more trusted advisor as they take on the challenges and opportunities of their later years.

CHAPTER 19

For Whom the Bell Tolls

Who, really, are these boomers who want to reinvent retirement—and can't afford not to?

The age wave has at last reached shore. In 2008, baby boomers began turning 62—old enough to draw Social Security. This horde born between 1946 and 1964, all 78 million of them, are the best educated and wealthiest generation ever. They've reinvented each stage of life as they've reached it, from emptying stores of coonskin caps to creating senior colleges.

If only that meant they had their finances in order.

A financial planner I know likes to say that many boomers have a one-word plan for retirement: "Don't." Noting that 80% of boomers say they'll continue to work, he points out, "Today, only 19% of people over 65 are actually working. Forty percent are too sick, and 41% can't find a job."

In a 2007 *Money* survey, 90% of boomers said they hadn't done a great deal of retirement planning. Yet 59% thought they'd be able to maintain their standard of living in retirement.

Similarly, when a 2007 Lincoln Retirement Institute survey asked baby boomers and retirees to imagine themselves in the future, 60% of those polled were confident they wouldn't run out of money in retirement.

It was the same story in 2005, when research sponsored by OppenheimerFunds found many

Who's a Boomer?

The term "baby boomer" is used to describe the generation born between 1946 and 1964, but there are in fact sub-groups. Leading Edge boomers, born between 1946 and 1955, were influenced by the Vietnam War, Beatles, and Woodstock. Those born between 1956 and 1964, dubbed Trailing Edge boomers or Generation Jones (as in "keeping up with the…"), came of age amid assassinations, Solidarity, and heavy metal. Some observers suggest that the youngest Trailing Edgers barely consider themselves boomers at all, but are Generation Xers at heart.

In reality, the boomer cohort spans a vast range of behaviors, values, orientations, and financial needs, from retirement to college planning, caring for parents, and managing inheritances. We need to be careful not to overgeneralize about this huge and diversified group.

boomers acknowledging that they would enter retirement with more debt than their predecessors, fueled by high credit card balances, more expensive homes, and luxury purchases—yet less than half of them wished they had saved more for retirement. "When it comes to baby boomers and financial planning, there is a striking contrast between perception and reality," dryly observed John V. Murphy, the fund company CEO.

You as the Bearer of Bad Tidings

Clearly, baby boomers need your help. But it won't be easy coaxing them into your office or persuading them to make changes that will ensure a more pleasant future.

One of the reasons why so many of them are woefully unprepared for their old age may be that they can't envision it. "In a recent U.S. survey," reports a *Today's Seniors Network* article, "when asked to define 'old age,' most boomers quoted an age three years above the country's average age of death."

Pre-retirees also tend to greatly underestimate medical costs in retirement—a scary symptom of what Heather Otto, president of the board of the Tucson, Arizona, YWCA, calls "our national healthcare mess." Otto e-mailed me that she and her husband, retired for three years, now pay 10 times as much for health insurance as they did while working. She wonders if there will be resources to help boomers when they need medical assistance in their old age, or if their children will be burdened with their care.

Boomers who do consult you are likely to be in a perilous financial position. They're spending more than previous generations and often caring for aging parents or supporting grown children as well. How will you tell one of these clients, "You can't afford to quit your job now. You'll have to keep working until you're 75"? Or "If you keep paying for your son's support (or your mother's at-home care), you'll have nothing left for your own future"? Or "Unless you cut your spending immediately and save four times as much as you do now, you'll probably go broke before you die"?

The Third Age: Achievement to Fulfillment

Sociology professor William Sadler views life as having four ages. The First Age focuses on preparing for adulthood. Achievement is the major theme in the Second Age, with an emphasis on security, belonging, and status. The Third Age centers on fulfillment, and the Fourth Age on completion.

How Others See Boomers

To get a better handle on baby boomers, I did a little not-so-scientific research by asking several advisors to tell me what terms they associate with this generation. They said that boomers are:

- "Profligate overspenders"
- "Overwhelmed by Sandwich Generation burdens"
- "Completely unprepared for retirement"
- "In real trouble financially"
- "In denial"
- "Overly optimistic"
- "Living in la-la land when it comes to their future"
- "Stubbornly attached to their unaffordable lifestyles"
- "Headed for disaster"

One exception was Holly Hunter, principal of Hunter Advisor LLC in Portsmouth, New Hampshire, who told me a boomer is "someone about to bust out and really live life!"

When I asked the same question of coaches, therapists, organizational consultants, and others who have studied boomers, it was a different story. While these professionals noted some negative characteristics, on the whole they were inspired by the opportunities for boomers to transform their Third Age into one filled with possibility, creativity, and vitality. They said boomers are:

- "Creative and inventive"
- "Reinventing every stage of life they enter"
- "Retiring the old concept of retirement"
- "Individually and collectively seeking new solutions to their life challenges"
- "Convinced they are immortal"
- "Living in the present"
- "Wanting to make a difference and leave a legacy"

Marie Swift, founder/president of Impact Communications in Leawood, Kansas, a marketing communications firm that works with independent advisors, said she associates boomers with a "search for significance." Other professionals in both groups noted that boomers are "fiercely independent," are open to change, and care about making a difference in the world.

Acknowledging the "terrible associations" that our society has with middle age, Dr. Sadler reminded me that recent brain research indicates that in people's later years, their minds often work better. If they stay mentally active, the brain grows new neurons and the right and left hemispheres collaborate more effectively. As a result, boomers can be expected to shape their Third Age with a high degree of creativity and productivity. He and James Krefft suggest ways to do it in *Changing Course: Navigating Life After 50* (Center for Third Age Leadership Press, 2008).

Finances are certainly an important factor in this equation, since boomers need to be sure they don't outlive their money. But as I heard from Dorian Mintzer, a personal and professional coach and psychotherapist in Boston who specializes in "boomers and beyond," "Financial planners need to be part of a more integrated life-plan model. Not only do they need to help their clients with the financial piece, but they need to [collaborate with] coaches and life planners so that they help their clients deal with the whole picture of their bonus years."

You can't do your best for boomer clients unless you're aware of your feelings toward the experience of aging, retirement, and boomers themselves. When I sat in on an online discussion organized and moderated by Mintzer, I found myself disapproving of boomers who retire and do nothing but play golf. In my view, they should be giving back to society in some fashion, not just enjoying themselves.

Several other therapists and coaches in the discussion felt the same way. We told ourselves that many burnt-out workers need to relax and just "be," after a lifetime of doing. In all probability, these folks would eventually be interested in making a difference. We weren't really at ease thinking that some boomers might just want to relax and not care at all about giving back.

If I were a golf-playing retiree, I would want my coach or financial advisor to be able to give me advice that wasn't colored by prejudices like these. So I encourage you to reflect on boomer and aging issues before you're faced with tough decisions involving boomer clients. Here are some of the questions to ask yourself:

- How do I feel about my own aging: positive, depressed, wistful?

- What are my fears and dreams for my 60s and beyond?

- How do I feel about my boomer clients? Am I excited to work with them, or do I dread the experience?

- Do I have any preconceptions about what they should be doing in their 60s and beyond?

Meeting Them Where They Live

Looking for ways to align with boomers' aspirations and passions, I explored the work of other coaches, authors, and researchers who have analyzed how members of this group are reshaping their future. Their work may suggest new ways for you to connect with boomers' hearts and minds.

Catherine Fitzgerald, Ph.D., principal of Fitzgerald Consulting in Bethesda, Maryland, and founder of Sagience LLC, a company that focuses on helping boomers optimize their vitality and intellectual and spiritual development, posits that as adolescents, baby boomers realized that their parents' recipes for success and happiness were no longer valid. Without role models, they were forced to redefine each phase of life as they entered it. The upside was (and is) tremendous creativity and innovation, but the downside was tremendous anxiety.

There's certainly cause for anxiety when it comes to boomers' financial security. The question is, how can you help them harness their penchant for innovation in order to create life changes that make their future more secure?

The "Work Till They Drop" Approach

The images of geezers and geezerettes strolling hand in hand on the beach, bicycling, or teeing off together are relatively recent, created by advertisers to sell retirement communities and cholesterol medication. I've found that most retirees don't buy into these pictures. Even those who have said they want to "do nothing" when they retire often find themselves bored and longing for more social, intellectual, and emotional stimulation.

As we know, work can give people a sense of purpose and meaning, and many boomers intend to be productive until their last breath. Even if they don't need the income, 60% to 80% of them plan to keep working during their "retirement" years. To assist these quasi-retirees, Jeri Sedlar and Rick Miners, a husband-and-wife team with 25 years of experience in helping people transition to more rewarding personal and professional occupations, have identified a five-step process to search for "fulfilling work that fuels your passion, suits your personality, and fills your pocket." In their book, *Don't Retire, Rewire!* (Alpha, 2007), they provide a list of questions to help readers identify what motivations drive them, then offer a guide to finding types of work characterized by those particular drivers.

Dealing with Loss, Embracing Change

Another concern that recent retiree Heather Otto often addresses in her blog (http://onretirement.blogspot.com) is the baby boom generation's tendency to deny aging and death. As time goes on, they must increasingly deal with disability and disease, the death of loved ones, friends, and colleagues, and rumblings of their own mortality.

As holistic physician Dr. Bernie Siegel used to say, even joggers and vegetarians die. This makes boomers laugh somewhat uncomfortably, reminded that all their efforts to live a healthier life won't really make them immortal.

Coping with life's losses is even harder for boomers because nothing has ever seemed impossible to them, from heart bypasses to moon landings to cars that park themselves. Hit with the death of a child or the illness of a spouse, they may well consult you in the throes of anger, denial, or another of the Kübler-Ross stages of grief. The better you understand the grieving process, the more successfully you can help them through their losses.

As a boomer journeying through retirement, Otto also mentioned her concern about social isolation. Many older boomers live in large houses separated from others, with long hours of work taking the place of neighborly interaction. After retirement, one member of a couple often resists moving out of their home to join a community where services, activities, and new neighbors could help minimize isolation. Widows and widowers, especially, often cling to familiar surroundings despite their new loneliness.

Balancing Urgency With Patience

Clearly, the challenges boomers face are widely diverse, since they're not a homogeneous group. Those on the later end of the wave may still have young children, while the oldest boomers are likely to be empty-nesters. Some are grandparents; others have adult children moving back home, and more than a few are the "sandwich generation," supporting elderly parents as well as their own children or grandchildren.

In speaking to advisors, coaches, therapists, counselors, and others who specialize in working with retirees and boomers, I heard over and over that it's critical to tune in to a client's personal mode of learning, working, and living. For example, when I shared with an artist friend of mine some of the planning steps I find useful, such as imagining what you want your "retirement" years to be like, she immediately responded, "That would make me anxious and shut me down. What works for me is having a lot of time and space to go inside, be with myself, and wait to see what the next right step is for me."

It's tempting to dive right into a situation to make the bleeding of assets stop or savings balances grow faster, and you may find it difficult to give a client like this the time to wait for clarity to emerge. But it's important not to get too far ahead of her. An overly structured approach with deep and probing questions could make her bolt, despite the good advice that accompanies it.

"The Number": Power... or Panic?

The words "aging," "retirement," and even "financial planning" strike most boomers with feelings of anxiety and dread, says Helen Dennis, a specialist on aging, employment, and retirement who co-wrote *Project Renewment: The First Retirement Model for Career Women* with Bernice Bratter (Scribner Books, 2008). She points out that far from spurring baby boomers into action, a warning about how ill-prepared they are can scare them so badly that they lose any motivation to act.

I tend to agree. In my experience, hitting someone with the news that they need to save $2 million (or any other mega-amount) is more likely to panic than empower them. There's a good chance they'll lose heart and sink into despair.

No matter how accurate your calculations are or how apt your proposed action steps, you risk losing your client's trust unless you build the relationship first. You need to understand where these folks are coming from, what motivates them, and what dreams fuel their imagination and their energy. My advice:

1. Ask what comes to mind when you say the word "retirement." Let them free-associate to see what concepts and images—positive or negative—emerge.

2. Take time to listen to them deeply, thoughtfully, and with compassion.

3. Ask what plans and ideas they have for their future. Help them flesh out the details as fully as they can.

4. What challenges do they see ahead for themselves? This can lead to a discussion about changes they may have to make to meet these challenges.

5. What concerns do they have? What is it that keeps them awake at night?

6. What is their most positive vision of their Third Age?

7. How do they feel about quitting work? How would they like their worklife to evolve?

8. What are their values? What truly matters to them?

9. What would they like the world to know about them after they're gone? What legacy would they like to pass on to others? If they don't have clear answers, suggest that they write an ideal autobiography or fantasy obituary.

In this conversation, try to tune into your clients' pacing. How slow or fast do they tend to move toward action? How do they process decisions about their goals? Ask questions that request feedback, such as "How is this going for you? Is the pace right for you? Are we going too fast, or not fast enough?"

Author, speaker, and coach Ted Klontz, Ph.D., teaches the art of "exquisite listening" to clients. When you give this kind of attention to boomers who talk about their fear of impoverishment, incapacitation, or abandonment, it can encourage them to heed your suggestions about how to minimize unnecessary stress, accept difficulties with grace and courage, and stay as vibrant and healthy as possible.

It may take some time to find out where a boomer client is coming from. But if you make compassionate and exquisite listening the cornerstone of your relationship, the rest will follow.

Reinventing Retirement

When I turned 60 last year, one of my close friends gave me a useful and fun book, *60 Things to Do When You Turn 60*, edited by Ronnie Sellers (Sellers Publishing, 2006), an anthology of advice from famous and not-so-famous folks about how to thrive in the next decade of life. The title reminded me of how diverse we boomers are and how much we yearn to explore our Third Age with positive energy. I have so many ideas and fantasies about my own future that this goal has at times seemed overwhelming.

With the prospect of 30-plus years ahead, coupled with financial resources that may not measure up to their dreams, many boomers are in real need of guidance. You'll be called on to help them prepare for the worst, such as a health crisis or difficulty finding well-paying work, while simultaneously urging them to envision and plan for the best.

When your advice calls for uncomfortable behavioral changes, different individuals will need different degrees of control and limit-setting to succeed. But as you learn about their fears, concerns, dreams, and goals, and discern how they operate internally, I believe you will be able to help your boomer clients create new life patterns for their retirement years.

CHAPTER 20

The Age of Enlightenment

Long-lived but short-sighted, optimistic but anxious, self-centered but altruistic, baby boomers badly need your help.

"Am I set for retirement?" the baby boomer client asked his financial advisor in their first meeting. "I've been writing checks for $3,000 a month ever since my CPA told me to."

After making out these checks, however, the client had simply been putting them on his dresser. "My CPA calls me up and yells at me because I don't send them in," he confessed sheepishly. "But I have a cash business. What if we run short?"

Instead of scolding him for this behavior, the advisor asked a simple question: "What does retirement mean to you?"

"Nobody has ever asked me that," the client mused. "I guess you go sit on a beach somewhere, and then you die." After a pause to consider this, he said in amazement, "No wonder I'm not sending in the checks."

To help this client let go of the notion that retirement meant death (no wonder so many boomers hate the word!), the advisor told him, "Retirement could mean doing what you want, when you want, with whom you want."

Reframing the concept set the client free. Soon he was contributing $20,000 a month to his retirement accounts. "I thought I didn't want to retire," he told his advisor. "Now I can't get there fast enough."

This fortunate baby boomer—a client of Rick Kahler, president of Kahler Financial Group in Rapid City, South Dakota, who told me the story—recently retired, having quadrupled his retirement nest egg since that meeting.

Advisors who, like Kahler, succeed in helping clients come to grips with the future typically use a process similar to one I've advocated for years. The first rule is not to impose your own agenda; find out why clients are coming to you. Then take time to help them plumb their innermost longings so you understand the deeper needs and desires to be built on. Listen attentively, and mirror their fears and concerns as compassionately as you can. Clarify their goals and dreams in specific terms. Finally, use all your expertise and resources to brainstorm ways to help them meet as many of those goals and wishes as possible.

That's how it should work. But the baby boom generation brings a unique mindset to the table. For instance, boomers feel "entitled with higher expectations of pleasure than any previous generation has known," as Diane Miller, a principal of Miller Financial Planning in West Somerville, Massachusetts, told me. Yet they are also "giving and sensitive to the poor," she added. "An interesting dichotomy." These apparent contradictions help explain why it can take special sensitivity to help them handle their financial issues.

More Than Money

"Retirement is about money and it's about more than money," says Helen Dennis, a specialist on "aging workforce" issues and co-author of *Project Renewment: The First Retirement Model for Career Women* (Scribner, 2008). "People are often pursuing what's most meaningful for them. Some have a religious calling; others a calling to build houses for humanity; others want to influence the political horizon. Retirees today have more opportunities than at any other time in history."

Given these possibilities, it may not take a fortune for some boomers to be happy. In fact, Kahler often reminds clients about a 2005 survey conducted by *Time* magazine which found that above the $50,000 annual income level there is no correlation between people's income and their degree of happiness.

Annual retirement income of $50,000 (or $55,000, adjusting for inflation) may be fine for clients who have a modest lifestyle. However, all too many boomers are accustomed to living large.

"Many boomers are living hand to mouth," Kahler says. "They don't have any money, which makes it hard for the average planner. We typically don't have the tools [or often the training, I might add] to help somebody who knows he ought to be saving but can't save."

But change is possible. Kahler cites the example of a boomer couple in their late 50s who were earning $350,000 a year but spending $400,000. At the outset, he says, they couldn't even talk to each other about money. It took him a year, working in tandem with therapist and life coach Laura Longville, to help them break this vicious cycle.

"At our last meeting, they were amazed at the progress they made," he says. "They'll be maxing out their retirement plan soon, which means they can retire with $65,000 a year. They'll still have to make some significant changes, but their future before this was living on Social Security. We've more than doubled their retirement income."

The Sandwich Generation

Many boomers are welcoming (if that's the right word) their 20- and 30-something children back home, sacrificing their own financial security and emotional health to support the kids. Others carry the burden of caring for elderly parents who can no longer look after themselves or have provided inadequately for their old age.

As appropriate as the principle of "Put on your own oxygen mask first" may be, you risk being thought cold, heartless, and completely out of touch with your clients' values and priorities if you urge them to put their own interests foremost.

Empathetic listening is a crucial first step. Hear what concerns them, and see if they're willing to consider changes that might free up more time, energy, and money. Reassure them that they're not alone. You could describe similar situations where making a few changes allowed other clients to take better care of their own financial security.

If you build enough trust, you may be able to help these clients realize that overgiving to their parents may leave them burdening their own children later on, and that prolonging their kids' dependency is unlikely to serve anyone well.

This is a slow, delicate process, with powerful emotions and needs underpinning boomers' actions. But if you proceed sensitively and cautiously, perhaps with the collaboration of a therapist, you may be able to create a little breathing space in your clients' squeezed financial and emotional lives.

Teaching Gratification Deferral

How can you inform boomer clients that if they hope to live comfortably in the future, they'll need to earn more or spend dramatically less? Many boomers aren't used to being told that they can't get what they want, the way they want it. They're likely to react with passive resistance, outright rebellion, panic, or shame.

To help them recognize and embrace the value of deferring gratification, I would encourage you to coach them on one of my core concepts: that superficially indulging ourselves makes it impossible to nourish our souls. You might begin a discussion by asking what one change your clients could make to begin treating themselves better on a deeper level.

If they're open to curbing their consumption, there are several tactics you can recommend. I'm sure you're familiar with the spending diary as a way to uncover areas of overspending. To make this tool more useful, ask clients to write down not just what they spend but how it made them feel, and see if it reveals anything about their choices, motivations, and new possibilities for saving.

Reviewing temptations to spend may also help. Do friends or neighbors push them to live beyond their means? Are there particular stores or restaurants where they tend to overexercise their credit cards? To the extent that they can avoid what I call "slippery places," they may be able to rein in their spending without feeling too deprived.

Spenders who need outside help may benefit from the support of a more frugal friend who would be willing to act as a money mentor or spending coach. If you recommend Debtors Anonymous, don't be surprised to hear a quick "no," no matter how solid your rapport with the client may be. Some people are too ashamed to admit that they could be damaged in this way. You may have to think of other solutions, such as a financial recovery counselor. (Karen McCall and her associates at www.financialrecovery.com and Bari Tessler's group at www.consciousbookkeeping.com are two valuable resources.)

Two more tips: Once you've developed guidelines for an overspending client, take care not to call it a budget—a word that free-living boomers mentally translate as "ball and chain." Refer to it instead as a spending plan, or a spending, saving, and investing plan, or even a financial growth plan.

Perhaps it should go without saying, but be sure the targets you set for overspending boomers are realizable. A client who has saved little or nothing can be thrown into hopeless despair by the news that he needs to amass millions of dollars for retirement.

Don't Blame Boomers

The worst strategy, I believe, is to blame clients for their inadequate savings or their excessive spending. Making people feel ashamed usually doesn't motivate them to change. On the contrary, they tend to lock into self-reproach, flagellating themselves over and over instead of moving forward.

Ted Klontz, Ph.D., who specializes in coaching professionals and clients in the process of change, is bothered by "articles I read about how the majority of boomers have acted irresponsibly…. [It's] a good example of taking a complex situation and making a simple solution."

The Charged Issue of LTCI

Baby boomers tend to be conflicted about end-of-life issues, especially ones that affect their choices. To many boomers, buying long-term care insurance may seem like accepting a sentence of 10 years to life in a nursing home.

When this coverage is appropriate, you might use the less emotionally charged term of "asset protection" to introduce it. If clients still feel anxious about contemplating their own or a parent's fragility, you may be able to calm them with stories of others who have faced this challenge and come through with flying colors. By tackling this difficult issue, you can help resolve one of your boomer clients' deepest concerns.

Klontz, president of Onsite Workshops in Nashville, Tennessee, suggests that boomers face new rules and shouldn't be blamed for operating under the old ones. He points out that when boomers started their professional careers, statistics suggested they would live only a few years in retirement. As average life expectancy has increased, so has the cost of health care—an annual retirement expense of tens of thousands of dollars that no one accurately predicted. Also, company-paid pensions were the mainstay of retirement planning when boomers began working. That secure income has largely gone by the boards, replaced by the risk of do-it-yourself investing. Finally, Social Security, once a reliable part of the "golden years," has been unveiled as a Ponzi scheme that threatens to implode.

To suggest that baby boomers should have anticipated and planned for all of this seems pretty simplistic, Klontz concludes. He feels it's fairer to say that boomers were blindsided by all this change in their later working years and are now blamed for being stupid about it.

I wholeheartedly agree with Klontz's view. If you approach your boomer clients without criticizing them for what they did or didn't do, but instead use empathy and compassionate listening, you'll find it much easier to get them on board with you.

Breaking Through Denial

Even though these "new rules" have received ample media coverage in recent years, many boomers still haven't stepped up to the plate. They may unconsciously think, "Something will come along to bail me out" or "I'll just keep working if I have to." These are examples of what Catherine Fitzgerald, Ph.D., of Fitzgerald Consulting in Bethesda, Maryland, calls "the weird optimism/anxiety, kind of magical thinking that we boomers tend to have."

How can you overcome this "magical thinking" to help boomer clients prepare for retirement's harsh realities? The professionals I queried use different approaches.

Larry Moskat, a former psychotherapist turned financial planner in Scottsdale, Arizona, takes a firm stance in overcoming denial: "I let [clients] know the situation is serious, but that we will explore any and all avenues in search of the best-case scenario outcome," he wrote me. "In the presence of further 'denial,' I may tell them that if they truly want help, they are going to have to decide to either go it alone, or align with a financial professional where they believe in the advisor's ability and integrity and feel a good 'chemistry.' Then I try to just shut up."

Daniel Wishnatsky, a financial planner who owns Special Kids Financial in Phoenix, points out that there may be something other than denial behind a client's resistance. "It may be that the client has already decided, for whatever reason, that they are not willing to make the necessary changes or that there are issues they simply don't want to share with you," he suggests. "Having come to that conclusion, it is easier for them to appear to be in denial than to try and defend a decision that appears inexplicable."

He adds that people who feel on the defensive will often say what they think makes the best defense, not what they're actually thinking. "Often the best tactic is to go in an entirely different direction, talk about sports or a hobby or whatever, and give them time to drop their defenses," he says. "It is absolutely crucial that you listen closely with an open mind. Because more often than not, they will start to drop subtle or not-so-subtle hints as to the real reason for their reluctance to plan. If you tune into that and nurture it a bit, without overdoing it, you may be on your way to a more productive dialogue."

Get Closer by Backing Off

Wishnatsky cautions not to expect too much right away. "The goal is to get you both sitting on the same side of the table. From there the rest is relatively easy." This is a great reminder that sometimes you need to back off from a client's resistance, waiting for an opportunity to move forward and "dance with" the resistance until you can touch the client's mind and heart.

Jim Ludwick, a planner with MainStreet Financial Planning in Odenton, Maryland, invites clients who are in denial to describe three scenarios: what happens if all their dreams come true; what happens if outcomes are just so-so; and what happens if they've made mistakes that force them to change their lifestyle. With each scenario, he asks, "What will your life be like? How will you feel? What will your friends and relatives say about you?" I suspect that when you get to scenario No. 3, this last question may unleash shame, regret, and a fair amount of pent-up feelings, requiring you to listen with extra patience and compassion.

"Hopefully the planning process gently stirs an awakening to reality," says Keith Newcomb, a financial planner and wealth manager with Full Life Financial in Nashville. "It's a delicate matter to help such a client understand the reality of what their situation requires, and to guide them through a process that leads them to reconcile their plans with reality."

In Ted Klontz's view, most, if not all, clients come to the table with significant shame around money, believing they have either too much or not enough. It's important to recognize that they're ambivalent to some degree about changing their financial behavior, he says; otherwise they would have already changed. That's why the planning process often bogs down in the face of client resistance.

"It is very clear what works and what doesn't" in overcoming this resistance, Klontz says. "Lecturing, providing more information and delivering more facts, threatening to 'fire' clients, cajoling, telling stories of how you can relate, asking questions, confronting, and all the other usual tools that seem intuitively correct are guaranteed to actually increase resistance and thicken denial." He draws a parallel with open-heart surgery survivors, only 10% of whom follow doctors' orders to change their heart-destructive lifestyles. "And planners are just dealing with finances, not life and death!" he adds.

To achieve better outcomes, Klontz teaches the technique of exquisite listening, which enhances a professional's ability to help clients clarify everything they are trying to say. It's a skill that his research has shown to be highly effective. "Typically, professionals miss much of what is being communicated because they stop listening too soon," he notes.

My experience suggests that there are a number of techniques for overcoming denial, each with its own advantages. I believe the most important, as Klontz and other empowering experts confirm, is attentive, patient, and empathetic listening.

Boomer Clients vs. the Greatest Generation

Planner Larry Moskat in Scottsdale, Arizona, believes that advising boomer clients is a "hugely different experience" than working with their parents' generation. Clients who came of age during World War II, he says, essentially trust professionals. Their retirement income is based on pensions and Social Security—"funds to which they feel entitled and which they do not care about having no control over," he points out. They typically intend to leave as much as they can to their children.

By contrast, "boomers are skeptical and generally do not accept most things at face value," he says. "They will Google planners and their recommendations as a matter of course." Accustomed to 401(k)s, they expect to have more control over their money. Larry also finds that boomers are less interested in leaving all they can to their heirs. "My impression is that they believe in giving their children the best tools possible to go out and create their own wealth, and in doing so feel they have done their part as good parents," he says.

On balance, Larry sees boomer clients as more aware and engaged in the planning process. In the long run, he says, financial planners may have more successful relationships with boomers than they did with many of their WW II-generation clients.

Changing Boomers' Attitudes

In mulling over ways to convert boomer clients' denial into greater openness and self-awareness, I'm reminded of the six stages of successful self-change, as described by professor of psychology James Prochaska, Ph.D. The first stage—denial of a problem—is what Prochaska calls precontemplation. I like the implication that there is a continuum between precontemplation and contemplation that we move along when we are ready to take a problem seriously. From there, we progress to preparation (getting ready to act) and then to action—the "busiest" phase of change. This framework helps me view denial as simply an early step on the path to taking action.

Holly Hunter, a planner and principal of Hunter Advisor in Portsmouth, New Hampshire, finds Prochaska's thinking very valuable. "As advisors we must be with the client as they move through the stages, changing 'for good' as in the case of overspending," she says. "Bribes and incentives are not likely to produce the desired long-term behavior modification that will be beneficial for the client. Having raised five children, I can attest to that."

Gayle Knight Colman, a financial advisor and wealth coach at Colman Knight Advisory Group in Carlisle, Massachusetts, sums it all up with her belief that an advisor's full-bodied presence, rather than specific techniques or tactics, makes the difference in helping clients overcome denial. "My short answer is to meet them where they are, in thought, space, and consciousness," she says. "At some core level, people know the truth about their overspending or lack of planning. At the same core level these people want to access that truth, which ultimately opens the door to freedom and making conscious choices. So I would not say I pierce the veil of denial, but I walk with my clients and allow them to unfold the truth with support, truth-telling, and inviting them to a whole new way of being and playing in the world."

The Compleat Boomer Advisor

William Sadler, Ph.D., has been one of the leading prophets of the new retirement for many years. Now in his 70s, he is an active speaker and author— most recently of *Changing Course: Navigating Life after 50* with James Krefft (Center for Third Age Leadership Press, 2008)—dedicated to helping boomers fashion their Third Age with greater consciousness and vitality. When I spoke to him recently, he suggested that boomers need to embrace the following guidelines to design what he calls a "life portfolio":

1. **"Dig deep and do mindful reflection."** Advisors can help clients in this part of the process by asking the right questions about what they really want, what moves and inspires them, what gives their life meaning.

2. **"Develop realistic optimism."** Clients rely on you for a realistic assessment of their situation. But no matter how unpromising it appears to be, you can encourage optimism by coaching them to build on their strengths and passions, manage their worries, and learn new skills to make their retirement years more rewarding.

3. **"Develop a positive Third Age identity."** Sadler characterizes the Second Age (one's working years) as a quest for achievement, while in the Third Age the focus shifts to fulfillment. To assist boomer clients in the transition to a "Third Age identity," you can help them

identify what used to motivate them, and explore new sources of inspiration that will guide them toward growing fulfillment.

4. **"Redefine work and play."** Sadler feels that in the Third Age, work may become more important for boomers, not less. Whether your clients want to keep working for love or money, or yearn to fully retire and relax, you can help them determine a productive and satisfying course of action.

5. **"Expand freedom and build deep personal relationships."** I believe you can have an important impact here when you help clients explore what more freedom would mean to them, and strategize ways to achieve it. You can also make it easier to develop new communities of support by steering them toward networks of people who share their interests.

6. **"Create a more caring life."** This means not just caring for family, friends, or worthy causes, according to Sadler, but also caring more deeply for oneself. You may want to become more of an advocate for your clients in this regard, encouraging them to find a variety of ways to manage stress well and stay connected to others.

This may seem a far cry from efficient portfolio theory or reading a balance sheet, but I believe that the more successfully you help boomer clients segue into their Third Age, the stronger your relationship with them will become. If you feel that you yourself need support in any of these areas, you might consider collaborating with a life coach or therapy professional.

Don't Just React—Act!

To capitalize on the tremendous need boomers have for your services and help them get past their resistance or denial, I urge you to reach out to them. Sponsor workshops and forums on important subjects such as the aging brain, managing the stresses of later life, nutrition and health, long-term care, new housing options, new avenues for fulfilling work, or volunteering choices. Topics like these can help boomers associate you with a holistic kind of life planning, making it easier for them to consult you in a climate of trust and openness (and shorten the time until you can inspire them to act).

If they have overly optimistic dreams of how much money they'll have when they retire, you'll need to be prepared for creative thinking about how to do more with less. As time goes on, I predict that you'll find yourself continually adding to your list of resources. New partnerships and new possibilities will emerge as more clients enter their Third Age and eventually their Fourth (the age of legacy, of passing the torch).

But now, as boomers flood into their 60s with the potential for a third of their life still ahead of them, they are at a turning point. They have a chance to move from achievement to fulfillment, to relax and savor long-deferred opportunities, to stimulate mind and body in new ways, to clarify their legacy, and to create a different life rich in meaning, pleasure, and purpose.

Money is merely a tool that facilitates this process. What your boomer clients need most is your wisdom and self-awareness, which can give them the confidence to believe that despite some unavoidable losses, the best is yet to come.

For More Third Age Insights . . .

Consider creating a library of resources to help boomer clients find help with unexpected issues of their 60s and 70s. These sources have been personally helpful or strongly recommended to me:

Print

- Marti Barletta, *Prime Time Women: How to Win the Hearts, Minds, and Business of Boomer Big Spenders* (Kaplan Business, 2007)

- Bernice Bratter and Helen Dennis, *Project Renewment: The First Retirement Model for Career Women* (Scribner, 2008)

- Gene Cohen, *The Creative Age: Awakening Human Potential in the Second Half of Life* (Harper Paperbacks, 2001)

- Gene Cohen, *The Mature Mind: The Positive Power of the Aging Brain* (Basic Books, 2007)

- Marc Freedman, *Encore: Finding Work that Matters in the Second Half of Life* (PublicAffairs, 2007)

- Marc Freedman, *Prime Time: How Baby Boomers Will Revolutionize Retirement and Transform America* (PublicAffairs, 2002)

- Brent Green, *Marketing to Leading Edge Baby Boomers: Perceptions, Principles, Practices & Predictions* (Paramount Market Publishing, 2006)

- Olivia Mellan with Sherry Christie, *Overcoming Overspending: A Winning Plan for Spenders and their Partners* (third edition, 2009)

- James Prochaska, John Norcross, and Carlo DiClemente, *Changing for Good: A Revolutionary Six-Stage Program for Overcoming Bad Habits and Moving Your Life Positively Forward* (Collins, 1995)

- William A. Sadler, Ph.D., *The Third Age: Six Principles for Growth and Renewal After Forty* (Perseus Publishing, 2001)

- William A. Sadler, Ph.D., and James H. Krefft, Ph.D., *Changing Course: Navigating Life after 50* (The Center for Third Age Leadership Press, 2008); also see www.changingcoursebook. com

- Nancy K. Schlossberg, *Retire Smart, Retire Happy: Finding Your True Path in Life* (American Psychological Association, 2003)

- Jeri Sedlar and Rick Miners, *Don't Retire, Rewire!* (2nd edition), (Alpha, 2007)

- Ronnie Sellers (ed.), *60 Things to Do When You Turn 60* (Sellers Publishing, 2006)

- Susan Krauss Whitbourne and Sherry Willis (eds.), *The Baby Boomers Grow Up: Contemporary Perspectives on Midlife* (Lawrence Erlbaum Associates, 2006)

Online

The following Web sites and blogs are also useful sources of insight (many references are courtesy of Dorian Mintzer, Ph.D., a Boston coach specializing in boomer issues):

- American Society on Aging (multidisciplinary organization of professionals in the field of aging): **www.asaging.org**

- BoomerTowne.com (a community of boomer-focused information, resources, and activities): **www.boomertowne.com**

- Center for Third Age Leadership (Dr. William Sadler, et al.): **www.thirdagecenter. com**

- Life Planning Network (life planning professionals focusing on the Third Age): **www. lifeplanningnetwork.org**

- Third Age Lifecrafting (coach, teacher, and facilitator Meg Newhouse): **www. passionandpurpose.com**

- Sagience (Dr. Catherine Fitzgerald): **www.sagience.com**

- The Boomer Blog (baby boom market specialist Carol Orsborn, et al.): **http://theboomer blog.com**

- Creative Aging for Women blog (personal coach Lynne Berrett): **www.creativeagingfor women.com**

- Klontz Coaching and Consulting blog (Drs. Ted and Brad Klontz): **www.klontzblog.com**

- On Retirement blog (recent retiree Heather Otto): **http://onretirement.blogspot.com**

- Professional Resilience blog (psychotherapist and life coach Marcia McConnell): **http:// resiliencepro.wordpress.com**

- 2 Young 2 Retire blog (life coach Howard Stone and coauthor Marika Stone): **http://2young2retire.com**

Passing the Torch

When I started specializing in "money harmony" work more than 25 years ago, talking about money was taboo in many American families. Since then we've become accustomed to hearing people bare their souls in public about everything from childhood abuse to erectile dysfunction, but the subject of money has barely begun to peek shyly out of the closet.

In some cases, younger parents are doing a better job of teaching their kids about money. But it's still rare for parents of a certain age to discuss their finances with their adult children. In particular, the younger generation often has no idea how their parents feel about leaving them money, how they want their financial legacy to be used, or what they want their life to have meant to family members and the larger community. In the absence of these conversations, adult children are left to wonder and worry about their aging parents' financial security and their own inheritances. Financial advisors and attorneys know all too many horror stories where a remarried parent leaves everything to a new spouse, without informing the children from his or her earlier marriage. These kids must then try to heal themselves of the pain of unexplained rejection before they can move on with their lives.

Advisors are well placed to help the generations talk with one another more directly and open-heartedly—sharing their fears and concerns and, more important, their hopes and dreams in a climate of love and respect. You can encourage older clients to write (or record) "ethical wills" in which they give each child their blessing and share life lessons about their principles, their accomplishments, their mistakes, their mentors.

With your help and guidance, adult children who will inherit large sums of money can be educated to understand where that wealth came from and to learn the basics of good stewardship. And children of almost any age are able to learn lessons in wise giving. The older generation can then have the peace of mind of knowing the family legacy will be passed on, along with their cherished values.

All this takes time, patience, and empathetic listening on the part of everyone involved—you, the parents, and the adult children who will inherit from them. Old wounds from the past do not have to be resolved in order for the generations to create a new, respectful dialogue with one another. Family members just need to be coached and mentored to share their thoughts and feelings considerately, to enter each other's worlds more deeply, and to build bridges between themselves so that the family's wealth—not only its financial assets but its values, traditions, cherished beliefs, and philanthropic goals—can be passed on with respect and good will.

CHAPTER 21

The Silent Generations

A huge chunk of our nation's wealth is in the hands of baby boomers' parents. Unless these generations start talking to each other about it, we may be in for big trouble.

As a baby boomer, I think of my generation as anything but silent. We're notorious for speaking out loud and clear in all directions. All our lives we've been telling our parents exactly how we feel and what we think.

Except for the thing that scares us the most: that they won't always be around and able to take care of us. The older they (and we) get, the harder it is to face the issues that inevitably arise at the end of life, including asking ostensibly mundane questions like whether they're okay financially, as well as profound questions such as what they want us to do with their values and assets when they're gone.

The havoc this avoidance wreaks can harm both generations, although its impact may be most obvious on the adult kids (or "grownchildren," a term I'm fond of). You've probably encountered the fallout in your own practice. The resentment dividing two siblings who learn after their parents' death that one has a free-and-clear inheritance and the other's funds are inexplicably in trust. The rage at a parent who enforces his kids' obedience by threatening to cut them out of his will, then dies intestate. The hurt and confusion of children trying to find out if their parents will need financial support, only to be accused of being greedy for an inheritance.

The only way to make progress in these situations is to open up communication. If you can use your professional clout to jump-start the process while both generations can still come to the table, there's hope for an easing of tensions and better resolution.

Why the Generations Don't Talk

Whether you represent older parents or a grownchild, better intergenerational communication is as important to you as it is to your clients. For adult children, an understanding of their parents' situation is a vital part of putting their own financial house in order. How can they plan for retirement without knowing whether or not they may have to support one or both parents? How will they know if they should buy long-term care insurance for the older folks to control their own financial risk?

On the other hand, they (and you) need to know if it's realistic to base life choices on a large gift or inheritance. Do they expect their parents to rescue them or make up for childhood deprivation?

For parents, communication can sometimes head off financial disaster when they don't have enough to live on. Beyond that, it offers an opportunity to develop warmer, more open relationships with their grownchildren. It will also give them greater peace of mind to know that the kids are all right—that everyone is on board with (or at least apprised of) their decisions and their desired legacy.

Why Kids Clam Up

Stereotypically, aging parents are reluctant to divulge their finances and shy away from matters relating to their mortality. However, recent research shows that many older folks are more at ease discussing twilight-of-life issues than their kids may think.

According to a 2005 survey by The Hartford, 76% of parents said they were comfortable talking about estate arrangements with their adult children. By contrast, a mere 45% of boomers felt at ease discussing this. So the blame for failing to communicate may well lie with Junior and Sis, not Mom and Dad.

Why are so many grownchildren conflicted, resistant, or downright fearful about bringing up these important topics? In my experience, emotions like these frequently come into play:

Denial. Some boomers resist growing up. (Not any of us, of course!) Many more hate to admit that they're already grown up or that their parents have aged, too, and may soon die.

Avoidance. Some "money avoider" children tell themselves that an older or more financially savvy sibling should deal with the matter. Others pass the buck to sibs thought to be closer to Mom or Dad. The Hartford research reported that "only children" were more likely than kids with siblings to be conversant with their parents' finances. This makes sense: an only child knows there isn't anyone else to step up to the plate, and parents don't have to worry about appearing to favor one child over another.

Financial fears. Younger people struggling to achieve financial well-being can feel overwhelmed by the possibility of having to support their parents as well. They may feel that if they ignore the need, it won't materialize.

Role conflict. It's human nature to dread that our parents may become emotionally and financially dependent on us. We want them to be there for us forever. If our relationship with them has been flawed, we hope that before it's too late they will give us the unselfish love, nurturing, and support we needed and never got. Keeping these turbulent feelings hidden is safer than confronting our parents' imperfections—and our own.

Why Parents Keep Mum

Financial planner Mary Malgoire, who heads The Family Firm in Bethesda, Maryland, cites half a dozen common reasons for parental reluctance to discuss or share money:

- They think they may need it.

- They want the children to make it on their own.

- Talking about money is "not done" in the family.

- They are embarrassed (usually by having saved too little).

- They don't want to be told what to do.

- They fear finding out that the kids are greedy.

When Mary has parents as clients, sometimes part of her job is complying with their wishes to keep the kids at bay. She points out, however, that it's important to prevent parental silence from producing devastating results. For example, I heard the sad story of a grownchild who lived on distributions from a family trust with no understanding of how it worked. When poor investments caused the funds to begin drying up, she came to a planner in panic. At that point, there was no way to avoid the consequences. Better upfront communication by the parents (or their advisor) could have saved her from having to take the kids out of private school, move to a smaller house, and go back to work to make ends meet.

Overcoming Obstacles

Advisors can play a crucial role in helping parents to think through the fears and concerns that keep them from sharing financial information. Some of these worries may truly apply to their kids, while others are rooted in money messages from childhood ("Money corrupts," "Talking about money is tacky," "All kids are inherently greedy"). It's essential to get these old beliefs out in the open before you will have any luck persuading the parents to initiate a dialogue with their children.

Sometimes more charged emotions such as resentment, anxiety, or shame need to be addressed before an intergenerational dialogue can begin. Consider teaming up with a therapist, counselor, or coach to facilitate these tricky situations.

For example, Ted Klontz, a noted pioneer in blending psychotherapy and financial planning, tells of an elderly couple of modest means who couldn't let their kids grow up. Overcome with guilt about not having been better parents in earlier years, the couple kept sneaking money to their now-adult children without admitting it to each other. Thanks to their handouts, the kids hadn't needed jobs for years. After working with Ted and financial planner Rick Kahler of Kahler Financial Group in Rapid City, South Dakota, the clients were able to stop this overfeeding, which improved their own financial well-being while helping their grownchildren become more productive and personally fulfilled. (For more examples, see *The Financial Wisdom of Ebenezer Scrooge* [Health Communications, Inc., 2006], which Ted and Rick wrote with Ted's son, psychologist Brad Klontz.)

Your efforts to educate a client can also be the first step in mending family bonds. Peg Downey, an advisor who is a partner in Money Plans in Silver Spring, Maryland, tells about a client who was bitterly disappointed when her parents gave the family-owned company to her brother. The lump-sum payment she received made her feel slighted and bought off. Once Peg understood these concerns, she explained that when one child inherits a business, it is normal and equitable to compensate other sibling(s) with the cash equivalent of the business's value. With a better perspective on the situation, the client felt more fairly treated. This led to an open discussion with other family members, improving the quality of their relationships.

Getting All Parties Talking

If it's the parents who are hesitant to talk, Mary Malgoire suggests that a grownchild approach them this way: "My financial advisor has asked if there is a chance you may need some financial support later in your life. I would like to prepare for that by setting something aside in case it happens. Would you be willing to share this information, either with my advisor or with me?"

Seven Questions

Essential issues for grownchildren to raise with their parents:

1. What legacy would you like to leave to our family? To the larger community? Have you written down your wishes? Would you like me to help you make an ethical will to share your principles and aspirations?

2. Have you planned how to manage and transfer your assets to the beneficiaries you've chosen?

3. Do you have a will? How recent is it? Is it still valid? Where can it be found? Who is the executor?

4. Do you have enough money to maintain your current lifestyle? Have you thought about how to pay for long-term care, if needed?

5. What if you get sick? Have you granted someone a durable power of attorney to manage your finances?

6. Who is legally allowed to make healthcare decisions for you if you can't? Do you have a living will expressing your desires about things like artificial life support?

7. Are your important financial documents in one place? Who knows where they are? Should I know?

Ideally, parents will discuss their situation with the children as well as with you. This gives you a role in learning and sharing, and possibly family healing as well.

If the older folks are headed for financial difficulty, embarrassment and shame may make them even more reluctant to level with their kids. However, the sooner the whole family can get together to strategize solutions, the better. You may be able to help them find an answer (a reverse mortgage, for example, or a private annuity) that both generations can accept.

If the kids are the ones with cold feet, you can initiate the communication process by inviting them to your office to discuss their parents' wishes and preferences. Coming from you, this invitation may be less emotionally loaded and have more professional weight than if the parents had sent it. Your office is also a neutral place, free of memories that might pollute communication in the kids' or parents' home. Ideally, these factors will work together to make the grownchildren feel less able to refuse the request.

You might mention The Hartford survey findings when they arrive, to let them know they're not alone if they feel awkward. Then sum up the ways this discussion can benefit them as well as their parents.

Introducing a Hidden Agenda

Sometimes a parent may appear to be investing unwisely, having trouble paying bills, or in the unhealthy grip of a neighbor or so-called advisor. How should you handle a client's request for help in getting them to change the way they manage money?

Since older people are often highly sensitive to any suggestion of impaired functioning, I would suggest a soft, gentle approach rather than confrontation. You might start by inviting the parents to contribute their experience and knowhow in helping you develop a financial plan for their offspring.

In situations like this, some planners prefer to tactfully usher the kids from the room and have a private conversation with the older folks. Once the discussion is underway, you may be able to win their trust and elicit details of their own money management that will indicate whether a change is really necessary. Sometimes the concerns are legitimate, while at other times you'll find they have been overblown by the children's fears.

A conference in your office can also be a ploy to get Mom and Dad to pay for the grandkids' education or help in buying a house—not that there's anything wrong with that! If your clients want to explore getting an advance on their inheritance, you can initiate a parental consultation without having to spill the beans upfront. Phrase the invitation in terms like this: "Your son/daughter, my financial planning client, suggested that you might be willing to help us strategize ways to reach their longer-term goals. Would you be able to join us in my office next Tuesday or Wednesday?"

After the meeting starts, it may be easy to discover if the parents want their money to make a difference to their kids (and how). If they have been assuming it's crucial to leave as large an estate as possible, try to educate them about the advantages of giving away some of those assets now. A current gift not only shrinks their potential estate tax liability, but also may be more appreciated while the younger generation is still struggling for financial security.

Speaking of estates, it's not unusual to encounter older parents who are denying themselves luxuries (or even necessities) in order to leave a larger inheritance. As in the situation Ted Klontz cited, this overgiving may be fueled by unresolved guilt at not having been there earlier for their kids. Encourage these parents to forgive themselves, apologize to their grownchildren, and perhaps ask for the kids' forgiveness, too.

"Mom, Dad, Let's Talk": A Guide for Adult Children

In our society, money means control and power. It's natural for parents to resist losing or giving up this control, especially if declining physical abilities have already made them feel resentful or alarmed. That's why clumsy inquiries about their finances by an adult child, even one they have always trusted, may be met with defensiveness and rebuff. Here are some ways for children to create a dialogue that reassures them their control is still respected:

1. **Don't wait for a crisis.** It's much more difficult to talk about plans and wishes in the middle of an emergency.

2. **Proceed slowly.** You may have to persist for several weeks or months, sharing pertinent articles and gently mentioning your need for peace of mind about your parents' plans, in order to win their agreement to talk.

3. **Respect your parents' right to keep their affairs private.** If they don't want to share their financial picture with you, ask them to have a qualified advisor give it a "safety check."

4. **Use language that isn't threatening.** For example, say, "What would you like to do with your estate?" rather than the more loaded "What would you like to do with your money?" Instead of a question about inheritances, asking "What would you like your legacy to be?" can open up a dialogue on values, wishes, and goals.

5. **Don't infringe on your parents' independence by implying that you expect an inheritance or gift.** If they feel like being generous with their money, that's up to them.

6. **If you're asking for help now, always give them an opportunity to refuse gracefully.** ("If you aren't able to do it, I can accept that. We'll manage another way.")

7. **Keep their wishes paramount.** If they would rather use their money to travel instead of helping you with a down payment on a vacation home, gently remind yourself that it's their money.

8. **Be sure to keep your siblings informed.** If they've designated you as the point person, try to head off problems by religiously keeping all of them up to date.

Getting the Generations Together

Overall, outcomes tend to be good when the whole family is involved in an intergenerational get-together. Such gatherings, reports Malgoire, can have "very powerful results, especially with the in-laws."

When you facilitate these meetings, be sure both generations have an opportunity to share their thoughts, feelings, and desires. You may need to occasionally interrupt information-sharing monologues to make sure everyone is still on board and paying attention.

Ted Klontz tells about a family meeting called by a client couple to update their grownchildren. The parents talked about their financial situation and wishes for a long time. A long, long time. The two kids' eyes began to glaze over. One finally left the office without a word. When Ted suggested asking the children about their own money preferences, the parents were taken aback. Apparently, the idea of a dialogue had never occurred to them.

Talking Through Their Hats?

In another extensive U.S. survey done by Allianz Group, most parents and grownchildren said they were "highly confident" talking about legacy and inheritance issues. However, less than a third had actually discussed such topics as values and life lessons, wishes to be fulfilled, personal possessions of emotional value, or financial assets and real estate. A good fifth of the baby boomers surveyed hadn't addressed any of these issues with their parents.

If we probed the conversations that did take place, I suspect the amount left unshared would dwarf the little that actually was said. How many other families resemble the one where the father left most of his wealth to a family foundation, stating in his will: "I can't get my children to work together while I'm alive—but if they want any say in where the money goes, they'll have to work together after I'm dead."

As more and more baby boomers are faced with the need to broach ticklish matters with their aging parents, you might consider developing special expertise in this area. Gather and share good articles on intergenerational dialogue. Identify therapeutic professionals experienced in money conflict resolution who can partner with you or serve as a resource for family members needing extra counseling. By all means, remind your boomer clients to "walk their talk" by discussing their financial plans with their own offspring as soon as the kids are mature enough.

With your understanding and support, there's hope that more parents and grownchildren will speak the whole truth to each other about legacies that can shape their family's course in the future. When that happens, the silence of the generations will truly start to become a thing of the past.

CHAPTER 22

Passing It On

A family retreat can take clients a long way toward defining their family and legacy values and imparting them—along with wealth—to the next generation.

The only people who are certain that inheriting wealth will solve their problems, I suspect, are those who have never been wealthy. Quite often, a large inheritance turns out to be more of a curse than a cure. As William K. Vanderbilt (grandson of the Commodore) reportedly grumbled: "Inherited wealth is a big handicap to happiness. It is as certain death to ambition as cocaine is to morality."

This isn't the fault of wealth managers, who spend a goodly amount of their and their clients' time setting up dynasty trusts, charitable trusts, and family foundations. But despite these well-laid plans, it's said that six out of 10 newly created family fortunes are gone by the end of the second generation. By the end of the third generation, nine out of 10 once-wealthy families are broke.

A major factor in this shocking 90% breakdown rate is parents' failure to communicate values that their children and grandchildren can absorb and thrive on. We all know instances of clueless kids squandering an inheritance through overspending, mismanagement, or self-sabotaging addictions. Parents also unthinkingly make estate-planning decisions that destroy family harmony, as when they give control of the family business to an inept son or daughter instead of to a better-qualified but less-favored sibling; or when children of a first marriage are blindsided by a parental will that leaves everything to a new spouse and kids.

In the next several years, an enormous amount of wealth is expected to pass to the baby boomer generation—$41 trillion between 1990 and 2044, according to the often-quoted estimate by John Havens and Paul Schervish of the Boston College Center on Wealth and Philanthropy. Wealth managers have an opportunity to help clients make this transfer in a way that can lead to personal and family harmony and empowerment and improve the quality of others' lives. Failure to meet this challenge, on the other hand, may promote more reckless spending, poor decisions, conflict, and pain.

Bringing Generations Together

To begin transferring an emotional legacy from one generation to another, it's crucial to have better, deeper, and more thoughtful communication about the things that truly matter. In recent years, clients have invited me to facilitate retreats where family members can discuss the kind of future they desire and the financial decisions they would like to see made for the next generation. Parents have the opportunity to communicate the deeply held values that constitute their emotional legacy, inspiring children and grandchildren to embrace this legacy as a basis for their own empowerment.

These experiences have been so satisfying for all involved, with outcomes far exceeding my own expectations, that I enthusiastically recommend family retreats as a vital step in planning intergenerational wealth transfers.

When to Suggest a Family Retreat

Some wealth managers are already firm believers in regularly scheduled family retreats. "To be stewards of the family wealth, it's important for the next generation to learn the technical side, the emotional side, and family values with regard to money," says John Waldron, chief executive of Waldron Wealth Management in Pittsburgh. His goal is to meet with client families twice a year, although he admits, "Realistically, it's once a year."

A retreat program can be started whenever the younger generation is ready. "We like to get involved early, as opposed to later," Waldron says. "I think it is extremely important that the kids start learning about money conceptually at an early age, around 12 or 14, when they are ready to understand the family's stated objective or 'mission statement' with regard to money. Then they can begin digesting the family's philosophy from an emotional standpoint when they are in their late teens to early 20s." As they reach college age, the process may step up. "We like to have interim sessions with the kids, or Web conferences, to keep the process going," he says.

If it's difficult to get clients together on a regular basis, a family transition is an ideal occasion for a retreat, says Susan Bradley, CFP, founder of the Sudden Money Institute and co-author with Mary Martin of *Sudden Money: Managing a Financial Windfall* (Wiley, 2000). A transition might be any big pivot point, she says, such as a parent's retirement, the sale of a family business, or the birth of a first grandchild.

Why Go to All the Effort?

Family retreats can be complicated and expensive to pull together, especially the first one. Work and schooling have to be put on hold and clients pulled away from commitments and leisure. Rod Zeeb, chief executive and co-founder with Perry Cochell of the Heritage Institute in Portland, Oregon, has learned that wealthy clients typically respond well to the idea of a retreat when he asks them, "If there's no training, and you dump all this money on the kids, what's going to happen?" He also notes that parents tend to embrace the opportunity to pass on their life lessons and values in a family forum.

In the early stages of organization, the clients and their advisor should agree on the goals of the family retreat. At Waldron Wealth Management, the focus is on raising the younger generation's awareness in five areas, according to Krishna Pendyala, Waldron's chief operating officer and coach. First, he says, they need to learn to appreciate their good fortune without being pounded over the head with it. Using real-life examples from their own age group— anecdotes about Paris Hilton or Lindsay Lohan, for example—helps them "get it" on their own.

Second, Pendyala says, it's best to inspire children to a calling—not just lecture them on the "right" things to do in life. As any parent can attest, children seldom respond well to preaching by their elders.

Third is helping them learn the fundamental role of money in their lives. "Basically, you can do four things with it: earn it, spend it, nurture it, and give it away," Pendyala says. ("We say money can be compared to alcohol," John Waldron adds. "It can be dangerous when you use it irresponsibly, and it can derail your life experience and the attainment of family goals.")

The fourth area of consciousness-raising is helping young people understand what it takes to sustain the components of their lifestyle. In one family retreat, Waldron asked the young adult participants how much they thought it had cost to fly them in on private jets. "Guesses were everywhere," he says. "When we told them the cost, they were flabbergasted: 'That's more than my two-month draw on my trust!' Next thing, we heard them saying, 'Dad, why did you fly us down here on our private jet? We could have flown commercial!'"

The final item on Pendyala's agenda is helping the younger generation become aware of taxation and the laws affecting estate distribution, which helps drive home the point of becoming responsible and knowledgeable. When all five areas are covered in a retreat, young family members usually come away with a more realistic understanding of their inheritance, improving the chances of a successful intergenerational wealth transfer.

Structuring a Retreat

Retreats run by the Waldron team usually last three days. The first two are dedicated to family business and the third to fun, featuring some group activity that promotes team-building. A recent retreat was held at a racetrack, with everyone learning how to be part of a racing team.

Older and younger family members have distinct roles in the "business" part of the retreat, Waldron explains. "First, the senior generations in the room tell the family story. Here's our history; here's what you didn't know; here's what we believe is our mission and our role as stewards of this money. Then senior family members leave the meeting, and we talk to the young adults about the 'facts of money.'"

With young people in their 20s, Waldron may introduce philosophical issues such as "How would you use the family resources to make the biggest impact on the family and the community?" or "What would you do differently?" These issues are explored in breakout sessions, and then everyone reassembles to discuss what evolved.

Family Council: the Heritage Approach

Zeeb, who wrote *Beating the Midas Curse* with Cochell (Heritage Institute Press, 2005), recommends a slightly different tack. In the Heritage training program for estate planners and other advisors, communication begins outside the retreat in a process called "guided discovery." The advisor interviews the family elders, inviting them to tell stories from their past that made a difference in their lives. They are then asked to explain what they learned from these people or events. Underlying values tend to surface in this process, while the advisor records and then edits their personal history into story format.

A second part of guided discovery is the creation of a vision statement, which essentially answers the question, "If you could look at your family 50 years from now, what would you want to see?" The answer to this can serve as a template for estate planning, helping to guide all of the family's advisors toward the stated vision.

To disseminate their views, the senior generation is encouraged to establish a Family Council. Typically, junior members of the family are selected to be its officers. "In the first retreat, the parents present their personal history and unveil their vision statement," Zeeb says. "They share these with the family, and we explain that the Family Council is the first step toward their vision." From then on, the council meets regularly on matters requiring a family consensus. Each year's event has a theme: in Year One, it's communication; then empathy; and next, leadership.

An unusual aspect of the Heritage Institute's approach is a "pre-inheritance experience." The older folks give the younger generation a sum of money—typically between $25,000 and $500,000—with advice to the effect that "Our goal is to help you learn how to work together as a group. For the first couple of years, we'd like you to learn how to deal with this money and invest it. If you do a good job, we'll match or increase the amount next year." Great investment returns are not the objective; what matters is that young family members learn how to communicate and work together well, establish relationships with their own team of experts, and devise an investment strategy. This educational experience promotes a better transfer of leadership to the next generation.

A Tale of Two Retreats

To illustrate how a family retreat can help resolve issues that may sabotage a wealth transfer plan, consider these examples from my own experience.

1. **Clarifying family consensus.** "Bill" and "Kate" suddenly found themselves very wealthy after Bill's business was sold. Among their concerns were how much money to give their adult children, and in what form (a lump sum? a monthly stipend?). Bill was worried about impairing the kids' work ethic and drive to succeed, but Kate felt this wasn't a problem and wanted to make the gifts substantial. They were also considering selling one or two family properties and were unsure how their children would react to this.

    To complicate matters, theirs was a blended family. Two of the four kids were from Kate's first marriage, and the other two were Bill's. Some step-siblings, all in their 20s and 30s, had difficult relationships with one another.

    We arranged a two-day retreat at the parents' home in Maine. Before this meeting, I interviewed everyone by phone and email, including the referring financial advisor, who would not be present at the retreat. These conversations clarified for me how the family members felt about the gathering, what they expected and hoped it would accomplish, how they felt about their new wealth, and how each of them "sat with" the others.

Mirror, Mirror

Listening and reflecting techniques may help free up communication among family members who have too much experience in pushing each other's buttons. My preferred tool is Harville Hendrix's mirroring exercise, which is done in pairs of a speaker and a listener. The ground rules are that the listener must empty his or her mind in order to enter the speaker's world. Only when it is his time to speak is he allowed to regain his own viewpoint.

The exercise begins with each person offering an appreciation of the other. It continues as follows:

Step 1: Mirroring

The speaker says a few sentences about whatever topic we are discussing. The listener "mirrors" this comment, playing it back as close to verbatim as possible and ending with "Is there more?" The speaker "sends" a few more sentences, which the listener plays back by saying, "You want to make sure that..." (repeating whatever the speaker just said). "Is there more?" Eventually, the speaker says, "No, there's no more."

Step 2: Validation

The listener enters more deeply into the mind and heart of the speaker by tuning in, in the most compassionate, nonjudgmental way possible, to what "makes sense" from the speaker's perspective. For example, if the speaker says, "I feel anxious about giving you too much money all at once," the listener validates this with a response like "It makes sense that you feel anxious about giving me too much money all at once, because in the past, I have been an overspender." Then the listener should ask, "Is there any part of your message you'd like to hear validated that I haven't included?" If so, try to validate it.

Step 3: Empathy

Once all the validations have been shared, the listener deepens her empathy about the speaker's emotions by saying, "I imagine you might also be feeling..." with an appropriate term such as angry, sad, hopeful or relieved. (This should be just one word—"angry," for example—not "angry because..." or "angry about...""). Then the speaker and listener switch places to create a climate of mutual respect.

This exercise may sound laborious, but it slows down family members' habitual communication patterns: failing to listen carefully, interrupting, injecting their own opinion or agreeing without fully grasping the emotional impact of the other person's perspective. In this safe space, they learn to listen more deeply when others are speaking to them.

I explained that in addition to the whole family getting together, we would meet in many different permutations: Parents together, children with their birth parent, children individually and so on. I also told them I would teach them "mirroring," a simple way to help create a safe climate for deeper, more empathetic communication. We would use it during the entire retreat, and, if they found it useful, they could employ it in their own lives afterward. I coached them on this technique as soon as we convened (see "Mirror, Mirror").

When Bill and Kate shared their vision and principles with the rest of the family, the feedback told them a lot about their children's values. The agenda evolved as the parents clarified their needs and concerns and the kids weighed in with their own issues. The discussion illuminated each child's maturity of judgment regarding expenditures, investments, and charitable giving, and helped lower any unrealistic expectations of each other. Bill and Kate decided to focus more on charitable giving as a couple, inviting the children to participate as they showed interest. They felt the retreat was a "complete success" and "better than we ever expected."

Several changes in financial strategy came out of the discussions. One example was the couple's decision to spend some of their new wealth on travel and other life experiences with their children, instead of trying to maximize their estate. But ultimately, I think the family benefited most from learning to listen empathetically to one another with the others witnessing the process.

"I believe the family feels they now have better information on which to base some of their most important decisions," their financial planner wrote me. He felt the meeting also succeeded in conveying the parents' sincere desire to handle the inherent challenges of their situation, and in laying the foundation for good communication in the future. Ideally, this blended family will continue to hold yearly retreats that allow them to revisit their values, goals, and issues, and see how well their money is helping them get where they want to go.

2. **Getting an estate plan back on track.** At stake in this case was a poorly functioning wealth transfer plan now in the second and third generations. "Elaine," a 70-year-old divorcee, and her brother "Ted" had inherited a fortune from their father, but they didn't have easy

access to the money. Elaine's younger son, "Mark," ran the family business and controlled the purse strings. Whenever Elaine or Ted needed money, they had to go to Mark. Although everyone got along quite well, the disbursements were unpredictable and communication about the money was unclear. Everyone was dissatisfied enough with the situation to agree to Elaine's suggestion of a family retreat.

As usual, I interviewed each of the family members before we arrived at the retreat site in Arizona. (The family didn't have a wealth manager to discuss the situation with.) At the first get-together, I taught empathetic communication to Elaine, Ted, Mark, and Elaine's older son, "Joe," who practiced it with each other as I coached and fine-tuned their mirroring and validation skills.

Several agenda items emerged in this initial discussion: first, to help Mark communicate more clearly with the others and disburse money more regularly; second, to get him the support he needed to be less overwhelmed and reactive; third, to figure out a better way for family members to communicate with one another; and finally, to determine whether parts of the business should be developed or sold off.

As Elaine told me later, "In my father's world, you just didn't talk about money. This process opened up all the lines of communication." Even Ted and Joe, who had started out with pretty strong doubts about the value of the retreat, shared their hopes and frustrations about their lives and the family business, in particular.

All in all, the meeting accomplished even more than the family members had anticipated. Mark learned that the others were interested in the business, appreciated his efforts, and wanted to help and support him. Joe ended up feeling more valued as part of the team. Ted's desire for financial independence eased as he became more knowledgeable about the business and felt more involved in the decision-making process.

Best of all, the retreat re-established channels of communication among close relatives who had nursed silent grievances for years. Mark now sends updates about the business to other family members, and the whole family connects in bi-weekly conference calls. "It's cleared the air so much," Elaine says. "The whole atmosphere is different when we talk now."

Things of Value vs. the Value of Things

When you propose a family retreat, be prepared to depart from your usual mode of thinking. "You're helping to integrate the financial side and the human side, which takes a new skill set, tools, and a lot of patience," says Susan Bradley, who trains advisors to coach clients through transitions. "It's immensely rewarding, but very different from the traditional financial planning approach." If you're unfamiliar with what's involved, or are uncomfortable with therapeutic techniques, you may want to partner with a therapist or counselor.

I encourage you to help more wealthy families communicate things of value to their children, rather than focus on the value of things (as Rod Zeeb puts it). By enabling your clients to share and pass on their mission and values and by teaching their kids how to handle their emotional and financial legacy responsibly, you will make them an enormously valuable gift: the preservation of a family legacy for generations to come.

CHAPTER 23

The Age of Giving

It's more blessed to give than to receive, but philanthropy is a practice your clients' kids may need to learn.

"I have seen how money ruins families," says Louise Marie Cole, CFP, principal partner of Heritage Group of Companies in Toms River, New Jersey, and an advisor for more than 26 years. "As an individual it's easy to decide who gets the money and when, but if you are part of a family, the dynamics change. The conversations about values and things they want to see are missing in today's fast-paced world."

Most parents hope that if they instill the right values in their children, the kids will grow up to be happy and fulfilled. But in many cases, we don't do a good enough job of teaching them how they can use money to make a difference in the larger world, and how philanthropy can add meaning to their life.

No matter how much wealth a family has, helping the younger generation learn these lessons is an important part of planning for the future. Tom Rogerson, managing director of Family Wealth Services at BNY Mellon Wealth Management in Boston, often refers to it as "the other side of estate planning." He says, "It's not so much how do you prepare your money for your family, but how do you prepare your family for your money?"

Strengthening the Family

"Families that stop and discuss their philanthropy with their children— whether it's helping at the local food bank or donating time in a myriad of ways—are far better off as a family," says Cole. "For me, there is nothing better than a good heated family discussion as to which charity should get this year's donation. It may be the only time the family becomes whole. It's extremely rewarding to me as a facilitator to see once-selfish individuals rationally discussing charities that may get the money anonymously."

She points out that instead of just telling clients to use charitable deductions as much as possible, advisors can suggest using these opportunities to teach children how families make decisions and how philanthropy benefits everyone. "If you know you are going to give a certain amount to charity, why not decide as a family where you want the money to go and then create a learning opportunity for the children?" she asks. "You can get your personal message across about which charities you espouse, and perhaps learn about others that your children would like to help. It may be the one thing you do as a family that will keep your kids there for you when you get older."

Parlez-Vous Philanthropy?

But how do you bring up this subject with clients? Here's a suggestion from Barry Kohler, an attorney and chartered financial consultant who works with a number of high-net-worth families at BDMP Wealth Management in Portland, Maine. "When clients are going to have a federally taxable estate, I start by telling them that they can leave what they have to their family, to a charity or charities, or to the government—and the bad news is, they have to choose two of these three," he explains. "Once the clients understand that, they say, 'Oh, tell me more about the charitable part,' because clients like to direct their social capital to causes that are important to them."

Kohler probes further during the planning process. What are the clients' values and attitudes towards charitable giving? Have they tried to pass these on to their children? If so, by instruction or by example? The result of this exploration, he says, is "a conversation that helps me understand the culture of the family around philanthropy."

"Many wealthy clients find out about family retreats and say, 'Let's have one!'" Rogerson says. "The problem is, they introduce philanthropy too early." He goes on to explain, "Many of these entrepreneurial types are used to making decisions and then telling

---

Experiencing the Power of Philanthropy

A family retreat can be a great opportunity to initiate clients into the power of philanthropy. Perry Cochell and Rod Zeeb, co-founders of the Heritage Institute in Portland, Oregon, once brought out a 12-pound box of chocolates at a retreat and passed the box around to all the family members. On the first go-round, everyone took a few chocolates. On the second pass, some people took one or two more. When it went around a third and a fourth time, no one took any. There were still 10 lbs. of chocolates left in the box, so Perry and Rod called over a woman who was refilling the coffee urn. They found out her name, inquired whether she had kids (she had four), and asked if she would like to take the remaining chocolates home to them. Her face lit up as she said she would love to, and they gave her the box.

After she left, Zeeb and Cochell asked the family members whether they had gotten more pleasure from eating the chocolates or from giving the woman the box to take home to her family. Virtually everyone said that giving it away was more pleasurable. This idea is a lovely way to introduce philanthropy to a group of people of all ages.

the family what their roles will be. That doesn't work. Before you introduce philanthropy, you've got to create a sense of 'we.'"

In the workplace, these business owners may know how to get a group of unique, strong, independent individuals to work together as a team. But they haven't built a team at home—a vital element in ensuring the family's survival.

At BNY Mellon, Rogerson follows a five-step process to help family members learn to work as a team. In step one, the entire family discusses issues related to their wealth: making it, losing it, and spending it and the impact of spouses, gender, and birth order. In step two, the group identifies family members' different communication styles and explores how to use these styles as an aid instead of an impediment to progress. Step three is a values test: "Now that we understand what the issues are and how to talk about them, what are the values we want to transmit?"

Step four (at last) is charitable giving. "Ideally, we get the children to participate in the design of a family philanthropy," Rogerson says. In step five, the family learns to engage in healthy self-governance, making decisions on such wealth-related issues as fairness and what lifestyle level should be financially supported. "We don't want them to try to deal with those issues on day one," he points out. "If they hold off these discussions until step five, they will generally be able to approach them with a more cooperative and long-term perspective."

How Soon Can Kids Start Learning?

Some authorities recommend waiting to encourage philanthropy until children are past the "me" period of the Terrible Twos. Rogerson, for example, finds that "the only time you can't engage family members in some kind of a process is from birth to three years old."

In my experience, though, little kids are often natural givers. Szifra Birke, a wealth counselor in Chelmsford, Massachusetts, points out that a common example is the baby in the highchair who wants to feed you her Cheerios and smiles as you enjoy the gift, or the tot who shares his snack with the dog. "Some studies suggest that primitive forms of empathy may begin at age one or two, such as kissing a parent's hurt finger to make it feel better," says Birke. "Pleasure in giving can start quite young."

Peg Downey, founding partner of the fee-only advisory firm Money Plans in Silver Spring, Maryland, notes that at the age of three her daughter Colleen decided to give away her holiday gift money to the county's elderly poor. Young Colleen's desire to "help grandmas and grandpas who need it" was quoted (and applauded) in the local newspaper.

"Philanthropy can be taught at a very early age," Louise Marie Cole says. "Experiences should be age-appropriate—multiple small lessons allowing a child to feel how good it is to give. For example, you might hand a young child two cookies and then ask, 'May I have one of your cookies?' Your acceptance of the gift, and the big deal you make of it, is philanthropy in action. That child will enjoy the feeling of having given, even if you choose to give the cookie back."

Anne Anderson, a therapist colleague of mine at the Washington (D.C.) Therapy Guild who has worked with young children for years, cautions that kids between the ages of two and five are developing an identity in relation to others, so parents shouldn't require them to give away favorite toys or clothes that they may see as part of themselves. However, parents can familiarize even very young children with giving by allowing them to put the family donation in a church collection plate, or to help make up a holiday basket for needy families.

Cole believes it's important to be open with your philanthropy, explaining your reasons to your youngsters and letting them participate so they can share the pleasure. "Most of what we learn as a young child—three to five years old—is by listening and paying close attention to adults," she says.

Bhaj Townsend, an advisor with Legacy Plus and TRGi of Kirkland, Washington, agrees. "Exposing kids who are two and three years old to what their parents, other siblings, and other people are doing philanthropically is good modeling," she says. "It's best to start with no expectations. Then between four and six, as children start to become their own beings in their own world, you can begin asking them questions about what they see, about what their parents and other siblings are doing. For example, 'How do you feel when we're going to the zoo?'... 'When you see me at a board meeting, how do you feel about that organization?' Get them involved in their own feelings."

For my part, I think the concept of sharing one's wealth can start as soon as the child is old enough to receive an allowance. I would suggest that parents get (or make) a special bank like the one I saw years ago in a toy store, with three compartments that are each of a different color and size. A portion of the child's allowance goes into the first compartment for spending money, another part into the second compartment for savings, and the remaining part into a compartment for worthy charities. In our instant-gratification culture, helping children see with their own eyes that money can be used for more than spending is a wonderful first step to raise their awareness.

Once kids reach the age of seven to 10, they can start getting involved in philanthropy more intellectually. Lisa Kirchenbauer, president of Kirchenbauer Financial Management & Consulting in Arlington, Virginia, observes that by this time, children should be getting an allowance or at least developing greater consciousness of the power and importance of money. At 11 or 12, depending on how mature they are, they will probably be old enough to start getting involved in the family philanthropy process. "I'm suggesting that they participate with their parents, not do it all on their own," she says. "But I have seen some exceptional children pursue low-level philanthropic efforts a little earlier."

Never Underestimate the Philanthropic Power of Kids

Krishna Pendyala, chief operating officer and coach of Waldron Wealth Management in Pittsburgh, and his wife Sangeetha have two children: a son, Nyan (which means "sight" in Sanskrit) and a daughter, Lehka (whose name means "writing"). About six years ago, Pendyala told me, he was sitting with Nyan on his lap while looking over a report from Orbis, a nonprofit humanitarian organization committed to saving sight worldwide to which he and his wife contributed.

When Nyan, then 4, asked about the caption on a picture of Ronald McDonald, Krishna explained that the clown was opening a pediatric eye hospital in India. Blindness in India is considered a near-fatal disease, reducing the average life span to only a few years. The tragedy is that simple eye drops applied at the right time can sometimes make the difference between shadowy darkness or a life of full-color clarity.

Nyan immediately said, "Papa, I want to open an eye hospital in India." His younger sister has shown similar enthusiasm, telling her dad, "Once children can see, they can read and write."

To date, Nyan and Lehka (now aged 10 and 8) have raised more than $21,000 for their eye hospital from friends at school, forgone birthday gifts, and nationwide donations. Their "Kids for Sight" initiative recently ranked 18th out of 1,190 projects entered in the American Express "Members Project" competition—a remarkable feat! (To learn more, see www.orbis.org/kidsforsight.)

Kirchenbauer adds that a child's coming of age may be an ideal time to bring them into the fold. A philanthropic project could become part of celebrating their confirmation, bat/bar mitzvah, or *quinceañero*.

Teaching Teens and Young Adults

Sally Rudney, executive director of the Montgomery County Community Foundation in Maryland, is a strong supporter of helping kids learn philanthropy. The parents she works with, many of whom are in their 40s or 50s, want their legacy to include charitable giving and involvement in the community. One group of five mothers and their daughters (students at the same middle school) have established a giving circle. Each family started by donating $2,500 to the circle, to be given away to deserving causes within the next two years.

Rudney's foundation is charged with helping the girls learn about philanthropy in this time frame. She explains, "It's not lecturing so much as encouraging the kids to examine the experience of giving and the tremendous rewards to the person who gives."

The girls played a Q&A game in one educational session, asking each other questions such as "How many kids get free or reduced school lunches in Montgomery County?" Since the area has a reputation for above-average income, the others guessed 2%, 5%, 10%. The actual answer—25%—shocked them and sparked a discussion about poverty in the county. They've also visited a farm where workers with developmental disabilities grow food for the homeless and indigent, and they have volunteered at a food pantry where the harvest is sent. At the end of this period of education and experience, the girls will vote on how to allocate the money their families gave.

Contrary to the public image of teens as spenders, many have a strong natural sense of generosity that can be reinforced by their parents' example. Anne Slepian Ellinger, a longtime proponent of giving away wealth, shook her head when I asked if she had raised her son, Micah, to be philanthropic. "Not really," she replied, but then added as an afterthought, "Well, one time when he was about 13, he gave away all the money he had in the world to help the tsunami victims." This story made me smile, because his family's emphasis on living their philanthropic values had obviously rubbed off on Micah.

From the age of 15 or so up to 25, children start to use their own voice and make individual decisions. At this point, advisor Kohler suggests, parents or grandparents may want to establish a donor-advised fund (DAF) and convene the family to decide how the money will be spent. "Maybe at first, the kids just come to meetings," Kohler says. He recommends encouraging them to talk about causes that are important to them, perhaps the environment, music, or a sport. Eventually, the kids may be ready to have more input into how fund recipients will be researched and chosen.

When the kids are 25 to 35ish, their concerns often include relationship issues. "You'll need to find a way to engage in-laws and significant others in your process," BNY Mellon's Rogerson points out. "How can you use philanthropy as a tool to bring these people into the family and help them learn what it means to be a member of the family?" From 35-up, the challenges typically include how to involve the new generation of children in philanthropy...and the cycle begins anew.

DAF or Foundation?

"Many of my clients have wealth that is newly made or created," says Lisa Kirchenbauer, head of Kirchenbauer Financial Management & Consulting in Arlington, Virginia. "When I'm helping them learn about charitable giving, normally we start with a donor-advised fund. I think it's a good place to practice more formal and conscious philanthropy. The process of naming your fund, thinking about who you might give grants to, how you will invest the money, how you will distribute (anonymously or not), etc., is a great experience for most of my clients. Once it's established and funded, I've encouraged several of them to get their children involved in 'grant making'—i.e., finding organizations and causes that they care about and using the gift fund to support these causes. Much to my clients' surprise, their children have come up with some great organizations to support."

All in all, she says, "I think donor-advised funds are a great way to communicate the value of philanthropy and give children an opportunity to actively participate in the process. They're also a great way to see how your children deal with money-related issues."

Barry Kohler, an advisor at BDMP Wealth Management in Portland, Maine, points out that while a family foundation can also provide this kind of experience, donor-advised funds tend to be less expensive and more flexible. Tom Rogerson, managing director of Family Wealth Services at BNY Mellon Wealth Management, observes that when family-office clients were asked to name something their family had done over the generations that was a good idea, as well as something that was a bad idea, one answer was on both lists: "Our family foundation." Prior experience with a donor-advised fund, he suggests, may help a new generation learn how to run a family foundation more successfully.

Giving Away an Inheritance

Anne Ellinger and her husband, Christopher, have spent most of their lives helping wealthy individuals explore their values and use their resources to make the world a better place. Co-founders of More than Money and now of BolderGiving.org, Anne and Christopher recommend an unusual approach for junior-generation adults in wealthy families. Anne explains, "If they and their family already have enough, we encourage them to talk with their parents or grandparents about putting all or some of their would-be inheritance directly into a charitable fund."

That's exactly what Christopher did. Made well-off by a legacy from his grandmother, he told his grandfather, "I already have more than enough money for my needs. The most meaningful gift you could give me would be to put my inheritance in a fund that Anne and I can use for causes we care about." His grandfather's gift became the Chutzpah Fund, which launched them into their life's work of promoting philanthropy.

This is one of the rare cases where a younger generation educates the older folks about philanthropy. Like the Ellingers, I wish it happened more often. Anne observes wryly, "One of the many things that holds people back from giving boldly is their fear that their kids will be angry with them for not leaving them more."

Whatever your approach, my conversations with advisors, dedicated donors, and community leaders have strengthened my own appreciation of the power of philanthropy and the usefulness of modeling a philanthropic life for children as early as possible. Helping families learn to function as a philanthropic team is a wonderful gift in itself—one that will help your clients strengthen their family legacy and pass on its values.

Authors' Note

Except as noted below, the chapters in this book appeared as articles in *Investment Advisor*.

All in the Family
Like Mother, Like Daughter	February 2007
Child Is Father to the Man	April 2007
Brother and Sister, Where Art Thou?	October 2007

Dealing with Differences
Typecasting	March 2005
Impersonal Finance	May 2004
Gender Matters	September 2005
Minority Report	July 2008
Minority Affairs	August 2008

Changes
Change of Heart	May 2005
Therapeutic Finance	July 2007
Emotional Rescue	August 2004
Sustainable Growth	June 2006

Managing Stress
The Present, Tense	November 2004
After Shock	
(original title: Five Years After)	September 2006
Thank Goodness	November 2006

The Right Thing to Do
Les Liaisons Dangereuses	July 2005
Pants on Fire	June 2008

Who're You Calling 'Old'?
Retiring Minds	April 2006
For Whom the Bell Tolls	
(original title: The Bell Tolls)	February 2008
The Age of Enlightenment	March 2008

Passing the Torch